The Destiny of the Mind

The Destiny of the Mind

East and West

by

WILLIAM S. HAAS

THE MACMILLAN COMPANY

New York

1956

Contents

7

Contents

Introductory Note

The insights of the mind occur variously. Some come as a final result of preparation emerging only after a long period of toil. But there are others, not so frequent to be sure, where this order is reversed. Here the insight anticipates the thorough preparatory work which logically is its condition precedent. In this case what really happens is that the material which ordinarily serves as the springboard, is out of proportion to the import of the revealed insight. It is in fact this revelation which lights the path to further progressive knowledge and in retrospect discloses the steps which normally would have led to it.

The theory developed in this book belongs definitely in the second category. And the reader should bear in mind the original significance of the word theory. It is vision. Indeed this book is the exposition and justification of a scientific vision. And it is an inherent characteristic of a vision that its origin can never be fully demonstrated. Thus neither upbringing nor outward influence can explain the attraction which the East and everything connected with it exercised upon the author who grew to maturity in a middle-sized town in Germany the life of which evolved within the limits of a prosperous bourgeoisie. In retrospect it seems even more strange that this addiction to the East for some time remained but a sentiment with only occasional substantiation through haphazard reading. So much was this so that during the author's university years philosophy and psychology overshadowed his systematic occupation with the East.

In these student years it was, that an experience occurred which left a decisive though by no means immediately visible influence. The author remembers being seated on the terrace of a country house overlooking a wide prospect toward a range of high mountains. He was discussing metaphysics with an Indian visitor. At that time the author's position leaned to the Kantian doctrine of the limitation of our reason by the space-time perception and the categories of reason. This contrasted sharply with the Indian's arguments, and the discussion seemed to have reached a deadlock. Suddenly the Indian, pointing at the flowers which grew in abundance in the garden before our eyes, turned to me with an unexpected and seemingly meaningless question.

'Against what background do you see these flowers?' he asked. 'Against the background of those shrubs,' I answered. 'And against what background do you see those shrubs?' he continued. 'Against the background of those trees.' 'And against what background do you see those trees?'

Again I answered, and so one question and its manifest answer followed the next until the query came: 'Against what background do you see those clouds moving behind and beyond the mountains?' The answer of course was—'Against the sky.' And then, came the final question uttered with the same calm as those preceding:

'And against what background do you see the sky?'

I was left stupefied—without an answer. The Indian turned to me and said with his soft voice:

'I will tell you: against the background of consciousness.'

This was certainly more than an escape manoeuvre. Nor was it an ingenious bluff. It was a counter-attack on the Western way of thinking, particularly a blow to the Kantian position. For it placed consciousness above reason as the ultimate and superior datum. And it intimated that the development of consciousness might lead up to quite other results than the investigation of reason.

Now here is a strange thing. Looking back over the years I am at a loss to locate that country house. Nor do I clearly remember the Indian. Equally I cannot determine the approximate date of the episode. And so reluctantly I have become increasingly convinced that the whole scene is my own, though of course, unintentional creation. In no way would this interfere with the significance of the story. On the contrary in the current of a biographical sketch it would assume quite another importance. For it would indicate that one of the basic ideas presented in this book—the existence of two clearly definable forms of consciousness—came not as a result of prior investigation, but had later to be and was confirmed

Introductory Note

by it. Again, the underlying idea that the difference between Eastern and Western civilization is founded upon clearly demonstrable structural principles, was not the result of painstaking research. Rather the idea itself opened the way to a deeper understanding of the phenomena characterizing each.

This new conception of the contrasting structures of the Eastern and Western mind was first suggested in an essay, *Die Seele des Orients, Grundzuege einer Psychologie des orientalischen Menschen*, 1916—The Soul of the Orient, Principles of a Psychology of Oriental Man. The corresponding idea with regard to Western civilization has been published under the title—*What is European Civilization?* London, Oxford University Press, 1929. This comprises three lectures delivered at the Geneva School of International Studies.

The definitive and final shaping of these ideas and of the views which are embodied in this book has grown over the years of an academic career, and also in connection with engagements in both official and private capacities in international relations particularly in relation to Eastern scenes and affairs and five years in Iran as advisor of the Ministry of Education. Likewise my writing and publishing in other fields such as psychology and ethnology and particularly another publication in this field—*Iran*, Columbia University Press, New York, 1946—is in line with this lifelong interest in the East.

The author wishes to express his sincere appreciation to Dudley C. Lunt for his collaboration in giving to the book its final form.

WILLIAM S. HAAS

11

CHAPTER I

Unity in Variety

A strange and significant relationship exists between Europe and Asia and their civilizations. The continent of Asia weighs heavily on the globe. Its huge and compact mass defies the oceans that wash its shores. It may be compared to some giant ancestral animal at rest, loaded with unknown energies. Europe presents another picture entirely. Itself a peninsula devolving into those of Scandinavia, Denmark, the Iberian peninsula, Italy and the Balkans, it plays lightly on the surface of the sea, inviting its waters. Europe resembles a living organism whose tentacles stretch out for balance and movement, giving and receiving. Thus its spirit, its structural principle of *unity in variety*, is expressed in its geographical shape.

Europe is the one continent without deserts. All the others harbour large stretches of barren land—stone, sand, or steppes. In the moderate climate of Europe fertility in varying degrees spreads everywhere. While free of those extremes which either subject man to an uninterrupted struggle for existence or emasculate him by luxuriant conditions, life in Europe requires a fair amount of regular labour. Communication has never been particularly difficult. Even the Alps cannot compare with the formidable barriers, insurmountable mountain chains, impassable rivers, impenetrable forests and deserts which on the other continents have blocked traffic and migration. In prehistoric and in Roman times, the Alpine valleys were inhabited while the Alpine passes were crossed by huge armies. The seaway to the other continents of the old world has always been within easy command. The inland sea of the Mediterranean—most glorious and fateful in the history of civilization—has by the law of nature ever been a European sea. The three great peninsulas of Southern Europe with their numerous ports protrude far into it, and its scattered islands invite

12

navigation. It is as if Europe, whose articulate parts are accessible each to the other, was reaching out toward the world. Thus in characterizing this smallest of the continents and the direct opposite of Asia there is no better formula than unity in variety.

The peninsular character of Europe is re-emphasized in the geographical origin of its civilization. For this reason Attica, a tiny peninsula projecting from Greece which in turn extends from the Balkan peninsula, may be termed mathematically a magnitude raised to the third power. This is more than an amusing observation. Between the great inland civilizations of Asia and Central America and the island continent of Australia, peninsular Europe occupies an intermediate and distinctive place. The radiation of the great Asiatic civilizations cannot be compared with the cultural conquest of the whole European continent by Greece and Rome. Chinese civilization spread only to Japan, Korea and to some extent to the countries of the South-East. The influence of India, which was mainly of a religious character, was limited to China, South-East Asia and the Malaysian archipelago. And the wide flow of Persian civilization to the Near East on the one hand and to India on the other did not transcend the religious, philosophical, literary, and artistic spheres.

To dismiss these geographical analogies as purely incidental would be difficult; yet it would be erroneous to credit them with a causative character. Here manifestly we face a relationship whose undeniable existence escapes clear definition. While the influence of concrete physical conditions on the psycho-physiological formation of man is largely understandable and even demonstrable, the connection between the physical shape of Europe and Asia and their civilizations almost defies comprehension. If this connection is not brushed aside as meaningless—an all too easy way to deal with a puzzling phenomenon—the geographical formations of the two continents are suggestive of a possible interrelation which is as yet unintelligible. Moreover, physical conditions of any kind explain but simple and general psychological attitudes—and even those only *ex post facto*. They do not establish a strictly causative relation. The higher the civilization the looser the tie between the geographical structure and the mind, until at the highest level of a civilization, the physical conditions are merely the raw material by which that civilization can realize itself. With this limitation in mind, the reference to geography and the implications drawn from it serve the valuable purpose of an illustrative introduction.

*   *   *

Greek and Roman civilization fanned out and gave to the European continent its lasting foundations and its intellectual tools. The weight and inertia of the Asiatic and American civilizations may be connected with their inland character, while the classic civilizations of Greece and Rome may to some extent owe their elasticity to their peninsular character. Other and more potent factors also contributed toward extending classic civilization to the whole continent. On the physical level there is the paramount fact of the racial homogeneity of the European peoples. The few ethnically foreign peoples such as the Lapps in the North-East and the non-Aryans of European Russia, live for the most part, and not only in a geographical sense, on the periphery of Europe, while others like the Finns have been entirely westernized. As a consequence of this racial homogeneity, the Greeks, Romans, and the later leading powers bequeathed their legacy to people of the same racial stock and presumably of essentially the same mental endowments.

One of the distinctive marks of Western civilization was its rise in one and only one clearly defined area. Whatever may have been the Eastern influence accompanying the birth of Greek culture, the Greek genius penetrated and assimilated it. In using foreign elements as stimulants rather than as values in their own right, the Greeks created their own world. And this was the matrix of Western civilization. Then the Greek spark sprang over to cognate Rome. Henceforth, this classic culture shaped the body of medieval civilization, Rome giving to the Church its visible organization and Greek philosophical thought permeating the structure of its dogma. Europe, thus integrated by westernized Christianity, at last proceeded to the scientific and technical stage, which was based on the secularization of the medieval world conception and conditioned by the interest of the Greeks in science, biology, and medicine.

This common origin to a large extent determined the texture

and consistency of Western civilization, and conferred upon it across time and space an inner continuity notwithstanding the variety of the Western peoples. And it is to this origin that Western civilization throughout all change owes its coherence and congruity. This life-stream, springing from this one source and widening and increasing its momentum throughout the course of history, flowed far out onto the delta of the various national cultures. This is the reason why there is in all European movements, intellectual, spiritual, economic or political, and wherever they may originate, an irresistible trend to extend to the Europe of their time and later to embrace the whole continent. This tendency takes the form of a more or less forceful expansion as in the spreading of Roman culture and the Christian creed, or—and this is more important—of a peaceful penetration as in the spreading of Greek culture. This flowing outward, this effort to cross national barriers and become continental is clearly exemplified in such modern movements as the Renaissance, which swept all civilized Europe with the exception of Spain, or the evolution of science which took root rapidly everywhere save in Russia and the Turkish Balkans; and the political and social movements which arose on European soil. Thus did the intellectual and emotional trends of the European continent and finally of Occidental civilization flow beyond their birthplaces and extend throughout the world.

A special relation to time corresponds to this form of expansion in space. This relation to time, which is peculiar to the West, does not refer to mere time-extension, that is to say the life-span of the civilization. For so far as age is concerned, almost all the Asiatic civilizations exceed those of the Occident. Rather it is a qualitative and not a quantitative distinction which is here involved. For in the development of Occidental civilization, time has a function which is totally distinct from that which prevails in the East.

In the Orient time is but a formal and extraneous condition to the unfolding of civilization. In the Occident, *per contra* time is one of civilization's great determining elements. It penetrates to the very heart of Western civilization, and it is a constituent part of that civilization, conferring on its development the distinctive shape of evolution. Time, then, in the West is not an indifferent medium in which events occur chronologically as things exist simultaneously in space. If science today has divested time of its absolute metaphysical character so that men speak—and by no means figuratively—of physiological and psychological time as distinct from time in mathematics and physics, it is appropriate here to describe evolutionary time as a specific form of time and the basis of a great unit of civilization.

Evolution, to be sure, is not the monopoly of Occidental civilization. In broken lines and limited fields it occurs in almost every place where man has left his mark, and of course in the great civilizations of Asia religious and philosophical thought, knowledge and art, took long periods to unfold. Nevertheless, Occidental civilization is the only one to which the term evolution can always be applied, and the only one where man, regarding history as an organic whole, visualizes time as essentially evolutionary.

Be it understood that evolution is not identical with progress. For the term progress involves a judgment of value. Evolution is naught but self-presentation in a particular form. It may and in human evolution it certainly does imply the achievement of certain values and ends. But it cannot be asserted that a civilization, by reason of this self-realization through evolution, is in any way superior thereby to one which unfolds its potentialities in a different form. Not only is there no connection between evolution and progress. Evolution as such is but an indifferent and neutral process unless indeed some positive value is imparted to it.

Genuine evolution is unity in variety perceived in the sequence of time. This is why a civilization founded on such a structure possesses an essential relationship to time and confers upon it a particular mode, that of evolutionary as opposed to flowing time. The comparison of an evolutionary civilization with the evolution of a living organism, though not wholly applicable, offers far-reaching analogies. Just as the human organism evolves through clearly distinct periods—childhood, adolescence, maturity and old age—so an evolutionary civilization passes through different stages, whether or not we are justified in speaking of it as aging. These decisive stages of an evolutionary civilization are closely interrelated because, like the parts of an organism, they do not function in terms of one another, but rather in terms of and for

16

the purpose of the whole. Hence, it becomes apparent that notwithstanding its several stages and their objectives, the structure of Occidental civilization is a unit. And it is this structure that rules the whole evolution of the expression of the Western mind.

*   *   *

The attempt to cultivate the individual marked the beginning of Western civilization. It was the great achievement of Greece to mould the body, the soul and the mind of man into a unified whole. To do this, the Greeks considered everything in theory and practice as being relative to man. Hence, their self-imposed limitations. They rejected extremes and in all those fields of knowledge where they laid the foundations, they kept within certain bounds.

To the Romans fell the task of dominating the world and organizing it into one realm and society, to the end of uniting and civilizing mankind. It then followed logically that the European mind, having tested its organizing capacity in the temporal world, turned to the world beyond. Whereas Greek philosophy lent its spirituality to the conception of an invisible Church as the mystic body of Christ, thus determining and formulating its theological system, the organizational pattern of the visible Church derived from imperial Rome. The next evolutionary stage in Western history was the investigation of nature. Though strongly attracted to this science, the Greeks never wholly abandoned themselves to it. And it was not until modern times that a systematic penetration of nature was undertaken with enthusiasm and the search fully rewarded.

Such then are the clearly distinguished stages in the evolution of Occidental civilization. Though the centre of gravity shifts, no clear dividing lines exist between one stage and another. One spirit, one mind accompanies the process throughout all its phases and thus pervades the whole. Despite her circumscribed interests, Rome preserved the Greek heritage to the limit of her capacity. The Middle Ages inherited not only Rome's idea of universality, but its universal language, so that Greek works in philosophy, mathematics and science, once they had been translated from their Arabic versions into Latin, came alive again. And this conjoining with the mighty current of the magic philosophy of nature prepared the new era. The study of nature prevailed over all others and under its aegis the various branches of knowledge flowered, receiving from that sovereign source a positive or a negative stimulus. In many instances the methods used in the investigation of nature were applied to these other disciplines.

The exclusive characteristic of Occidental civilization is that its history is composed of stages, each possessing a clearly discernible objective. While in the ascendant each stage aspires to embrace the totality of human existence and to be perfect in itself, yet it brings forth the very force that eventually destroys and replaces it. Whoever looks back at this tremendous pageant will recognize that these consecutive stages present facets of the Occidental mind—a mind that is ever striving to organize according to its own structural law all the provinces of human existence in a logical sequence. This consecutive organization of life according to one pattern constitutes Western history. More than that, the process of this construction is itself the history of the Western mind.

All the European peoples have contributed to this process. Or at least they have been receptive to its results. The Greco-Roman culture was received by the barbarians just as Christianity was everywhere assimilated. Eventually all members of the Occidental civilization joined in the adoption or creation of science and techniques. Though not all of them contributed equally to the initiation of this last stage, all could understand it and were eager to incorporate into their lives the applications of its new ideas.

This intellectual and moral community finds its parallel in general history. It is as if the Western nations had been summoned in turn by destiny each to take the lead—each manifesting itself to the others, having its aptitudes and talents tested, and being educated for the community and its common causes.[1] To be sure,

---

[1] The organic evolution and co-operation of the European people despite their national differences and continuous warfaring was not only an unquestionable fact. It also lived as a God-ordained duty in the consciousness of illustrious minds. *The Chronicle of Jordanus Teutonicus* (thirteenth century) expressed it in these truly magnificent words: 'As among the great nations to the Italians the papacy (sacerdotium) has been assigned as their singular task, and to the Germans secular rule (imperium), so to the French the studies (studium), and the one Paris suffices as the seat of studies.'

18

political leadership does not always coincide with cultural predominance. Following the Greek and the Macedonian hegemony Rome assumed supremacy, after which the power passed to the Teutonic imperium. Then the struggle between imperial and ecclesiastical authority was supplanted by the competition between France and England until, at the end of the fifteenth century, the Italian states appeared like comets in the sky. Spain and Austria rose to paramount power. For a time the balance was kept between France under her great kings and rising England. Small countries founded on economic and military strength like Holland, and Sweden, came to the fore. Finally, in the nineteenth century, France, England, and Germany assumed world leadership, yielding that role in our day to America and to Russia.

If ever a metaphor was justified, it is that the evolution of Occidental civilization is organic, and that this Western civilization itself is a highly developed organism. Indeed this civilization has a structure. The interdependence of its relatively autonomous parts depends upon the relationship of those parts to the governing whole. And at the same time the whole is ever realizing itself through the evolution of its parts. Western history is therefore evolutionary history. It is a history which less than any other can be comprehended in terms of cause and effect, or as a chronological process. The significance of Occidental civilization is in its evolution, each stage of which has its preordained place. Here time is no longer a mere external condition. Rather it is an inherent element in the process that is both qualitative and concrete. Historical consciousness is often considered the monopoly of the Western mind. If this be true, this prerogative is but the consequence of an evolutionary form of history which is itself the reflection of the historical sense. Only an evolving mind can take more than a chronological interest in the past, an interest which transcends that past and is ever recreating its picture.

The Occidental mind cannot approach any sphere of existence without moulding it according to its own structural principle of unity in variety. Thus, if the form of its evolutionary history exemplifies the structure of the Western mind, the same thing must be true of the consecutive stages which compose that history, their respective themes, their individual manifestations and the cultural creations contained in those themes. In demonstrating the anatomy of these fundamental ideas and their realization, completeness cannot be attempted. Such a task belongs to a history of civilization. Our argument requires rather a selective choice for the sake of illustration.

*　　*　　*

In the perfecting of the personality of man the Greeks sought to achieve a balance of all of its parts and the complete harmony of each part with the others. This was their supreme preoccupation and in pursuit of this ideal they had to resist the temptation to develop any particular part at the expense of the whole. For the preponderance of one field would not only distort both balance and harmony, but might well end in subordinating all education to that favoured field. A radical example of such corruption was the sophistic movement. This made education subservient to the power motive and in so doing perverted the spirit and meaning of the ideal.

Education is hardly conceivable unless it be directed to a specific end. This end determines from the outset the form, means, contents, and method of education. The aims may differ greatly, for example—preparation for life in general or for one of the various professions; the training of character and will or the sharpening of the intellect; the preparation of the citizen; the salvation of the soul, and such standards may be isolated or more or less blended. Now harmony is not one-sidedness, or mixture, or even balance. Most educational systems, particularly the liberal and humanistic, insist on a certain balance between the fields of study. However, lacking a clear fundamental idea coupled with a scale of values, this principle of balance loses its creative force and retains only the negative meaning of avoiding one-sidedness. Yet a mere arbitrary co-ordination of the chosen branches of knowledge does not present an ideal of education. The same frustration occurs when a paramount educational aim such as training for the professions is augmented by additional studies. Not even balance will be thus achieved. Neither the human mind nor the educational idea is a mechanical system to which the principle of balance can be mechanically applied.

Unity in Variety

This at least was the conviction of the Greeks. Harmony they viewed as the building principle of man just as they considered it the soul of the universe. Unlike balance, harmony involves a hierarchical order. To achieve and to maintain this order, a supreme value is needed which will impart rank and function to the other values. The Greeks esteemed reason as presiding over the harmonious formation of man. But to them reason was not just the thinking power. It was that capacity by which ultimate reality could be known in a clear and intelligible form, the best-known example of this being Plato's Ideas. Reason, thus conceived as capable of grasping ultimate reality, transcended the world of experience. And through this transcendence it was alone capable of comprehending the world below. In the formation of man, reason acted as wisdom and moderation assigning to each human faculty its place so that each was organically disposed to its own function.

The human body was the visible paragon of this organic concept and it too was intrinsically included in the formation of man. But the body, no less than the psyche and the mind, had to undergo a process of training and education for the sake of the Greek ideal. Gymnastics, sports, the Greek contest in athletics, chariot racing—all served this purpose. Characteristically the highest specialized achievement was looked down upon and the mere athlete was despised, for harmonious development was the ambition and the aim. Music was a prominent part of education for it constituted the natural link between poetry and the rhythmic movements of the body, and there was also its humanizing influence and its relationship to mathematics. In its classical form sculpture expressed the harmony of the body, the soul and the mind,—in philosophic terms, of sensuous desire, will-power and reason. None of these three was permitted to disturb the architectural unity of the whole.

The Greek theatre, far from being either a place of entertainment, or of aesthetic pleasure, or an institution for moral purposes, served another and a higher aim. This Aristotle described as purification—*catharsis*. His famous definition may be interpreted either to mean that the effect of the tragedy was to arouse pity and fear in order to purify these emotions, or—as is more

21

likely—to free the spectator from both passions. In either view the purpose and the result of the tragedy were what may truly be called a psychological liberation, a mind cure. Borrowing its main plots from legendary heroic history Greek tragedy depicted man as the victim of the most formidable passions both in his misdeeds and in his sublime acts of sacrifice. Here was a tragic figure fighting his solitary fight against fate and against the heavenly and infernal powers. In this drama the Greek saw not only the ancestral world so near to his heart, but he saw *himself* with all his destructive urges and his sublime potentialities. He passed open-eyed through the vicissitudes of fate, experiencing many of the human complications rediscovered in our time by psychoanalysis such for example as the Oedipus complex. In the end he emerged from the trial delivered from the weight of this heritage. He was a free and more harmonious being.

Particularly interesting to our argument is that part of the tragedy by means of which this result, if not brought about, was deeply enhanced. The Greek chorus is a kind of detached spectator on the stage yet performing an integral part in the play itself, It takes part by making general observations or giving advice to the characters, thus investing the play with a sort of higher reality. Thereby another level of consciousness is created and in it as in a mirror the deeper significance of the action is glimpsed. This spectator-chorus, though part of the play, reflects on the scenes as they pass, and by reason of this it is never lost in the action, never completely carried away. Thus, audience and play were fused in a remarkable organic whole, and thereby the soul was purified and purged of its anarchy of psychological perplexities in the fulfilment of the supreme task of tragedy.

The Greeks did not differ substantially from any other highly gifted people. Their virtues and their astounding intellectual endowments were matched by proportionate vices and shortcomings of which the history of Athens alone bears ample testimony. Their greatness as a people consisted in the fact that they produced so many men of genius who achieved supreme harmony in their personalities and whose creations gave the people an ideal. There is an almost paradoxical phenomenon that the Greek mind, which discovered the scientific approach to practically all branches of knowledge, was never tempted into developing any of them to the detriment of the rest. This restraint is particularly remarkable as regards science where the Greeks not only first discovered the fundamental attitude required for inquiring into nature but also developed pure and applied mathematics. If this path was not followed to its natural end, the reason can only have been that they felt the destiny of man centred on a higher value.

The Greeks sensed the tremendous danger to which the Promethean goal of a science of nature could expose man and his development. Dominated by measure and the idea of harmonious limitation, their great minds were aware of man's tendency toward the infinite, the limitless, and they foresaw the perils of excess latent in a science of nature pursued for its own sake. No better illustration of this can be found than in Plato's attitude toward mathematics. The words he inscribed over the entrance to his Academy: 'No one who has not studied mathematics may enter here' do not mean that for him its value lay in mathematical science as such, whether it be used for the investigation of nature or in solving practical problems. For Plato its supreme value was that here was an incomparable instrument for diverting the mind from the world and elevating it from the spheres of changing phenomena to the realm of pure thought and the contemplation of true reality.

The Greek attitude toward religion does not differ in principle from their attitude toward science. Despite an incomparable talent for metaphysics and a marked tendency toward the transcendental, the Greeks did not lose themselves in fruitless speculation and unworldly mysticism. Nor did they even grant religion a high importance. They had no priestly caste or class and no highly developed theology. Here too they sensed the danger of religious aspiration growing into a power strong enough to jeopardize the balanced unfolding of human nature.

The autonomous city state of the Greeks—the *polis*—was an adequate expression of the mind which created it and a form in keeping with all that grew out of it culturally. Its main external feature was that it comprised both the city itself and enough land around it to feed the population of free citizens with their serfs and slaves, and to provide for the needs of the armed force consisting of free and able-bodied men. Out of this consciously restricted area where everything and everybody was within reach there rose a commonwealth of free men who, unhampered by any overwhelming religious or political autocracy, decided their own destiny, wrote their own laws, and changed and probed political ideas and institutions. These achievements have ever since served as patterns for political theory, and more particularly for democratic evolution in the Western world.

The *polis* is a creation unique in human history. Equidistant from the tribal state and from primordial, natural kingship, both of which reigned longest and over the widest area in the history of mankind, the *polis* was not a natural growth. On the contrary, it was a product of the mind at its highest level, an intentional creation that sprang full-armed from theoretical thought. The supposition that the *polis* evolved from the tribal state or from original kingship is baseless save with reference to chronological sequence. For neither in its structure nor its prerequisites did the *polis* resemble any preceding political forms. The spiritual and physical heart of the *polis* was the market place or place of assembly where public buildings like the theatre and the gymnasium were concentrated.

No greater apotheosis of the interrelationship of man's individual and political life exists than in Plato's ideal State where the three estates constituting the political body represent the three parts of the soul. The legislators and regents are the equivalent of creative reason or wisdom. The guardians who defend the state against its enemies foreign and domestic correspond to will-power and courage. And the mass of the people, peasants and craftsmen, represent the vegetative part of the soul. From this coincidence with the psychological structure, the state derives its legitimate claim to absolute authority. Neither an absolute monarchy with its class society, nor a totalitarian state in which man and society become an amorphous mass, the *polis* represents a super-soul or super-ego. The omnipotence of the state inheres in its structure, and is not arbitrarily superimposed creating thereby a tyrannical Leviathan. Thus the idea of the *polis* and the *polis* itself are intended to fulfil that end which Aristotle attributed to the State when he asserted that it came into being to permit existence, but that it existed to assure the perfect existence.

Unity in Variety

The human ideal of the Greeks was the invention and monopoly of an urban aristocracy. The *polis* is just as much the creation of political man, that is to say the civilized being, as it is his guardian and guarantor. It is the frame within which the harmonious personality alone can arise and prosper. However it is precisely this connection between the *polis* and the forming of personality that implanted and determined its limits. True it is that Greek individualism was in almost constant revolt against this wisely constructed balance of the *polis*. But a more important consequence of this balance was that the Greeks never succeeded in extending their power over wide areas. The only example of an imperialistic policy, the Delian confederation, was doomed to an early end because the Athenians were unable to organize their domination effectively. This shows how heavily the spirit of the *polis* weighed upon them and how incompatible its inner extent was with external power and empire policy. The Greek form of imperialism was essentially cultural expansion and this is amply demonstrated by its penetration of Rome and of the Near and Middle East during the Hellenistic centuries.

*　　*　　*

Where Greece failed, Rome took over and arrived at the gradual and systematic organization of a conquered world. In creating the *polis* Greece had stressed the formation of the individual, whereas Rome on the other hand regarded the commonwealth as the embodiment of all of its virtue. The spirit which permeated the political life of Rome was born and kept alive in the patriarchal family from which the Roman state had developed historically.

This spirit has been admirably characterized by Mommsen in his *Roman History* as that 'which held the son in awe of his father, the citizen in awe of the ruler, and both in awe of the Gods, that demanded and expected nothing but the useful and forced every citizen to fill every moment of his short life with ceaseless work, that made the decorous clothing of the body a duty even for the child, that condemned as a bad citizen whoever wished to be different from his fellow, for whom the state was everything, the extension of the state the only higher idea which was not despised ... the deep feeling of the general in the particular, the devotion and

25

self-sacrifice of the individual, the firm belief in their Gods, is the rich inheritance of the Italic peoples.'

The family was a superior entity of which the living family was only the transitional representative. Thus the paterfamilias held his position not in his own right, but as the representative of those who had passed and as the trustee for those to come. And all these were integrated in the worship of the Lares and Penates, the spirits of the ancestors and of the household. If ruling oneself is the prerequisite for ruling others, the virtues qualifying a people for a world-order were certainly fostered in the Roman patriarchy which filled city, state, and empire with the same spirit. The substance of this spirit, which prevailed until Augustus, was condensed by Cicero into the three words—*gravitas, pietas, simplicitas*. Even etymologically, *gravitas* expresses the weight carried by all public affairs for the Roman. And as practically everything was judged from the standpoint of the interests of the state life itself became grave. In none of its forms did the Roman commonwealth in so far as organization and institutions were concerned show any tendency toward totalitarianism. But with its pre-eminent qualifications, Rome realized the totalitarian ideal more perfectly and in an infinitely nobler way than have any of the modern totalitarian states with their spurious implementations. Because of its supra-individual character, the religious mind of the Romans regarded the commonwealth as a *numen*, that is a divine power. Thus there was conferred on all public actions and ceremonies a halo of solemnity, and to this there corresponded in the individual soul *pietas*—reverence and devotion.

The limitations of the Roman mind as compared to the Greek are obvious. Whereas the Greeks' concern was the restraint of their all-embracing interests and capacities for the sake of harmonious development, the Romans, in identifying the perfect man with the perfect citizen, eliminated important aspects of man and the world. Theirs was a real simplification for the purpose of concentrating on the one ideal, the eternal commonwealth and on the one task, the expansion of that commonwealth to the bounds of the known globe. For centuries the greatest representatives of this spirit sensed the threat to the Roman mind and tradition lurking in the Greek culture and they tried by example and word of mouth to stem the rising tide of its influence. This resistance to the speculative and theoretical thought of Greek philosophy and to the *bel esprit* of Greek rhetoricians sprang from the sound instinct of a mind which left to posterity unique models of individual and national greatness. The Roman mind discovered for itself and gave to civilized mankind the answers to certain fundamental problems.

One such answer, and it is the outstanding one, is the Roman law. This autonomous system of rules by which permanent relationships could alone be established between individuals and groups is imposed neither by divine or human authority, nor is it the inarticulate recognition of custom and tradition. If it seems to derive its validity from the commonwealth, this is true only in so far as law itself is an integral part of the commonwealth and its chief support. If it can be called man-made, the man who makes it is not the individual but the *Civis Romanus*. The bare fact that Roman law enjoyed an organic evolution undisturbed by political changes for a thousand years from its historical beginnings until the composition of the Justinian Code, is evidence of its autonomy. Indeed, of the great achievements of Rome, 'the art of government and expansion, the reconciliation of local diversities with imperial unity, the approximation of a world-wide peace'[1]—all are based on and accompanied by legal conceptions. This can be traced in the process by which the Roman civil law, originally the law of the city of Rome and applied only to its citizens, was gradually completed and to a large extent supplanted by the *Jus Peregrinum*, the law valid for non-citizens and used in intercourse with foreign peoples. Then out of the *Jus Peregrinum* rose the *Jus Gentium*, the International Law, law common to all the nations of the Empire. The idea which with increasing clarity inspired the work of empire building was set forth by Virgil:

> *Tu regere imperio populos, Romane memento,*
> *Haec tibi sunt artes, pacis imponere mores,*
> *Parcere subjectis et debellare superbos.*
> *Remember Thou, O Roman, that thy task is to rule*
> *in one empire the people of the earth!*

[1] The Rt. Hon. H. H. Asquith in his introduction to *The legacy of Rome* edited by Cyril Raily, Oxford A. T. The Clarendon Press, 1923.

Unity in Variety

These are thine arts: to impose the morale of peace,
to spare those who surrender and to fight
to the bitter end the supercilious.[1]

★   ★   ★

The medieval world conception united the people of Europe under a single idea. Thereby there were fused barbarian society, the continuing influence of antiquity, and the Christian creed and outlook on life. Then for the third time the centre of gravity shifted again. Having tested its power first in the harmonious development of man, next in the organization of a world-empire and society, the European mind now turned to the world of the supernatural, the sphere of religion. Here too its method of necessity was the same. It grasped and moulded the materials at hand according to the law of its being. The organizing power of the European mind was perhaps never more impressively expressed than in the medieval conception of the world. For here it dealt with every phase of existence from the idea of God to the smallest details of human life.

If ever the term organic unity can be appropriately applied, it is to the medieval conception of the universe, that sum total of all conceivable existence. From the created but non-creating nature, that is inanimate and unorganized matter, all created beings ascended in a clearly demonstrable order to God who embodied the creating but non-created nature. This same gradation prevailed in the inviolable order of human society which consisted of sharply separated classes with their respective functions, duties and rights. It was a true hierarchy with the Pope and emperor at the top and everyone else constituting in a descending scale a unified order under God.

At the height of its evolution in the time of Pope Gregory VII (1073–85), the Church ceased to recognize the earthly power as an independent body and established its ascendance over the emperor, referring to him as the mere arm of the Church. With its own constitution, largely the heritage of the Roman Empire, its administrative bureaucracy and international organization, its own law code and absolute authority, the Church was well qualified

[1] (*Aeneid* VI, 852 ff.) My translation.

to impose on state and emperor. This however was but its bodily aspect.

The spiritual reality was the invisible, the sacramental Church. The physical aspect mirrored the soul in form and expression in so far as the imperfect could mirror the more perfect. If therefore the visible Church as an expression of the invisible, was a well-developed organism, the invisible Church itself was still closer in the purely spiritual sense to the ideal of an intelligible living organism. According to the classical teaching of the Church, the Church is a supernatural body, the totality of its members being nothing other than the mystical body of Christ. This is a necessary consequence of the sacrament of the Eucharist in which, as St. Bonaventure teaches, the faithful partake of the living Christ. The real presence of Christ in His Church and the daily repetition of His sacrificial death make of the invisible Church something transcendental, not merely a supernatural community of the faithful like Calvin's idea of a community of the elect. The invisible Church is rather a body permeated by so peculiar a life that it can only be described by the term *corpus mysticum.*

The power of this Western mind-structure does not even end here. Indeed it reaches into the idea of the supreme being itself. The conception of a divine trinity is not a Christian monopoly, for it can be found elsewhere, for example the Trimurti of Hinduism. However, to compare other conceptions of the trinity—conceptions signifying at best a threefold aspect and expression of the God-head—with the Christian trinity, is to ignore the totally different structure of the Christian idea. This is the unity of the trinity in the personal God Himself. Moreover, it is important for our argument to appreciate on the one hand the astounding intellectual effort required to bring this supreme example of unity in variety, this idea of an organic deity, nearer to our comprehension. It is equally important on the other hand, to understand how the triune God supports and fills the whole life of the Church. To realize what the first point meant to the Western mind one need only think of the space occupied by and the dialectical sagacity brought to bear upon this problem of the trinity in scholastic philosophy. The second point concerns the doctrine and the road to salvation—how God assumes human form; the drama of the God-man crowned by His sacrificial death; the foundation of an invisible and supernatural Church in which He is forever present, in which He rules, and by means of which He united man with Himself and His eternal Father; the significance of the liturgy; the Church year as nothing but a dramatic repetition and presentation of the whole history of salvation, not in the form of an enthralling drama or an absorbing memory but so that all the faithful are united and elevated in a mystical community of action. Once this mysterious life of the Church is appreciated, it becomes evident that it is from this idea of the divine trinity that the stream of spiritual life flows through the Church.

*   *   *

With the passing of medievalism the European mind entered on its fourth stage. This time nature was its object. The scientific penetration of nature which has resulted in our technical civilization is thus the latest and most mature manifestation of the Western mind. Now maturity does not necessarily imply a positive evaluation. As a term stemming from biology it means merely a state of full development, the preceding stages of which have been assimilated and overcome. Indeed in any intellectual and cultural development, a stage preceding maturity may well be superior to it in vigour, creativity, and also value.

The ground work for the study of nature was prepared by the Greeks by their keen interest in all that surrounded them and their conception of the intellectual tools needed for the task. This also contained the will to power and domination that characterized Rome. But strange as it may seem, it is to a large extent to the Middle Ages that the study of nature owes its development. And this despite the fact that modern science is antagonistic to all that the Middle Ages represent. Indeed, the spirit of modern science must be understood as the secularization of the spirit of the Middle Ages with nature and the conception of nature taking the place of God and the conception of God.

At the outset the conception of nature as the sum total of eternal and mathematically demonstrable laws harmonized with the idea of God. These laws were believed to express God's greatness as Creator. In this new idea of nature and in man's relationship to it essential attributes of the Divine as well as man's religious attitude came to be secularized. Even self-abnegation, the moral ideal of the Middle Ages, now characterized those who were the initiators of this scientific outlook. This was evident from their unconditional devotion to scientific truth for its own sake, quite disassociated from any thought of its practical application, and from the lack of any egocentric motive.

The modern science of nature started, as did all great discoveries of the mind, not from some pallid and bloodless theory but from what the Greeks called a genuine *theoria*. This word derives from to gaze, to visualize. To them theory was vision, intuition. The vision in this case was nature embraced and comprehended in a single glance as a cosmos, a harmonious entity determined by perennial mathematical laws. This attempt to organize nature, to mould its phenomena so as to constitute unity in variety, assumed two major aspects.

These aspects correspond not to the work itself but to the underlying philosophies and they may be characterized as the philosophy of discovery and the philosophy of construction. As the sky yielded its secrets, the initiators of modern science stood in deep humility before the momentous yet simple laws according to which God built and ruled the universe. Fully conscious of the revolutionary importance of their insight, they felt themselves to be the discoverers of truth eternal and divine. They were convinced that thenceforth one discovery after another would unfold before their eyes and they felt bound by these imperishable and unchangeable laws which they had discovered.

In time, this view came to be contested and it was finally replaced by the conception that scientific thought, far from seizing and comprehending things as they are, constitutes on the contrary an arbitrary system of signs and symbols, consistent in itself and therefore infinitely applicable. Hence, it was a network flung over the necessarily unknowable reality. In this conception, of which Thomas Hobbes was the first great representative, science ceases to be discovery. It becomes invention and construction. So long as man had felt and acted as the discoverer of nature and its laws, he was in an objectively real world, God-created, and permeated by divinity. And he knew himself to be limited by the eternal order of things. However, as soon as he thought of his effort as a spontaneous constructive activity, he was freed of his bonds. While he lost faith in objective truth and while he might even deny such an idea any meaning, he could now claim sovereignty over his own mind, and be proud to impose the rules he invented on the phenomena of the world. Here started the great adventure of the Western mind in its latest stage. The infinity of this task is apparent and so is its correlate—the mind that conceives of itself as unbounded and absolutely free from authority.

Fundamental to both these conceptions of science is the vision of a demonstrable unity in nature, and the resulting effort to proceed toward that unity by means of scientific methods. Obviously the conception of mathematics and mathematical physics as an *invention* of the mind is more closely connected with power and domination than is the conception of law as *discovery*. While the conception of science as discovery corresponds to the theoretical elaboration of nature, that of science as invention combines theory with the factual reconstruction of nature, and so arrives at harnessing and directing the forces of nature to human ends. Thus the inventive aspect is far more conducive to the application of science for practical purposes.

Of the four stages constituting the history of Western civilization, the scientific organization of nature is the only one whose task is endless. For its aim can never be consummated, at least within the time-dimensions we know. The objectives of the preceding stages on the contrary were necessarily limited. External limitation holds good for the organization of a world state. There, the extension of the known globe in Roman times and of the whole globe today is the manifest boundary. In the formation of personality on the other hand, which was achieved during the Greek, humanistic and neo-classic periods, the mind was satisfied when it found that it could attain that ideal and arrive at perfection. The extension of this achievement, that is in the forming of an ever larger number of such constituted personalities, was merely incidental and extraneous to the achievement as such. The same thing is true with regard to the supernatural. For self-realization in the sphere of religion, it sufficed that one religion be created whose structure presented in all its aspects the mark of the Western mind.

Unity in Variety

But no such limitations mark the theoretical organization of nature and its application. This is a process without end. There is nothing external to stop its evolution since the science of nature embraces everything in existence, be it infinitely large or infinitely small. Nor can it be said, as it can be of the Greek formation of personality or of religion in the Middle Ages, that science contains its own internal limits. It is not so much that scientific theories are in constant flux and change. Rather the point is this. There is the central fact that no field of nature can ever be scientifically penetrated so that it represents the organization of nature in the same manner and with the same perfection as did the Greek formation of personality, and as did the satisfactory organization of the supernatural by the Church. Neither of these latter two realizations points to anything beyond. But this is precisely what happens to the modern scientist. Here the physicist, investigating the last constituent elements—atoms, molecules, electrons and the like—inevitably reaches a point where, unable to proceed alone, he turns to inorganic chemistry. Then this in turn leads him into organic chemistry. The process proceeds leading through physiology into biology and ending up with the science of psychology. Once in the realm of the mind, the scientist again finds his efforts barred. He falls back on physiology, and thereupon the whole process starts over again in inverse direction.

New insights are won, but there is no hope that this circle will ever come to an end. There is no fulcrum, no place of rest, let alone any definite conclusion. Thus the organization of nature, unlike the objectives of the preceding stages, reaches towards its objective in infinity.

* * *

No one who is not blinded by the prodigious progress of science and technique can ignore the danger, unprecedented in history, which is concealed in the illimitability of this venture. For it diverts men's thought, will and emotions and estranges them from their natural and adequate aims, subjugating them narrowed and distorted to its own purpose. Faced with this imminent threat of impoverishment of the Western mind and the perversion of its civilization, it becomes increasingly important to ask what would balance and canalize this scientific process so as to make it serve man as a whole and assume its due and beneficent place in the world. There are those who would reinstate Greek and humanistic ideas as the leading forces in our educational system. There are others who believe in a revival of Christianity. Both seem unaware that the formation of personality and the structuralization of the supernatural as well are sovereign ideals that belong to the past. The time of their uncontested ascendancy in Western civilization is over. They still may and indeed they should contribute their share, but to hope for their reinstatement now when another power holds sway is to ignore the very structure of Western civilization. Thus, since neither an insight into the needs of the situation, nor the resuscitation of the past is powerful enough to cope with this danger, from whence might the nostrum come?

According to the structure of Western civilization, a great and effective countermove would occur only if a new stage with its new objective were called forth to compete with and eventually to supersede the present stage, becoming in its turn the paramount power. It is not inconceivable that such a new stage may even now be rising above the horizon. Conceivably this might take the form of a reorientation and reconstruction of Western society which would not be based, as was that of Rome, upon the political domination of a single people. Useless it is to wonder what peoples of the Western world might be destined for the main part of this task; what price would have to be paid; whether the old continent of Europe would be instrumental in finding the definitive form of Western society; and whether the initiative would shift to Russia or rather to America, since the rigid monotony of the Russian system is in complete contradiction to that great structural principle of the West, unity in variety. And equally unprofitable is it to speculate whether war and destruction will have to pave the way for the creation of such a new society or whether it can be worked out through peaceful co-operation.

Though such a tentative anticipation of the future is an extrapolation of the structure of Western evolutionary civilization, it lies beyond our immediate argument. For our purpose is the demonstration of this structure as it appears in an objective view, characterizing its stages as well as its evolution in time. With respect to time, it has been shown that in Western civilization it plays a vital part as evolutionary time. In this civilization the idea of evolution achieves its clearest and highest expression. Not only is there a succession of meaningful stages, but each stage, while resting on its predecessor, produces something entirely new and unpredictable. And the whole evolutionary process is based upon and upheld by that one structure: unity in variety, as mirrored in an organism. Against this background the Oriental mind and civilization must now be presented and understood.

CHAPTER II

Juxtaposition and Identity

The physical features of that part of Asia which gave rise to Eastern civilization reflect the architectural plan of the East in the same way that European geography expresses the structure of European civilization. Separated by a huge mountain-wall from the Near East, Persia is barred in turn from India by desert and mountains. To the eastward the massifs of the Eastern Himalayas constitute almost insurmountable obstacles between India and China. Then the ocean separates China and Japan. Albeit these natural barriers are not prohibitive, they have seriously obstructed land communication on a large scale between these cultural zones. For a sea route never compensates for the lack of convenient land communications.

The coast-wise trade between China and India and between India and Persia dates from a remote past. Though at various times Buddhist monks went to China by sea, it was Chinese pilgrims like Fa Hsien and Hiuen Tsang who in the early fifth and seventh centuries A.D. returned to their country with the Buddhist message. They were the men who penetrated Indian life and brought back both the Holy Scriptures for translation and assimilation and works of Buddhist art which became sources of artistic inspiration.

Persia proved her cultural power and magnetism by the transformation she effected on her invaders. Her own ephemeral conquests of parts of India never amounted to much until the Persianized Mogul emperors succeeded in establishing dominion in the first half of the sixteenth century. Penetrations of this kind were insular and the most important was the impingement of Chinese civilization upon Japan. No universal and perennial interchange of culture ever existed between these four regions. This lack is peculiarly evident from the fact that throughout Eastern history the main stream of influence ran in an easterly direction from Persia to India, from India to China and from China to Japan. No corresponding cultural movement ever ran in the opposite direction—a phenomenon which defies satisfactory explanation.

In every way the Eastern scene is the opposite of the Western. In the East there is neither a natural and continuous interpenetration of the national cultures nor a collaboration in their achievement of common objectives, nor their combination into a single evolutionary process. This lack of interchange cannot be attributed to the racial differences between the great members of the Eastern world. For they all belong to a sphere of civilization possessing the same structure, and within that sphere they have all reached the highest achievements. Indeed the relation between these great members of the Eastern world corresponds with their geographical regions. They stand side by side each in juxtaposition to the others.

Thus in precise contrast to Western nations those of the East, though belonging to one great type of civilization, have developed in relative insularity. If their lives as nations and their cultures display so many deep affinities, the reason lies solely in their structural homogeneity. And this is unsupported by either a common historical origin or a continuous mutual adjustment and collaboration. This participation in the same structure by itself gives to their juxtaposition the appearance of co-ordination. Such is the general aspect of Eastern civilization in space. And to this aspect its appearance in time also corresponds.

Among higher civilizations the relation to time is exemplified by the mode in which their past and contemporary existence is conceived and recorded. Indeed there is no safer, nor more enlightening approach to the problem than the forms of historiography which have sprung up within the different areas of civilization. In this field history—as a branch of knowledge—when measured by the standard of Western historians, the East has produced little comparable to the achievements of the West. For the scientific form of Western historiography there are several requirements.

A clear delimitation of the objective which will remain the centre of interest comes first. Then there is need of conceptual thought as the instrument of expression. This differentiates historiography from loose presentation through myth, legend, and poetry. The application of the critical method and consequently the resorting to original sources is also prerequisite. Later Western historiography requires a sense of development and a systematic context, which must establish a causal connection between events. This may take either of two forms—that is where extra-human factors determine the course of human events, or where there is a causality of psychological motivations. To these a final point may be added. This causal context could be supplanted by the teleological view. This teleological or purposeful mode of looking at history is based on the conviction that in the course of historical events aims of a more or less universal character are being realized which may or may not be perceived by their human agents. Thus this teleological point of view leads from historiography to the philosophy of history, introducing that inherent significance into history whereby the historical process as a whole, or prominent parts of it, can be understood.

Of these requirements it would be difficult to discover more than a few traces in Eastern historiography. The Eastern history is one of annals—the mere relation of events in chronological order, and even that, not always with a well-established selective principle. It might be objected that in the West too, history was restricted to annals and chronicles for a long period during the Middle Ages. Ages. While this is true, two factors are usually overlooked which compensate to a large extent for this exception to the classic rule. One is that the best of the Greek historians in the Byzantine Empire upheld during the Middle Ages the great tradition of Herodotus and Thucydides. The other is that, naïve as it might seem, a philosophy of history in the form of sacred history tried in Byzantium and the other European countries to embrace the history of humanity in one great idea. This was a clear manifestation of that universal and systematic historical sense which is peculiar to the West.

If we drop this Occidental standard and identify the historical with the chronological sense, China unquestionably developed a positive relation to time and thereby a marked historical sense. The histories of China cover a period of approximately three thousand years and if translated into English, they would constitute a library of about 450 volumes of approximately 500 pages each.[1] But they are mere annals enumerating facts of a varying character in chronological order, interspersed with interesting anecdotes. Not even Szu Ma Chien, who is considered the greatest Chinese historiographer, transcends this general model, though his presentation is more elaborate and his anecdotes are more pointed and illustrative. The enormous bulk of these chronological records constitutes invaluable material for a potential historiography and for a sociological and biographical history of China.

As for Persia, what is left in fragmentary Arabic translation of the only historiographic work—*The Book of Kings*—which stems from pre-Islamic Sassanian times reveals that it did not differ in principle from the rock inscriptions in which the Achaemenian kings immortalized their deeds. It was only after the rise of Islam with its assimilation of the Hellenistic tradition that Persian and Arab historians produced works which transcended the chronological records of royal dynasties thus widening the scope of their interest and developing a form of history nearer to the Western approach.

India's relation to time has been uncertain. Therefore her chronological recording of events is infinitely less marked and accurate than that of China. Indeed Alexander's appearance on Indian soil constitutes the first reliable date in Indian history. It is only since the Mogul conquest that the Western historian is on safe ground. Thus it is no coincidence that the three volumes *The Cultural Heritage of India*[2] which faithfully and comprehensively present the great achievements of India in all fields, from religion and metaphysical speculation to science and literature, do not even mention historiography.

Such briefly are the Eastern attitudes toward historiography. The particular relations to time concealed in these attitudes must now be interpreted from a twofold point of view—first, with regard to the psychology of the Eastern nations; and second, in order to throw into clear relief in spite of national varieties the fundamental difference between the relation to time in the West and in the East.

[1] Homer H. Dubs in *The Far Eastern Quarterly*, Nov. 1946, Vol. VI.
[2] *The Cultural Heritage of India.* Sri Ramakrishna centenary memorial. Belur Math, Calcutta, Sri Ramakrishna centenary committee, 1936.

Juxtaposition and Identity

Time as it is here considered is, of course, not abstract time. Rather it is the time-experience of distinct human groups. These time-experiences are the concrete modes in which the members of great civilizations are embedded in the time-dimension. They condition their outlook on history and consequently their different ways of writing history.

Time is the arch-enemy of all living. While over limited periods it may assume the friendlier guise of a condition wherein creation and fulfilment are possible, in its entirety time is the great annihilator of all being. The broader the consciousness, the more it perceives with despondent clarity the negative aspect of time. Against the limiting and destructive nature of time which dooms aims and creations to a haphazard death, mankind revolts. The pathetic means by which societies and civilizations rebel against time in vain efforts to neutralize its devouring effect vary according to their personalities and cultural levels.

Primitive societies pit their stubborn sameness against time's disruptive power. Fearful of being drawn into the whirlpool of time they dare not deviate from a traditioned pattern. They feel that change means handing themselves over to the fatal spirit of time. This impression of duration adduced by stagnating societies is a specific time-experience which is intended to hide its annihilating function. It is no accident that this experience of time as pure duration approaches Newton's definition of mathematical time, and gives it concrete expression: 'The absolute and mathematical time . . . is called by another name duration.'[1] Indeed, these immovable primitive societies resemble those objects of the inanimate world to which Newton chiefly referred. And this equally-flowing time earmarks their sense of time just as it inheres in the unchanging motion of the heavenly bodies.

Since in a primitive society the element of change and thereby the destructive aspect of time is thus ignored, the dramatic character of time peculiar to all higher civilization is vastly reduced. Translating this qualitative experience into quantitative terms, one may say that the sense of time in a primitive society is

[1] Newton, *Philosophiae Naturalis Principia Mathematica.* Def. VIII Scholium I. Tempus absolutum verum et mathematicum in se et natura sua sine relatione ad externum quodvis aequabiliter fluit, alioque nomine dicitur duratio.

reduced to a minimum. This finds expression in the fact that primitive man's measure of time is limited to three living generations—at the time when grandfather was a child—or it extends vaguely from some momentous event which lacks any distinct location in time—at the time of the great earthquake. Primitive society therefore is before and beside time. Its stagnation cannot even be called a negation of time since there is no clear conception but only an ignorance of time.

At the other end of the scale stand the great civilizations. A great civilization can be conceived as the result of a gigantic effort-the struggle of the mind to erect a bulwark against time's annihilating forces, until victim in an uneven battle the magnificent edifice eventually collapses. This is a positive, creative attitude which attempts not only to neutralize but to overcome time. Western and Eastern civilizations differ radically with regard to the ways and means of achieving this goal.

Western civilization not only admits time it posits time in order to vanquish it. This paradoxical attitude conditions and to a large extent explains the intricacies to which Western civilization has been subject from its beginning. The Western mind penetrates deeply into time—it takes time onto itself. In so doing, Western civilization is thus bound to time and it readily accepts it as the condition of continual change, conceiving continual change as the payment to time for survival, and survival as the retention of identity. This conviction that it is possible to remain the same in the midst of change, and more, that change constitutes the only means of maintaining one's identity, lies rooted deep in the Western mind. Moreover this conception is in harmony with the structure of Western civilization—unity in variety.[1]

Western history has fulfilled itself through successive stages each characterized by a new objective. This is a clear demonstration of a great civilization working in conformity with the idea that nothing less than continuous transformation guarantees identity with itself. This unique affirmation of time springs paradoxically from the will to defeat time by time itself. The grandeur of this attitude consists in the refusal to surrender to time or to be a

---

[1] Kant's definition of time as 'the possibility of contrarious qualities in the same object' is an abstract definition of this mind structure.

victim to the natural process of change. Western civilization assumes time's Janus-faced role of creation and destruction and implements that blind force in the building of a cosmos by an orderly process of progressive rejection and recreation.

This is the most dangerous adventure ever embarked upon by man. Only a mind foreordained by its structure to function ultimately in the study and organization of nature—an enterprise so remote from man that no other civilization has ever dreamed of it—only such a mind had the capacity, by a supreme effort at abstraction, to deal with any imaginable subject by means of conceptual thought. And this involved in the face of apparent change and self-negation a sublime faith in its own power not only to preserve but to reaffirm its identity with greater certainty. Furthermore, only a mind as flexible and insatiably curious could, in an evolution of indisputable momentum, have spun out its own self-made history.

All these factors which are so closely interwoven explain the vital interest taken by the Western mind in its own history. They also make it clear why historiography could only have originated as an essential branch of intellectual and scientific enterprise in Western civilization. However, this untiring effort of the Western mind to penetrate its past and find out its relation to other cultures draws its strength from a hidden source. This is a deep uncertainty as to itself, a doubt that recurs again and again particularly in the decisive periods of Western history.

The attraction and even fascination which the East has always exercised for the West would perhaps not carry much weight if Eastern thought had remained merely a stimulus as it did at the time of early Greek philosophy. However both the influx of Eastern creeds during the Hellenistic period and the West's adoption of an Asiatic religion with all its implications reveal a deep uncertainty in the central sphere of existence. Prolific mainly in philosophical systems and incapable of producing a great religion the Western mind bordered on religion but it had to rely on another power to open the door to that inner sanctum. This inability to create a religion, and the adoption of a foreign one coupled with the gigantic effort to assimilate it by recreating it are the deeply rooted causes of this deep uncertainty in the West.

Such doubt could emanate only from the depth of the spirit and it is unknown to the East.

It might be assumed that Western civilization would have rid itself of this uncertainty in the course of its growth. But the contrary has happened. Since the eighteenth century at least, Western civilization has become increasingly enigmatic with regard to itself—doubtful as to its essence and value—uneasy as to road and objective. In this predicament Western man turns repeatedly to history and the philosophy of history in search of equilibrium and a fulcrum. From history he hopes to learn the process of his formation, from the philosophy of history his place in the world and his significance to humanity. All this he seeks to the end of securing and stabilizing his own relation to himself.

Thus for about two hundred years the evolution of science has paralleled that of historiography. This correspondence is no mere incident. The choice of nature as the object of investigation by the West is an orientation so disparate from man's being and his concerns and so alien to his innermost needs, that it was inevitable he would become estranged from himself and a prey to those metaphysical uncertainties so apparent in the world today. Also it was almost as inevitable that history, the counterpart of science yet a recognized branch of scientific knowledge, would be regarded as the counterpoise which would lead the mind back to itself, mirroring man and thus restoring his self-knowledge and confidence.

Indeed this is the psychological origin and background of modern historiography, which is so involved and so full of significance, and has its only counterpart in the simultaneous launching of science and historiography by the Greeks. The untiring effort of modern archaeologists to extend the knowledge of man into the remote past; the research done by anthropologists and psychologists into primitive races; and the widespread interest taken in these enterprises by the public at a time when we are all involved in present-day problems and the domination of nature —the interpretation of these two seemingly incompatible developments takes us to the very heart of Western civilization. Only in Western civilization could genuine history have arisen and grown as it did.

*   *   *

Juxtaposition and Identity

From the standpoint of Eastern civilization, the attitude of the West toward time is immoderate, not to say nefarious. It is an attitude inviting retaliation. The East's attitude toward time, on the other hand, is one of pronounced discretion and wariness. The Eastern mind rarely embarks on the venture of time, and when it does it reduces the risk to a minimum. It refrains, so to speak, from provoking time's hostility. The two Eastern civilizations whose relation to time is most significant are the Chinese and the Indian.

In China, time is viewed and is experienced as succession. Succession however is naught but juxtaposition applied to time. Thus it is that China is the classic land of the chronological recording of history. In no other place has this form of historical writing been carried on so persistently nor assumed such gigantic proportions. Nowhere else have the consequences which flow from the conception of time as pure succession been so meticulously observed by the annalists. Not only did they limit their field to the events of their own lifetime, they also tabooed the records of their predecessors, never submitting their statements to criticism or amendment.[1] This conception of time as unconnected succession is at variance with that of the medieval chroniclers of the West who even when their main object was the recording of contemporary events, almost always started with a chronology of previous happenings often commencing with the creation of the world.

The relation of the Chinese to time is also revealed in the paramount factor of Chinese life and civilization—the family. The Chinese patriarchal family is distinctly characterized by its feeling for and experience of succession. An existent family possesses as it were no life of its own. It is yet it is not. Regarded as the point of intersection between the generations that recede into the dim past and those that extend into the future, the family acts as the bearer of a legacy, a trusteeship. It possesses all the dignity and responsibility inherent in an institution representative of something infinitely superior to its transitory aspect. Thus the authority invested in the patriarch is not of a personal nature. It is his because he is a potential ancestor and a trustee for his successors. The ancestors themselves are viewed as protective spirits irrevo-

[1] Cf. e.g., Ch.S. Gardner, *Chinese Traditional Historiography*, Cambridge, 1938.

44

cably connected with the family and they are therefore reverently commemorated.

Despite this overwhelming evidence for the category of succession, both in family life and in the form of history writing, the other component of the Eastern mind structure—identity—is not hard to establish. This exists in the formerly deep-rooted conviction that ancestors are continuously reborn in the living generation. More important still, the eldest son is the re-embodiment of the great-grandfather. This idea which derives from a belief current in animism is by no means a Chinese invention. But its significant aspect here is that not only was it adopted and retained by one of the highest civilizations, but assigned a significant place within the frame of its most cherished institution—the patriarchal family. The existing family is not merely a continuation of the preceding generations. It is the ancestral family itself, reborn in the one living.

The metaphysical interpretation of this belief is peculiarly interesting in connection with Chinese philosophy. This assumption that the same ancestral family is reborn and fulfilled again and again in the consecutive families imparts to the latter a deep meaning and cohesion. An insight into their metaphysical identity brings the endless generations of the family to a standstill, so to speak. Thus this ceaseless movement reaching out from the remote past into the unlimited future is before the understanding eye suddenly arrested. Past and future are now absorbed in the eternal presence of this ancestral family.

As regards the relation of the Chinese to time, this conception is of primary importance. It represents nothing less than the Chinese way of overcoming time and it epitomizes the subtlety of the Eastern mind, the Chinese mind in particular. In thus emphasizing the paramount importances to human life of the unbroken family chain, the Chinese seem to surrender unconditionally to time. However, the reincarnation of the ancestral family down through the ages introduces a deeper level of comprehension. At this level the endless continuity of time is transcended by the fact that one and the same ancestral family is ever-present.

A truly metaphysical conception this when translated into philosophical thought, and it is precisely what happens in the philosophy of Taoism. Before the eyes of the sage the iridescent scene of history to whose recording generation after generation of annalists have devoted their efforts, dwindles away into nothing. The sage penetrates the illusion and the futility of all human doings and human misdoings which result from the fallacious interplay of pairs of opposites. His is the insight that truth exists where these opposites meet and in meeting refute and annihilate each other. This knowledge, immanently realized, unites the sage with Tao. To him, doing is as not doing. He operates without effort. Good and bad, beauty and ugliness—every pair of opposites —loses its meaning. He rises above time, beyond change and outside impermanence.

Different as are the social family sphere, and the metaphysical one of Tao, the Chinese relation to time manifests itself equally in both. Just as the successive generations are revealed to the discerning mind of the sage as the eternally recurring ancestral family, so the endless drama of the world with its pairs of opposites disappears before him and he perceives behind it the immovable reality of Tao. This then is the way that the Chinese mind with infinite subtlety neutralizes the ghastly power of time. And it is achieved by means of the category of identity.

Among the great civilizations, India is the only one of which it may be said that it almost completely lacks any historic sense. No dates or events in Indian records can be taken at face value. Whatever historic material there is in such voluminous holy writings as the Smritis and Puranas, it must be unearthed and separated from poetic descriptions of a fantastic cosmology, the legendary history of the gods, the expounding of ritual, and the explanation of the caste system and its social consequences. Nonetheless, if a people of such astounding achievements and contributions to world civilization have utterly discarded anything approaching our idea of historiography, this ahistorical attitude cannot be dismissed as a mere deficiency. There must be powerful motivations for this attitude. And indeed there are. India's penetrating insight into history's lack of significance is one of them and her trenchant evaluation of the individual and his fate as the only historical reality is the other. With regard to the first, the Indian attitude toward history is well expressed in the words of Arthur Schopenhauer:

Juxtaposition and Identity

'The true philosophy of history consists in the insight that in all these endless changes and their confusion we have always before us only the same, even, unchanging nature, which today acts in the same way as yesterday and always; thus it ought to recognize the identical in all events, of ancient as of modern times, of the East as of the West; and, in spite of all difference of the special circumstances, of the costumes and customs, to see everywhere the same humanity. This identical element which is permanent through all change consists in the fundamental qualities of the human heart—many bad, few good. The motto of history in general should run: *Eadem, sed aliter*.'[1]

If the same play is performed always and everywhere the historical interest is scarcely more than a spurious, a fallacious and a useless curiosity. For a single look at the plot, the motives and aims of the ever-changing actors, is enough to reveal the emptiness of the anarchic effort we call history. People, nations, humanity are the agents of history and the subjects of historiography. But in India their aims and actions are considered futile and doomed to destruction. What reality there is in this world resides in the individual, not as a link and member of the historical process, but in him as such.

There is another process in which the individual participates and where his fate is worked out. This is the karmatic or causal process of reincarnation. Whereas history and the historical process are essentially concerned with groups, the subject of this karmatic process is the individual. Here on his erratic way to salvation the individual lives out his real history and before the solemnity of this road to eternity history in the usual sense evaporates into naught. But it cannot be assumed that two individuals share the same fate on their wanderings through incalculable incarnations.

Thus India, it may be concluded, is interested not in world history but in the specific histories of individuals. It is this inner process, not the chain of activities and events in the outside world, that constitutes the true history of the individual. In this karmatic

---

[1] Arthur Schopenhauer, *The World as Will and Idea*. Translated from the German by R. B. Haldane, M.A. 7, Kemp. M.A. 8 edit. London, Kegan Paul, French Trubner & Co., Vol. 111, p. 227.

process, the individual is no longer the exponent of social and other conditions, nor the product of hereditary influences. Here, the circumstances of his birth and life are pre-ordained, determined by the karma acquired and accumulated by him in his past existences.

But this does not exhaust the subject. From the fate of the individual, India, ignoring historiography and the fate of nations, rises straight and immediately to the cosmic spheres. In the Indian view these are those boundless and numberless worlds which coexist with the known universe and succeed each other in an eternal and unchangeable rhythm. According to their belief all these worlds unfold in four unequal stages of decreasing moral and spiritual value which range from 1,728,000 years to 432,000 years.[1] The cycle composed of these four stages, or yugas as they are called, is a great yuga and it covers 4,320,000 years. A thousand of these yugas is called a kalpa which is a single day of Brahma. And at the end of this the universe disappears. But even the lifetime of a Brahma is limited. It consists of 100 Brahma years, each measured by the length of the Brahma day or kalpa. At the end of this vast period all existing worlds are absorbed into the Absolute. Then the gigantic cycle of 311,040,000,000,000 human years starts anew. Assuredly this conception of sublime grandeur involves a conception of time which competes with the time measurements of modern astronomers.

★   ★   ★

To return to our main topic—the relation of the East to time and its consequent attitude toward history—it is clear that India, far from lacking a passionate interest in and an intense feeling of time, is fundamentally preoccupied with it under the aspect of the impermanence of all that exists. Whatever is, is the victim of time and the true nature of time is victimization. Now time everywhere presents itself to immediate experience as filled, qualified time. But the prime characteristic of India is that the interpenetrating phenomena of perceived and imagined reality which constitute this experience deluge the mind with a force so terrifying that

---

[1] Cf. Heinrich Zimmer, *Myths and Symbols in Indian Art and Civilization*, edited by Joseph Campbell, Pantheon Books, New York, 1946, pp. 15–19

vast systems such as the cosmic cycles, the wheel of karma and reincarnation have had to be invented to resist the assault, to save man's consciousness, and to secure to him a place amid this pandemonium.

India, spellbound by the spectacle of existence and the splendour of creation, was all the more repelled by the blind cruelty of destruction. It is the endless revolution of the universe, the worlds of gods and men—not the minute, the confused, and the meaningless history of mankind—with which she is concerned. Instead of a philosophy of history conferring significance and purpose on the doings and fate of mankind, there evolved there an ever-recurring cycle of boundless worlds in which and from which a rational being might work out his own salvation.

India stands as a monument to the general fact that to the Eastern mind time is ever filled—concrete time. Time is experienced and recognized as adhering to phenomena—as undetachable a quality as extension or colour and the like. Since it is the phenomena either external or mental, which are significant, time consists in the course of man's natural experience in the happening of these phenomena, as they are present or remembered or expected. At this point the Eastern mind leaves off. The idea of an abstract or absolute time never develops, never has a life of its own in philosophical and scientific thought.

In so far as the notion of an abstract and absolute time was formed at all, as in the *Zervan Akerene* of Zoroastrianism, it did not transcend the nature of a vague metaphysical idea subservient to the religious realm. Never did it capture the attention of pure philosophy, mathematics, or science. The efforts of Greek philosophers to penetrate the mystery of time are just as alien to the Eastern mind as are the time-intuitions and conceptions of Western mathematicians and physicists. The Eastern mind perceives and weighs only what time effects with the phenomena. It does not possess the disinterested and dispassionate attitude of the West which truncates its emotional bonds with the phenomena in order to build up systems of thought which lack immediate relations with human needs.

Time, then, in the East has no reality in its own right independent of time experienced. For there a basic aversion exists to those abstractions of a purely conceptual character which constitute the life and essence of Western philosophy. Their place is to a large extent taken by symbols or personifications inspired by religion and destined for spiritual practice. The temptation to regard this aversion as incapacity is not easily resisted. However, at the metaphysical level, incapacity and unwillingness merge. Where the spirit of a great civilization is born, the opposition of knowledge and will, and of will and capacity, does not exist. This is why the relation of the East to time exemplifies a deep disinclination on its part to have the wholeness of experience dissolve into independent parts. The Eastern mind strives rigorously to prevent the decomposition of knowledge into elements of a purely theoretical nature. It tries to keep it within the boundaries of man's manifest spiritual and material needs. The approximation of knowledge to application and its coordination with action confer on it a human character irrespective of its content and despite those forms which to us at times seem strange and abstruse.

Whatever the idea and form time takes, be it conciliatory or inexorable, it always remains near at hand, full of meaning, and close to man's nature and destination. To the Chinese and the Far East in general, time exists in the uninterrupted continuation of society through the patriarchal family. Here it is essentially one-dimensional, without any visible beginning or end and unchangeable in that it neither progresses nor deteriorates. In Zoroastrian Persia, the idea and experience of time is bound up with the metaphysical struggle between the powers of good and evil which ends in the definitive subjugation of evil. Since the Persian king is entrusted with the mission of rallying in this fight all men of good will, the atmosphere is religious and political. In this light, while time is limitless, it proceeds, so to speak, in a diagonal ascending line until the final victory of Good, whereupon it continues eternally on the same plane.

In India two entirely differing times co-operate to constitute the picture of the world. First, there is curved time. This is exemplified in the enormous cycles of existence which start from and return to that timeless state when the godhead is at rest with itself. On the other hand, there is the time of individual man whereby he fulfils his predestined path of karma, now approaching, now moving away from the final goal. This last may be called zigzagged time to express the ups and downs of fate.

The link between these two differing, if not incompatible, conceptions of time lies in their function for the goal of salvation. The never-ending cycle of creation and destruction which is both inhuman and superhuman fills man with terror and desolation and with the inevitable desire to escape from such an inferno. By contrast the karmatic way pictures man tangled in the whirlpool of existence but at the same time presents him with the possibility of putting an end to the process.

* * *

The relation to time of the West when viewed against that of the East, presents certain similarities. On investigation however these instances cannot be regarded as expressive of the core and substance of the Western mind. For example, the North Germanic tribes created a myth of rare grandeur in the destruction of the world of gods and men—the twilight of the gods—out of which a new world was to be born. But here there is a striking difference. The cycle occurs but once. The world comes into being, is destroyed and replaced by another, and then the process ends. In the 'Edda', we likewise find a few examples of the idea of reincarnation, but here also it occurs but once, and is unconnected with moral or spiritual issues.

The Greek scene offers the characteristic variety. In ancient times the prevailing idea seems to have been of a world process degenerating in four stages, from the golden to the iron age. Heraclitus introduced the conception of an endlessly recurring world creation and destruction. But he looked at the cosmic process of rotating cycles from the angle of a scientist and metaphysician. From it he drew no religious implications, and he brought into his description thoughts of a speculative depth and dialectical power which make his philosophy the true precursor of the Hegelian system. The theory of reincarnation is also clearly expressed by Anaximenes and by Plato in his *Timaios*.

Whatever the origin of these ideas—whether they grew on Western soil or were introduced from the East—their influence on Greek life and time-experience was negligible, nor did they influence the main trends of Greek thought which followed other roads. The rejection of these ideas testifies with even greater force to the unswerving self-assurance of the Greek mind than if they had never appeared at all. As to experience the Greeks, until the Periclean era, lived time with full consciousness as evolutionary time, which as has been noted, is by no means necessarily connected with progress. Moreover, to the Greeks, the notion of progress scarcely conveyed more than the connotation 'to be worthy of the forefathers'. To the Greek in the flowering period, the evolution of the world was a unique process, one-dimensional and linear, with a beginning but no indication of an end—its distinctive mark being a rapid conversion from the mythological period into consciously lived and recorded history.

Here then we find the three main elements constituting the West's relation to time—the one-dimensional and linear aspect— the evolutionary and historical character—and coupled with these two elements the stress laid on man in the temporal process. For the distinctive place thus assigned to man in the evolution of the universe clearly conditions both the linear aspect of time and its predominantly historical character. Again while their superior evaluation of man confers upon his acts and fate an importance which warrants their recording and elaboration, the conception of linear time guarantees the uniqueness of man's appearance.

Now it is this uniqueness which is denied by the idea of time in ever-recurring cycles. In the endless repetition of ever the same phenomena, the Indian has indeed invented a grandiose and ghastly system to demonstrate to himself the futility and nothingness of his own, as of all, existence. True, the cosmic myth of the North Germanic people does not concede man the pre-eminent place in creation, and the Nordic worlds of gods and men with their tragic atmosphere and traces of reincarnation only vaguely recall the Indian scene. But the significant fact remains that in the Nordic creed the creation and destruction of the world and the birth of a new one is a cosmic drama which happens only once.

The conception of the Middle Ages follows in its great lines the Greek paradigm. It even stresses the essential features—time, linear and limited, moving between well-determined events, the creation of the world and the reappearance of the Saviour announcing the world's end. Medieval time is eminently historical time, so much so that God by His incarnation exalts man's history, just as the creation of the world for man's sake increases beyond any conceivable measure man's importance and value.

Starting with the Renaissance the modern period emphasized man's central place in the universe. Despite the discovery of the earth as but a planet among others, this concept continued, enlarging the scope and value of history and historical consciousness, while time, retaining its one-dimensional character, became infinite. Not even Darwin's theory of descendance, which was a far greater blow to man's unique position in the universe than the Copernican revolution, was able to shake this conviction of man's supremacy. Indeed, while theoretically undermining the earth's and man's privileged place in the universe, the age of science has not destroyed man's inherent belief in his ascendancy.

It might be suggested that China and Persia as well recognized a one-dimensional time process. Persia, at least in the spiritual realm, conceived even time as an evolution consisting in the progressive triumph of the Good. Such a comparison, however, only throws into further relief the trenchant difference in line with our last argument. For in Persia the great actors in the dramatic struggle between Good and Evil are the divine principles themselves. Man is but a helper in this metaphysical battle. In China, it must be remembered, the exclusive place is held by the family and the individual exhausts his life and its significance in the service of the family. Finally in India, man as he subsists in the cosmic cycle, shares with all creatures the need for salvation, and only in so far as he strives for and achieves this goal does he participate in reality. Here in a sense is an over-emphasis on individualism, but for the fact that Indian individualism is restricted to the realm of salvation.

Indeed, that conception of the individual and his place in the universe which most closely approaches that of the West, exists in the Near East and more particularly with the people of Israel. The desire of the Near Eastern peoples to record historical events and hand them on to posterity matches that of the Chinese. The great number of peoples of various races and languages which since prehistoric times have invaded and settled in the Near East, seem to have fostered the birth of national consciousness by the pitting of one against another. Israel it was, however, that in restricted form developed a view of history and man which contained elements similar to the Western conception. True, while there is in the Old Testament the constant interference of God in world affairs, and the only subject of historiography is the chosen people, yet there is also an unfailing endeavour to explain events and to understand the motivation of men and their fate by psychological means or with reference to God's intentions. But above and beyond this is the emphasis laid by the Old Testament on individual personality, the value assigned to it, and the perfect psychological characterization of all the main figures. And this characterization brings them to life in a way and to a degree unknown in the records of the East.

* * *

Albeit this presentation of the Eastern mind and civilization against the background of the West is the most illuminating approach, it does suffer from a natural disadvantage. For the East in many respects lacks what the West cherishes as its most valuable possessions. Furthermore it lacks them without offering by Western standards any necessary equivalents. The net result is that our first outlook suffers from a certain incompleteness. The reader will do well to bear in mind that only by steady progress into the study will this impression be corrected.

The basic fact is that the Eastern mind and civilization pose difficulties of description and analysis greater than those of the West. The first obvious reason for this is that our approach to the East is by necessity conditioned by our own mind structure and the intellectual patterns that derive from it. Then again there may be objective reasons for these difficulties which are inherent in the structure of the Eastern mind and civilization. Let it be emphasized, however, that each structure by itself and by its nature is clear and simple. It is in their application to and their penetration of the visible and invisible worlds that world conceptions are evoked which are strikingly different from each other. In this respect it is true that the civilization of the East, though spreading out in powerful splendour across space and time, does not reveal its architectural principle to us with the same ubiquitous clarity as does that of the West.

Juxtaposition and identity—this is the structure of the Eastern mind and civilization as contrasted with the *unity in variety* which is the characteristic structural principle of the West. Juxtaposition implies the positing of data—thoughts, emotions, attitudes, institutions, and the like—which data the Eastern mind feels no need to interrelate in order to establish a unit or an order. This capacity that the East has for leaving the data insulated and accepting them as such is evident from the way the Eastern mind deals with contradictions. Far from wanting to dissolve them, to bridge them by interpolating links, or to subordinate them to superior data as the West always strives to do, the East seems to a high degree unaware of or at the least indifferent to the clash of the contraries. The single may be left single, multiplicity and variety may subsist, and pairs of opposites may remain untouched.

However, when and if it is felt necessary to free the solitary from its isolation, to do away with all the multiplicity and above all to overcome contradictions and the pairs of opposites, then the instrumental category applied by the East is identity. The East is the virtuoso of identification. *Identification* plays the same decisive role there as does *unity* in the Western structure. Just as organic *unity* is the principle by which the undetermined multiplicity of the world is overcome in the West, so *identification* is the counterpoise of separateness, multiplicity and contrariness in the East.

It should not be difficult to comprehend how intimately identification corresponds to juxtaposition. The clear separation implied by juxtaposition excludes compromise and transition. Thus identification necessarily emerges as the sole and radical means of establishing unity. Nothing but the fundamental operating procedure of the Eastern mind has been characterized in these statements. Needless to say many manifestations of Eastern civilizations, while bearing this structural mark, do not express this structure to perfection and this applies equally to Western civilization.

This structure, juxtaposition and identity, appears simple, yet at the same time radical. If to us it seems an over-simplicity and to evidence a lack of initiative to let things and ideas—even contraries—subsist in insulation and then to redeem them from that insulation by identification, it would be imprudent to abide by such an impression and then to pass judgment accordingly. True, the Easterner may go a long way either in the realm of the mind or in the affairs of the world before changing this attitude and acting. And this attitude may verge on indifference or *naïveté*. But it may also assume the proportions of a superior tolerance and endurance, a deep modesty, a remoteness from or an almost religious reverence toward all that exists. And thereby there may be realized not only particular insights into the nature of things and man, but exalted forms of human dignity.

Complementary to and contrastable with this attitude, there is an extremism in the East which resolutely reaches beyond things given, to a position from which, regardless of phenomena, identification sets in, undermining the single, absorbing multiplicity and fusing the contraries. All this may be done with a sovereign contempt for intermediary links. There is a tendency in this toward what we would consider short circuits, or even violent solutions— a strange and unexpected counterpart of the indulgence inherent in juxtaposition. Thus at first glance the East appears a realm of superlatives and extremes, iridescent and unseizable, earthbound and transcendental, uncertain and inexorable.

In thus illustrating the operation of the structural principle in Eastern civilization psychological terms have been used. However no general psychological characterization of the Easterner should be implied. In the description of Western civilization it has been amply demonstrated that the structure realizes itself in the form and in the main aspect of a civilization, in its outstanding creations and its great individuals. While the psychology of the mass of people also bears the mark of the structure in varying degrees, it is not formed by it as are the higher expressions of the civilization. This is why all that has been said about the structural principle in action, though it points to psychology, must not be taken as describing the psychology of the Easterner as such.

CHAPTER III

State and Society—I

The embracing in one vision of two structurally different civilizations is a delicate task and its difficulties can be neutralized only be constant caveats. There is hardly a term which can pass without clarification and redefinition. In a strict sense and in the absence of a common background and yardstick, comparison and evaluation are, save in exceptional instances, impossible. The structures themselves, the main creations fully expressing these structures, and such fundamental phenomena as the concrete architecture of the two civilizations cannot really be compared and evaluated. One can only set one alongside the other.

The man of the East accepts his social conditions and the established political form as natural and unalterable in principle. They are gifts from above and a liability. He is not, as the Westerner is, urged to disengage himself from what his experience tells him is the given data of existence in order that he may question and change them for the sake of other conceivably preferable data. In this conservative attitude of the East there is enormous power, and it is not only the power to stand, endure and abide.

The first evidence of this is the sudden force with which the Eastern civilizations burst into being. They had their incubation period, a period almost completely lost in the dim light of prehistory. But unlike Greek civilization which reached its peak through a clear and logical evolution, these civilizations seem to have achieved maturity at a rate far exceeding that of the Greeks or of Western civilization in general.

To the West, Eastern civilization appears conservative and stagnant. This is a rash and superficial judgment. It stems from a blind transference of Western standards, and an incapacity or unwillingness to admit of the Eastern form of mind and existence. In Eastern civilization there is inherent a power that is no less remarkable and efficient than that of the West because it operates in a subtler and less conspicuous manner. The East's reservoir of forces constitutes a concentration of intense power which is at variance with the West's power which moves by extension and the distribution of energy.

Thus it follows that Eastern man will adhere with pious fidelity and intensity to and persevere in whatever he creates in the material and immaterial sphere including the idea he has of himself. His creations are part of him and he is part of them. The Westerner, on the other hand, will at any given moment take his stand intellectually and emotionally outside his creations and in so doing he prepares the way for replacing them by others.

There is an outstanding example illustrative of the contrary functioning of these two types of mind. All human groups, be they primitive or civilized and particularly the politically united, think of themselves as superior to all the rest. If this be true of the Western and Eastern nations in relation to their sister nations, it stands out with even greater clarity in the relation between West and East as entities. However, in these contrasted attitudes the psychological character of the East's point of view is totally different from that of the West. At all times the West's conviction of its superiority has been compatible with its interest in the East. Beginning with the Greeks, the Western people evinced a marked curiosity as to other men and civilizations. Though Eastern ways and customs differed from and contradicted their own, rendering comprehension extremely difficult, they recognized though to a rather lesser degree in the Middle Ages, the achievements of the East.

This appreciation of foreign merits however in no way interfered with the West's conviction of its own pre-eminence. Hand in hand with an elementary desire to extend its horizon went an equally irresistible urge to reveal itself to the East. Indeed, the West not only lacked any inhibitions concerning its innermost thoughts but it invited the East to share in its ideas, its intentions and its institutions. Albeit this was a truly human attitude, it bore, due to the West's assumption of superiority, fatal fruit. The West insisted more and more on its right, nay moral duty, to introduce into the East its own products from religion to cheap merchandise. According to their nature the Eastern people failed to reciprocate. Aware of the threat to their life and ideas implicit in the West's attitude, they offered a passive resistance to this type of holy zeal, opening neither their hearts nor their ports. And to a certain extent this very resistance kindled in the West an aggressive fanaticism prompted by the will to power and embracing all spheres, religious, cultural, economic, and political.

The East's sense of superiority assumed another form altogether. This involved a complete independence of everything outside its own world. The West had always stood in need of contact and communication, gaining thereby a deeper confidence in its own being and essence. But such exteriorization and interchange were never of importance to the East. The East, with the exception of Buddhism, had little inclination to proselytise. Only the Semitic people of the Near East—Phoenicians, Jews and Arabs—possessed the indomitable interest in the surrounding world characteristic of the West. This self-containedness, this self-sufficiency of Eastern man invested him with a dignity and aristocratic reserve which had never failed to impress the Westerner. And this regardless of whether or not this attitude was accompanied by corresponding human values. Even in its aspect of deference and humility, this attitude may be compared to the British talent for understatement—the tendency of a people so rooted in the conviction of their own superiority that they can easily afford a gesture of obliging politeness.

Before the East began to change under Western influence there is no doubt that it considered the Westerner's attitude childish, uncouth, indiscreet and shameless, not only lacking in respect and reserve, but betraying by that lack a strange want of self-confidence. The East's self-esteem, more solidly entrenched than the West's because it subsisted without feeding as it were on foreign capital, was a bad soil for the missionary spirit, religious and cultural. Nor had the East any desire to admit the West into its own sphere of life and thought. In this connection a striking and characteristic fact must arrest attention. The East certainly had its full share in warfare and conquest. However, neither of the two world-conquerors who appeared on the soil of Asia, Jenghiz Khan (d. 1227) and Timur (d. 1404), belonged by origin and tradition to any of the great Eastern civilizations or religions. Jenghiz Khan adhered to the Shamanistic creed of his nomadic ancestors, Timur embraced Islam. The Eastern mind as a whole wants to remain within itself. From this form of existence it gathers its own specific energies. In any case, the Eastern peoples, by their instinctive or fully conscious reactions, indicate clearly that they have always been fully aware of dangers threatening their congenital existence.

In their relations to outside influences, these secluded and self-sufficient civilizations differ basically from the Western. In so far as they allow any influence from without, they are careful to limit its radiation even at the price of depriving it of its original meaning and productive value. Examples of this typical reaction abound, particularly since the time when the Eastern nations could no longer defend themselves against the impact of the West. They felt that in order to survive, they had to receive certain Western ideas and inventions. Yet they shrank from acknowledging the importance of these innovations in the vain hope of limiting the West's influence to the periphery of their lives.

However, once a large enough breach had occurred, the consequences were of necessity infinitely greater than they would have been in the West. This was due to the absence of a habitual and quickly operating assimilative power. And since the cleft once made could not be closed, the traditional order suffered a shock which for a time threatened its creative power and blocked the march of traditional life. In this connection there come to mind the experiences of not a few primitive peoples who, upon coming in contact with Western civilization, paid for their inability to adjust to it with a rapid racial decline or collective suicide. The defenceless primitive was struck the roots of his bare existence. Not so, of course, the man of the East—child of a great and old civilization. Even when the very fundaments of his civilization are being questioned and parts of it are beginning to crumble, he is protected by that inalienable endurance and self-confidence which preserve the vital forces of existence in the face of tomorrow's uncertainty.

Be it emphasized, there is no indication whatsoever that the stagnation apparent in Eastern civilization during these last 150 years results from a natural decline—an exhaustion of vitality or creative force. On the contrary, it is due rather to a long process of corrosion beginning with its contacts with the West. Increasing and intensifying, these opened the breach and slowly ate away the marrow of Eastern civilization. Indeed one may assume that had they been permitted to continue their traditional life without interruption from the West, all Eastern civilizations would have proceeded to unfold values worthy of their past. Even as late as the Emperor Ch'ien Lung, 1736–1796, China passed through a period of efflorescence, while Japan in the first part of the nineteenth century did not betray the least sign of decadence. Persia, under Fath Ali Shah, 1797–1834, recovering from a long and unfortunate term of wars, civil wars and misrule, might have reached her former heights had it not been for constant interference in her domestic affairs for the benefit of foreign powers. As for India, she survived greater hardships than the decline of the Mogul dynasty without suffering the loss of her vital creative power.

We may therefore conclude that it was not their own stagnancy which delivered the Eastern peoples into the hands of the West. On the contrary, it was a stagnation that developed inversely as a result of their contact with the West. And this was not a fateful contagion of Western customs and vices. Rather the significant fact is that the structure of Eastern civilization had caused a pre-determined reaction to intrusion by the West. This closed and self-sufficient system with its unwillingness and incapacity to assimilate foreign elements suffered from a susceptibility which in due course paralysed—not its powers of defence, because it had none—but, as it were, its central nervous system. It is significant that the distinctive but not indigenous civilization of Japan alone was able at the last moment to defend its independence by assimilating, though with a remarkable inner reserve, the essential elements of the modern world.

Such are the two types of civilization as distinguished by the two forms of energy pervading them. These may be termed extensive energy and intensive energy. Its form of energy determines not only the life of a civilization but also the way of its death. Accordingly just as the ways of life differ in both civilizations, so do the causes of potential death. If death occurs, Eastern civilization will die from an inherent incapacity to ward off the onslaught of a civilization opposed in structure to hers. Without such an onslaught, there is no innate, no discoverable reason for the East's death. Consequently, if its death occurred, it would be due to the coincidence of two different factors—an outward challenge, and an inexpedient and injurious reaction to that challenge.

On the other hand, if Western civilization should ever come to an end, or if the process of decline be assumed already to be under way, no such external causes are needed to account for the catastrophe. It would die, not from an inadequate response to external challenge, but from the actualization of an intrinsic danger—one concealed in its extensive form of energy. It might happen that the stream of this energy, having coursed through the changing objectives of successive periods, should be suddenly arrested at one and the same objective and utterly exhaust itself in the effort to perform an impossible task.

If this be now true, the Western mind, belying appearances, may run the risk of losing its unity and its inner connection with the past, thereby emptying its structural principle, unity in variety, of living significance. It cannot be denied that the possibility of such a fate threatens Western civilization at the present time, a time that envisages the organization of nature. On the other hand one might consider the organization of society to be the next possible stage in the Western process, the logical and preordained end of Western civilization. Whatever view be taken in this matter, the cause of the death of Western civilization would be concealed in its own organism.

Admitting these deductions, we are faced with an apparent paradox. The closed system of Eastern civilization with its intensive form of energy is theoretically immortal—to end its life the death-blow must be delivered from the outside. Western civilization, *per contra* with its readiness to expand and to master one great objective after another, is doomed to die by the principle inherent in its own nature. This paradox, however, dissolves in the face of the simple, pertinent fact that the number of objectives is naturally limited and that for this reason Western civilization must sooner or later reach its apogee, whereas Eastern civilization, with its intuitive aversion to abstracting the distinctive spheres of existence from the whole and dealing with each separately, preserves its claim to potential immortality.

* * *

The background just outlined is essential to a full comprehension and appreciation of the concrete aspects of western and eastern civilization. The remainder of this chapter and the next one will now be devoted to their social and political forms, leaving the intellectual and spiritual spheres to be dealt with later.

The social and political institutions of the East cannot compare in number and variety with those of the West. But what they lack in this respect is compensated by their binding force, their endurance and their commanding weight. And they owe this weight to the fact that they are deeply rooted in elementary, instinctive life. Furthermore, they remain so throughout the whole march of civilization, with the Chinese family and the Indian caste system on one hand, and autocratic kingship, the dominating form of political existence, on the other. The objection that all civilization is founded on instinctive life is relevant only in a broad biological sense. Applied to the present problem it is invalid.

All civilization starts with a definite, a decisive move of the awakening mind. Thereby that mind confronts the whole sphere of instinctive life, weighs its value, and determines its stand in regard to it. Whether civilization be assumed to emerge or to develop from the instinctive level, it is this mental awareness, this intellectual independence which gives it a significant autonomy and distinguishes it from the primitive and the barbaric. At this critical awakening a new chapter opens in the history of the mind. Consciousness makes a revolutionary move forward. Then with that decision which establishes its future relation to instincts based life, a great civilization appears.

Adopting the word nature for the sum of instincts, which is the foundation of precivilized group life, it is this taking of a deliberate attitude toward nature that constitutes the change from primitive to civilized life. This decision is, as it were, the simultaneous coming to birth, the legitimization, and the first creative act of civilization. Particularly is this true of Eastern and Western civilization where this truncation is clearly visible. This coincides with the first appearance of either structure, that is to say with the momentous phenomena by means of which each of these two minds unmistakably express their respective structures, the structures themselves both containing and determining their relation to nature. At present, this relation alone is our preoccupation particularly that aspect of it evidenced by their social and political institutions.

In principle a choice exists between two attitudes with regard to nature, the positive and the negative. While such radical positions are unrealistic and therefore not likely to be taken at the start of a civilization, the main trends of the two civilizations in question point clearly in these opposite directions. In the East the relation to nature is distinctly receptive, appreciative. In all Eastern countries the patriarchal family, as it was handed down from earlier times, remained the basis of society, sanctified by religious ritual and moral philosophy in China and strengthened in India by the caste system which was also to a large extent rooted in the instinctual plane. As to political forms, Eastern civilization inherited that most ancient institution, the tribal or magic chief, and elaborated it into the powerful institution of autocratic kingship. And this became almost the only form of government known to the East. There is, then, in the East a deep confidence in nature. No urge is felt to deviate from its ways or to question its function as the basis of society. Thus the social and political institutions of the East assume a twofold force. One derives from the natural power of instinct, and the other from the unquestioned value conferred on these institutions by the conscious mind.

Starting with the Greeks, Western man took a reserved and critical attitude toward nature. This attitude accompanies him through history. It finds expression in his uncertainty as to what nature really is, and what the elementary drives of men are and how they should be evaluated. Equally apparent is it in his resulting confidence in reason as the power qualified to question nature and to substitute for it his reason-made institutions. While the man of the East rose above the natural plane only to confirm and thereby dignify it, the man of the West stepped out of that plane, and in so doing abandoned the ground from which he could view and reflect upon it. In his scrutiny of the natural basis of group life, he became aware not only of the threat to the foundations of his social and political institutions, but also of the hazards involved in his choice of reason as the sole determinant. Lost to the innocence of the primitive and despising the cautious wisdom of the East, Western man proceeded with his reason in search of a solution capable of restoring that balance which reason itself had destroyed. In this paradox the West thus pays with a life of unrest and adventure for the unbounded freedom of what the Greeks termed the *logos*. This is man's reason and the splendour of its creations.

This uncertainty of the West with regard to the natural foundation of civilized life finds its first expression in the Greek heroic age. There man's mythical ancestry unfolds a vast pageant. His crimes and perversities are barely matched by acts of generosity and sacrifice. The picture is one of flagrant injustice in which even the gods participate, impelling men to evil to no apparent purpose. And over this drama of terrible confusion there towers the inescapable power of fate, the master of gods and men, making puppets of each. Greek tragedy mirrors and projects this legacy.

Regardless of how far the *catharsis*, the purging intended by these tragedies, succeeded in freeing the spectators from this legacy of horror, it is clear that, even after obtaining their inner freedom, the Greeks still bore this mark of their past. Their consciousness awakened, they looked back in awe on such a pandemonium of instincts and passions. Seen in this aspect, Nature could no longer be relied upon, and though its power was never ignored and remained the source of Greek vitality and creativeness, inspiration was sought elsewhere. There followed a reserved, an even critical attitude toward nature and this stamped its character on Western life and thought.

This pessimistic view of life and of the nature of man, which is evident in the oldest poetry and philosophy of the Greeks, never entirely disappeared. It is proof of the deep inner uncertainty of the West. The most conspicuous symptom of this, however, is the instability of Greek social conditions and political forms. What distinguishes these shifts from anything which might appear to correspond to them in the East, is their irreverence toward tradition.

The East strove for improvement within the framework of existing institutions. Rarely was there thought of turning against the values of tradition. While in the East discontentment in many cases was appeased by the correction and reform of actual conditions, Greece, and the West in general, did not refrain from radical measures. The overthrow of traditional institutions was always accompanied by elaborate ideologies. Since the time of the great social and economic reform of Solon social revolution marked the domestic history of both Athens and the West.

In Greek terms the classic formula of the fundamental controversy was 'what is *physei*' and 'what is *nomo* or *thesei?*' These questions—what is the natural endowment of man, and what is posited by his rule—perfectly summarize that perplexing problem —what is natural in man and what has been imposed on the natural in man, by man himself? Immediately there arises the next question. Must the natural be identified with the best, or should man substitute for the natural the superior values of his creative reason? These questions appear with even greater clarity in the political sphere.

When the Greeks left the Homeric period of petty tribal kingship, the power of which was limited by the council of elders or by an assembly of the people, they did not transform this tribal kingship into absolute rulership. Or if they did, this transformation was isolated and of short duration. This is certainly true of the Athenians. Even in olden times the rule of one was seriously questioned. Otherwise the author of the verse 'not good is the rulership of many; one must be the ruler . . .' would not have found it necessary to emphasize the superiority of the monarchic form of government.

The unrest pervading political life and thought inevitably gave rise to a search for the perfect form of government. The Athenians in particular tried one form of government after another. Aristotle constructed a cycle of potential constitutions recognizing three forms, monarchy, aristocracy, democracy with their corresponding degenerative forms, tyranny, oligarchy and the rule of the populace. This cycle began with monarchy and ended in the rulership of the proletariat, after which the cycle started anew. Whereas Plato's ideal State derives from the *a priori* foundations of his philosophy, Aristotle is said to have consulted seventy-five existing governments before propounding his theory of the perfect state.

The Romans too, after the abolition of kingship, did not agree upon a new form of state until the commission which had been sent to various countries for the establishment of a new constitution, had returned with the collected material. In the Middle Ages the Church doctrine of a god-ordained world order did not prevent social unrest. Neither did it arrest the struggle between two different forms of government under Pope and emperor, and the rise of the national state. Republics of so antagonistic a character as Venice and the Swiss confederation added variety to the picture. The transition period between the decline of the Middle Ages and the firm establishment of absolute monarchy was filled with Utopias describing the perfect state and society. Since the eighteenth century social and political theories have achieved a closer union with their realization than ever before. And this in turn has caused as much unrest in the life of states and societies as there has been perplexity in the realm of thought.

Viewed against these violently agitated waters of Western social and political history, the situation in the East was an ocean only stirred on the surface by gentle winds. To say that the framework of Eastern social conditions was sufficiently strong to ward off attack, or that reformatory ambition did not aim at the overthrow of that framework, is actually to express the same thought. The only remarkable parallel to the West is Persia. Indeed, the attempt of Mazdak around A.D. 500 to introduce a radical social form based upon communistic ideas is the only secular reform movement which originated in the East. His activity, however, did not go beyond the initial stage of success, and it ended in disaster for him and his doctrine. True, had the religious and metaphysical systems in the East been given time and liberty to spread out and bear fruit, they might in due course have caused a social revolution. But the East rarely thought of social reform as an immediate aim, nor for that matter as a value in itself.

The greatest example of this attitude is Buddhism. Although one of the intrinsic elements of Buddhism is the equality of all men, the Buddha never directly attacked or even criticized the caste system. Asoka, who in the third century B.C. established Buddhism as the state religion, did not attempt to abolish the caste system. Rather he declared that it was not birth but the way of acting which made a Sudra, a Sudra and a Brahmin, a Brahmin. It was expected that the convert to Buddhism would necessarily detach himself from caste and then with the spread of Buddhism the caste system would come to an end. However, there has existed in India since ancient times a religious complement to the caste system. Just as the high caste man, having provided for his household and progeny, was supposed at the age of forty to leave his family and the world to dedicate himself in solitude for the rest of his life to the attainment of salvation, so any man of a lower caste, the moment he assumed the life of asceticism, was freed from his caste mark and became an object of universal veneration.

A deep conviction underlies this view. This, however dimly felt, is the belief that the world which is man's centre of gravity is not self-sufficient. It is not, therefore, mere lack of interest or passivity which prevent the East from interfering with social and political conditions. The innermost desire is to keep a solid order which permits human affairs to go their way undisturbed by revolutionary measures. For such an order enables a man to return at any moment to his true aim and, the door having thus been left open to spiritual rehabilitation, to endure on this earth injustice and discrimination. Imbued with this faith, not even Gandhi opposed the caste system. Rather he sought a solution to the problem of the untouchables by receiving them into the system's framework.

While permeated with this same fundamental belief China's social and moral philosophy added to it the realistic theory that human conditions will not be improved by the mere overthrow and change of existing institutions. Improvement can only be achieved by "redefining names", that is to say by a clearer insight into respective functions and duties and their mutual delimitation, by improving the men in high office, and by setting up moral paragons for the people.

In the East, social and political institutions are rooted in the natural, and to the natural they cling throughout their history.

The natural is identified with the original. This identification, however, is by no means self-evident. A clear example of this is the Christian doctrine of the Fall of man where as a result, the natural is a corruption of the original. It is to the original with all the connotations included in the term, that tradition which is the preserver of the natural owes its sacrosanct character. The East admits of no reason, or *logos*, in opposition and superior to the natural. The natural possesses, so to speak, its own reason. And it is the part of human wisdom to recognize and to submit to it.

In Eastern religions the natural is likewise accorded its right, and perversions violating this rule are phenomena existing only at religion's periphery. The caste system is the natural social order. A man has but to see its true meaning to find himself in harmony with it.[1] The same concordance exists between the Chinese family and its intrinsic values on the one hand, and Confucian philosophy on the other. Taoism points to nature both as its source and as the place where its principles are realized. True, the natural in Taoism is not what common sense considers the natural. Looking deep into the workings of the instincts and passions, the Taoist sage discovers that the ways of nature are different from what they are generally believed to be, and on this insight he founds his theory of government and society. Nowhere in the East is there a conception of origin as independent from and foreign to nature—nowhere a claim to that competence which seeks to dethrone the natural.

* * *

In developing the patriarchal family of earlier times, Chinese civilization conferred on it a deeper significance and wider functions. The coexistence of family members within the same compound was preserved. Then with the rising level of culture the responsibilities of the absolute authority of the patriarch began to increase. For example, there was the division of labour within the practically autarchic family, the determining of the profession of those male members who could not or would not be employed in the agricultural economy of the family and the like. At the same time the

[1] A. K. Coomaraswamy, *The Religious Basis of the Forms of Indian Society*, New York, 1946.

family extended its natural scope to include the social and charitable functions which elsewhere would fall to state or community.

In this way the Chinese family became a great educational institution and the birthplace of specific virtues particularly of reverence and love for old age in general and parents in particular. Accordingly, the relations between father and son, man and wife were stressed, the superiority of the male members was considered indisputable, and the woman as wife and daughter took a subservient part.

The ancestor cult gave the family supreme sanction. Psychologically rooted in animistic times, it underwent a long evolution before taking the form by which it is now known. While the dim belief in the continued existence of the deceased in some form or other, their permanent presence, and the propitiatory rites connected with this belief, came down as an almost universal tradition, there is a purer Chinese form of ancestor worship. The rationalistic reverence for the ancestors which caused their names to be preserved on tablets in the shrine, seems to have started within the aristocracy. There, the right to vow a cult to a certain number of ancestors was granted by the emperor with the conferring of nobility or promotion to higher rank.

This custom is one of the many cases where the Chinese way of thinking, paradoxical as it may seem, is more logical and penetrating than ours. In the West, the giving of rank means the creation of an officially recognized ancestor, the originator of a line to which coming generations will look back as their grandsire. In China, the conferring of nobility constituted an immediate right to possess and revere ancestors to a number varying with rank, which was limited by imperial edict. Thus, if the right to two ancestors had been granted, the spirits of the grand- and great-grandfather might be the objects of the cult, but after the father's death, the great-grandfather's tablet had to be removed from the shrine. Regardless of whether or not the life-span of the deceased ancestors was fixed by imperial decree, it would seem more sensible that the man honoured by rank should possess from the beginning even a limited number of ancestors and, in case of promotion, see that number increased, than to have to wait the slow accumulation of ancestors in the course of generations.

In its purified form ancestor worship seems to have spread to every stratum of the population. The worship of the family ancestors must be evaluated as the keystone of the Chinese family. It constituted a private religion with which not even the cult of the deceased emperors could compete in importance. While the patriarchal family was not only the primary cell of Chinese life, it remained its centre, an all-embracing and in its way perfect unit which focused both the energies and the emotions of the Chinese people. The dark side of the picture is obvious. The family acted as a state within the state. True, its very separatism deprived it of any direct influence upon the government of the state. But hostile by its nature to any interference with its sovereignty, or curtailment of its traditional rights, the family viewed with distrust the growth of a strong central power. Hence, it successfully paralysed the evolution of an almighty administrative bureaucracy such as that which rose in the West.

For this reason quite a few leading representatives of modern China such as Kang Yu-wei, Hu Shi, Lin Yu-tang, and others, pass a rather severe judgment on the patriarchal family and its role in Chinese history. Understandable as this judgment is, it does not do sufficient justice to the great human aspect which Chinese civilization owes to this system. In order to build his moral and social philosophy, Confucius had only to extract the values and ideas inherent in the patriarchal family, relate them to each other and bring out their full significance.

A word remains to be said about the Chinese patriarchal family as compared to that of the West. The Roman family which was the most powerful example of this system in the West seems in every respect to resemble the Chinese. But on analysis, differences so fundamental are revealed as to give a deeper insight into the divergences between the structures of the Eastern and the Western mind. Regarding first the position of women, the *matrona* in the Roman family was not only mother and wife. She was likewise companion and partner to the man, and her influence transcended the narrow limits of the family. The history of the Roman Republic offers not a few examples of women who appeared in public to defend cases and who exercised a decisive influence during times of political stress. Nothing in the Roman family suggests the Chinese devaluation of women, an attitude which rendered the Chinese daughter and daughter-in-law unhappy creatures, and found expression in the time-honoured custom of female infanticide.

Still more revealing with regard to the spirit of the Roman family are its religious and political aspects. The Romans too worshipped ancestral spirits—the *lares*. In conjunction with the *penates*—the spirits of the household—the *lares* protected the life and continuity of the family, thus holding a place dear to the Roman heart. These spirits, however, were never given ascendancy over the deities of the national cult. The Roman family never had nor claimed the kind of omnipotence which fell to the Chinese family. In sharp contrast to the latter, the Roman family, from its first appearance in history, aimed at something more general and greater than itself, something whose superiority it never questioned. Hence it was that the virtues cultivated within the Roman family were easily transformed into civic and political virtues, while those of the Chinese family remained distinctly social.

The historical and sociological cause of the difference in behaviour between the Chinese and the Roman families lies in this contrast. While the Roman family took its place as the essential constituent of city life, the Chinese remained what it was from its origin, the dominant product of an agricultural society.

Wherever it appears, the patriarchal family is a natural phenomenon. But in the West, as is clearly illustrated in the Roman paragon, it pointed at something beyond itself, namely, the state. In the East on the other hand it maintained its natural form and developed into a creative centre of human values. The state rose and unfolded beside it, even against it. Indeed, the Chinese family always constituted more an obstacle to political life and thought than a source of political strength and good will.

Here, then, we face a highly important example of the opposed ways in which the two structures work and express themselves. The East tends to move within a given frame, creating, shaping, and improving existing conditions. It remains refractory to any revolutionary act which would end in the overthrow of that established frame. In contrast, the Western institution points beyond itself to something new or to what is considered new.

Neither the Chinese nor the Roman state grew out of the patriarchal family. The Chinese state was a phenomenon in its own right with its own implementation. A psychological and ideological rivalry resulted between it and the family. It is perfectly compatible with these conditions that the state in China should have been regarded as a kind of national family, a view which did not contribute to the state's strength. On the other hand, the Roman family went a long way toward meeting the prerequisites of the state. The rising state had only to take and shape what was offered it by the family to strengthen its own political virtues. This of course did not make of the Roman family a state, any more than the reverse conditions made of the Chinese state a family. Yet the fundamental difference remains that the Roman family was oriented to something beyond itself of a higher order.

Hence we arrive at this seemingly paradoxical fact. The Roman state attained the power of its inner organization and outward force because of its deep psychological relation with the family. This relation, however, in no way obliterated the boundary line between the two institutions. In China, the state and the family faced each other as strangers. But this separation, far from shaping the idea of state in the Chinese mind and strengthening its factual position, tended to make it difficult for the state to assert its full authority. In Rome, despite the difference between family and state, a certain organic link between the two was achieved. These two widely different relations between state and family apply not only to China and Rome, but with few exceptions and in varying degrees to the East and to the West in general.

In all higher civilizations the upper levels in the social hierarchy were monopolized by the clergy and the military nobility, both groups competing for the leading position in state and society. Chinese civilization was the only one to reverse this order. To the social stratification it applied a unique standard. Here too China remained faithful to the natural order. Nowhere else did the farmer enjoy on the social ladder the place of distinction awarded to him in China. True, he had to compete in the general evaluation with the scholar but the fact that precedence was given to the latter, far from impairing the esteem in which the farmer was held, threw it on the contrary, into clearer relief. These two groups, seemingly so distant or even opposed to each other, were linked by the idea that they alone, each in its respective field, constituted the productive classes.

True, the artisan stood on equal terms with them, but socially he constituted a considerably smaller influence. The farmer owed his high social rank, elsewhere granted only to the great land-owner, not solely to his economic importance. Also there was the fact that the patriarchal agricultural family represented the traditional virtues. On the other side, the scholars and the higher officials of the Chinese bureaucracy were chosen by the well-known rigid examination system, and were equally rooted to tradition. Their function as administrative leaders on the one hand, and as guardians of the intellectual tradition and creators of ideas on the other, secured them the supreme rank in the social hierarchy and they were followed immediately by the peasantry, the other productive group.

Characteristically enough, the merchant class, since it did not increase the amount of goods, was considered unproductive and therefore did not rank high in the social view. This disregard of the merchant class was bound to have great consequence in the history of China. Whereas in the West the merchant class and the liberal professions formed the rising bourgeoisie which initiated and carried the cultural, social and political movement of modern times, no such powerful middle class ever developed in China, and the scholarly intelligentsia kept aloof in its own privileged position.

The military profession, still more than the merchant, suffered from a lack of social appreciation. But this was of little practical moment since it did not prevent military activities. Like any other nation, China had her wars, not all of which by any means were of a defensive character. Wars of conquest and civil wars in particular fill the history of China. It may be precisely on this account that China came to disregard the military. At any rate, the Chinese seem to be the only people who have dared devaluate a profession which enjoyed a prominent and at times an undisputed social position everywhere else and certainly in Western history. Undoubtedly, the very spirit of Chinese civilization revolted against the destructive aspect of the military profession.

Indeed, whether the term social hierarchy in the Western sense is applicable to China at all is a question. Since by its very nature Confucianism lacked religious functionaries, and since neither the Taoist nor the Buddhist priesthood developed into a socially important group, the clerical caste was entirely deficient in that respect. Nor is it correct to speak of a military nobility in China. In any case, there was no such thing after the early disappearance of the feudal state. And feudalism in China as in Asia in general, never compared with the highly elaborate form of that social system in Europe. If a military nobility ever existed at all, it did not enjoy that confidence of the people which had accrued to it in Europe.

Thus in the absence of a clerical estate and military nobility as top ranking classes, the social order in China took on a unique and a more elemental character. Regardless of the fact that the principle adopted proved an obstacle to evolution, the unconditioned estimation of the farmer introduced a standard of productivity matched only by the scholarly class. The whole system subsisted at the price of the social devaluation of the merchant class with its accumulation of monetary capital. And this devaluation probably began to change slightly when the trade with Western countries yielded unforeseen wealth to those Chinese merchants who had been granted a monopoly on dealings with foreigners.

* * *

In India the patriarchal family was also the foundation of society. India however did not elaborate and perfect the family as China did. As a result of the coincidence of various incentives and influences, that peculiar and complicated social structure known as the caste system was superimposed on the original Indian society. It is not the purpose of this argument to go into the history of this system. Rather the point is to demonstrate that it also is rooted in the natural instinctive life. To reach this conclusion, one must reconsider a fact that is basic to group relations.

A primitive tribe meeting another unknown tribe reacts instinctively with fear, distrust and hostility. In human history the stranger is the enemy. This negative reaction to the alien, however, is not in itself the basic fact. It is the expression of a deeper experience. In such a meeting each group instinctively asserts its own existence and withdraws as it were into itself. The alien group is sensed as the other pure and simple—the absolute object. The cause of this reaction, which is not limited to the human race but extends to the whole animal world, transcends the emotional sphere and is evidently of a fundamental character. Fear, distrust and hostility merely give it an emotional expression. If triumph over this elementary reaction between groups is one of the main tasks of civilization, nationalistic experience of modern times teaches us that this primitive reaction is by no means limited to the primitive and that it is ever ready to break forth.

India is the one civilization which has recognized with relentless sincerity the fact of this elementary separation of human groups and has given it its full due. Moved by the same realistic spirit which is almost always overlooked or misunderstood by the West, India has at the same time sought the antidote to this in an unequalled solidarity of the groups within themselves. The combination of these aspects reflects the importance and significance of the Indian caste system.

Just why the caste system sprang up in India is a matter of conjecture. Evidently the Aryan invaders were a people penetrated by a sense of superiority and particularly sensitive to race and colour distinctions, and this sensitivity must have been stimulated by the different physique of the aborigines they met in Northern and North-Western Punjab. This reaction, coupled with the natural disdain of the nomad for a sedentary people and the equally natural superiority felt by a conqueror over the conquered, may account for the implacable severity with which the Aryans cut themselves off from the native population. Starting with this discrimination between the conqueror and the vanquished, the Aryans reserved to themselves the priestly and military castes, and a social system then rose up composed of four main castes which in the course of time divided into subcastes. Outside of this system and apart from the main castes, were the untouchables.

With the impenetrable partition walls set up between castes there came a feeling of homogeneity and solidarity among members of the same caste—among the conquerors on the one hand, and the native population on the other. Whatever may be the reasons for the origin of this order which established such strong barriers between human groups—at first between Aryan invaders and the non-Aryan aborigines and then between the four castes themselves and finally between the four castes and the outcasts—it must be recognized that the caste system worked. More than that, it has subsisted unshaken over a period of 3,000 years because and only because it is rooted in the depth of instinctive life.

A comparison with medieval Western society—a social order which seems to approach the caste system—brings out all the differences between the two and establishes the uniqueness of the Indian institution. The caste system consists of strictly separated social strata, each distinguished by an inherent value. But medieval Western society was a true hierarchy. Although the distinctions between the classes and their privileges and obligations were thoroughly maintained, ascent to a higher class was not exceptional. Members of the bourgeoisie rose to the nobility. And in the clerical estate, no obstacle barred the lower clergy, recruited mostly from the bourgeoisie and the peasantry, from attaining the highest ecclesiastical offices. The position of serfs and slaves in the West offers no parallel to the discrimination against the untouchables.

Thus, contrary to the rigid caste order and despite class distinctions a stream of life flowed through the body of medieval society which was alien to India. Nor could this have been otherwise since an organic structure is the monopoly and heritage of the West. The hierarchy of medieval society represented a pyramid, the apex of which was the Pope. The Pope's supremacy over the emperor, though almost always a matter of dispute, was ordained in a society conceived as an organized unit directed to God. For the same reason there had to be one spiritual and one secular head to the Christian society. In India, the Brahmin caste, though its members and sub-castes differed in importance, remained unorganized, and as to the military caste, there was always a plurality of kings with no overlord overshadowing the rest. What gave Western hierarchical society its weight was the idea that it constituted a part of that great hierarchy of the material and immaterial universe directed to God as it had been created by him.

Medieval society was an edifice to whose construction Rome had contributed the universality of her Empire and the legal spirit of her institutions, the Germanic people the elements of a feudal order, and Christianity, with its patrimony of Judaism and Hellenistic harmony, the breath of life. Thus, medieval society was a creation of rare complexity and the elaborate product of various civilizations. It was an achievement of the rational consciousness—an artful and artificial creation. But such a social order, though making a powerful appeal to the natural drives, without which no society can subsist, was not immediately rooted in the natural and instinctive sphere.

The respective relations of social order and religion illumine perhaps better than anything else the difference between the Western and the Indian phenomenon. The Indian caste system was and it had to be incorporated into the fundamentals of the Aryan religion, it having been established by the conquerors as the basis of their domination. In the so-called laws of Manu, it received its theological justification—it stemmed from Brahma Himself. Thus religion both strengthened and preserved the system as it had received it from the political power. However, if this gave to the caste system a deeper significance, its fundamentals remained untouched.

In the West, *per contra*, religion assumed quite a different role. True, the feudal system, the backbone of the medieval social order, grew up independently of the Church. But the Church built the body of its own hierarchy—and this involved its values and ideas no less than its administration—and knit it so closely with that of the secular, that the two fused. And they fused to so great a degree as to entitle the Pope to claim to be, and at times to become, the supreme feudal lord. Thus in the West, religion, as a creed and as a Church, was intensely instrumental in the shaping of the social structure.

These conditions and relations demonstrate with unmistakable clarity the difference between the Indian system and the Western. But they also do more. They again lay bare the basic fact that the social forms of Western civilization recede from and set themselves up against the natural and the instinctive, whereas the natural, though remoulded and reinterpreted, remains the foundation of the social forms of the East.

A survey of the political forms of East and West will still further emphasize this fundamental contrast.

CHAPTER IV

State and Society—II

The creation of the *polis* was the decisive step taken by the West toward a high level of civilization. The *polis* was a unique creation. No people, save under Greek influence, have ever achieved a similar institution. It neither derived from nor can it be explained by any preceding forms of social and political life. No road leads to it from the primitive community of the tribe, or from the petty patriarchal kingship of Homeric times. While these ancient forms may be said to have paved the way, this is true only in the indeterminate way in which heredity, environment and education influence the emergence of a genius.

With the establishment of the *polis*, the Greeks, socially and politically, left the shelter of the natural for a power other than the instinctive. The *polis* was a product of the rational in man. It embodied an idea extraneous to nature, and the will that created it bore no resemblance to the impulsive forces of natural drives. As a sovereign political unit of free men determining their own fate, creating and enforcing their own laws without divine or human bias, the *polis* stands as the paragon of Western history. It is not without significance that our word politics derives directly from the Greek *polis*.

Although the Greeks often betrayed this creation and, save for a comparatively short period, failed to live up to this ideal, they never lost sight of it. Conscious of its significance, Plato and Aristotle considered the state, in the scale of values, as existing before the individual, and by no means only as an idea exists before its realization. This view must be appreciated under a twofold angle. It raised the state once and for all above being a mere function for sustaining life which it had been before men emerged from their collective mentality in the community of the tribe and in primitive kingship. And it impressed all citizens with the knowledge that in founding the *polis* they had recognized an eternal idea in a free act of vision, and further that in substantiating that idea they had obligated themselves to strive for political and individual perfection.

The *polis* gave to the Greeks their feeling of superiority over other nations, whatever the endowments of those nations or their merits in other fields. The Greeks recognized the power and splendour of the Persian Empire and they appreciated the qualities and cultural achievements of the Persian people, but they could not forget that they lived under a despot's rule. In the eyes of the Greeks, the *polis* had a very concrete and ever present shape. It was evident in the *agora*, the market place of the city where the temples of the gods stood beside the government and public buildings, in the theatre and the gymnasium and everywhere that free citizens discussed and treated the affairs of the city state. What Pausanias, the Greek traveller and topographer of the second century, A.D., said of Panopus, a city of the Phoceans, can be applied still better to the Eastern towns: 'Panopus, a city of the Phoceans—if we can call it a city when it has no public buildings, no gymnasium, no theatre, no *agora*, no waterways guided and channelled to a spring . . .'. Strabo,[1] the Greek geographer, who died in A.D. 21, qualified the town of Soatra in Asia Minor ingeniously as *komopolis*, a village-town.

Indeed, this is what all the towns in the East were and still are when they are untouched by the West—great, sometimes enormous agglomerations. It is true of the towns in China, many of them gigantic in size and population, and it applies no less to India. Even Persepolis, the residential town of the Achaemenian empire, consisted of a great palatial centre forming the royal residence, which was surrounded by humble dwellings of a peasant population and the tents of nomads.

The market place of a Greek city differed from the Eastern bazaar, each in its way the life-centre of the city. The first was an open square conspicuous for its edifices where public affairs were dealt with, the other a noisy colourful business centre entirely involved in trade, barter, and the exchange of information. Not before the conquest of Alexander did cities in the Western sense

[1] Book XII, 5.

spring up on Asiatic soil.[1] With their public buildings, theatre, and gymnasium, they then imitated the *polis*. It was deprived, however, of its essence because, as parts of the Hellenistic kingdoms, these Eastern cities lacked the sovereignty of the *polis*. Indeed, what they always lacked was the burgher, the free citizen.

The *polis* accompanied the Greeks through the most brilliant period of their history, marking the height of their outer and their inner freedom. The intellectual intuition from which the *polis* originated and of which it was the concrete expression, conferred on the Greek mind another kind of freedom as well. It has ever been a characteristic of the higher intellect, the *logos*, that not only does it rise and discern that which is below and outside itself, but that it possesses this same detachment with regard to itself.

Paradoxically, however, this light shining back on itself casts a shadow. Thus the unruly and at times licentious mind of the Greeks used reason lavishly to criticize and disprove reason by reason's own power. Possessed of this capacity, they more than once deserted the idea and the reality of the *polis* to try other political forms. In addition, they suffered the difficulties familiar to modern democracies—the questioning of what freedom means and what it should mean, and the temptation to redefine it in terms of the social and economic movements of the day—symptoms of uncertainty which shake the foundations of the state. None of these vicissitudes of course impaired the greatness of the *polis* as an idea, the splendour it conferred on Greek life and civilization, and its lasting influence on the political evolution of the West.

Acting with greater caution and inspired by a circumspect wisdom, the East kept man within his natural bonds. Even when the speculative flights of the Eastern mind seem to carry it an infinite distance from the natural, its social and political institutions remained close to the natural. Never was the East guided by a new and revolutionary idea of man destined to interfere with actual conditions in order to mould and reform them. However, it is quite another thing when the founders of religious creeds who are indifferent to social and political forms preach the ascetic ideal as did the Buddha or again when Mani, the creator of the Gnostic

---

[1] M. Rostovtzeff, *The Social and Economic History of the Roman Empire*, Oxford at the Clarendon Press, 1926. Cf. vol. 1, p. 509, vol. II, p. 1055 *et al.*

system of Manichaeism, who was born about A.D. 215, thought of creating an entirely unrealistic society wherein the upper class was formed by the elect who were bound to a life of extreme austerity, including a vow of celibacy.

To the West alone belongs the *logos* which, having established a chasm between itself and nature, the bridging of which is the conscious or unconscious effort of our civilization, differs radically from nature by origin, essence and power. Though contradicted, albeit not by the most representative and influential philosophies, this separation from nature is just as much a component of the Western mind as is the lasting effort to bridge the gulf and achieve an organic conciliation.

The *polis* introduced the *logos* into the political and social sphere. A product of pure reason, it sanctioned the free citizen as the only adequate agent and representative of civilized life. Thus, only in the West was man considered to have inherent rights by natural law. This idea that man, by virtue of his rationality, possesses inalienable rights, is the monopoly of the West, and it exists nowhere in the East. There, on the contrary, man is concrete. He is as he stands in his traditional, social and political stations and relations. The rational in man gives him no innate rights, and thus does not reflect *a priori* on his legal status.

To the East the Western position seems an abstract and fictitious invention, endangering man's empirical and concrete unity. According to the Eastern conception, what is inborn in man is an ethical endowment and a desire for salvation, there being an immediate way which leads from the natural to the ethical and to salvation. Tradition and custom in the East occupy the same place in the social and political spheres as do those conditions and theories so freely created by reason in the West.

This severance of reason from the natural coupled with the ensuing activities of reason in its own right have given to the West a life of almost uninterrupted political and social unrest. Despite tradition and custom, individual minds in the West looked on existing situations as phenomena that not only could but perhaps should be changed. Starting with Solon in Greece and with the abolition of kingship in Rome, social and political movements, upheavals and revolutions were planned and put into effect with an ever increasing intensity in the name of principles, elaborate theories and fundamental rights.

When in the sixth century B.C. Solon solved the critical situation in Athens by imposing a new distribution of land, thus alleviating the condition of the landless proletariat, he did not act in an arbitrary manner. On the contrary, he was guided by high rational principles which he expressed in immortal lines. Thenceforward in Europe there were few philosophers and philosophical schools which failed to deduce social and political theories from their fundamental convictions. And since the fourteenth century in almost all important countries upheavals called forth by social or socio-religious ideologies have succeeded one another. At an accelerating rate and with increasing success these movements have altered the social, the political and and intellectual framework of the continent.

To this, there is no parallel in Asia. In India, political theory and reality remained strictly traditional just as the caste system has until our day held its own. Not even so powerful and revolutionary a heresy as Buddhism ever succeeded in gaining a firm foothold on the Indian mainland or in corroding the caste system. The attempt of Mazdak in Iran to revolutionize society by preaching the equality of all men and therewith an equal distribution of property ended quickly with the putting to death of Mazdak. China demonstrated her freedom of spirit in the invention of ideas of man and of theories of society and the state which in variety and originality may well rival those of the West. However, there is this trenchant difference. In the West from the time of Plato and even the Pythagoreans, there have been unyielding attempts to convert the theories of state and society into reality. Not so in China. There, philosophers and reformers wandered indefatigably from one court to the other in the hope of finding the understanding ear of a benevolent prince who would put their ideas into practice. It never entered their thought to organize movements in order to realize their ideas. Whatever the particular reasons which prevented the Chinese from following this line of effort one fact results clearly. And this is of primary importance in the line of our argument.

Since classic times ideas have assumed in the West a life of their own. Once they leave the mind of their creators they become independent entities. They now are facts and they are dealt with as though they exist outside the minds which positively or negatively receive them. Of this the numerous 'Isms' which surround us as so many quasi-autonomous entities are an all too living proof. Nothing could be more remote from the Chinese mind and from Eastern mind in general than this hypostatization of ideas. To the East the things of the mind, whether in live activity or just routine, remain the phenomena and experiences of the minds in which they occur. They do not aspire to and they do not reach that quasi-independence which they easily attain in the mind of the West. Such an autonomy is the condition of the scientific mind. So likewise is it a condition of the evolution and revolution of social and political forms.

Thus in the East while revolutions were certainly not unknown, they usually were satisfied with a change of the personal or dynastic rulership. With few exceptions, the East limited itself to the changing or improving of social, economic or political situations within the traditional frame, and refrained from tampering with the established order itself. These efforts remained natural struggles for a better life or for an increase of power and influence. In the social and political sphere, the East lacked the great flights, the soaring inspiration of the West but its institutions were less affected by the fierce resentments and dangerous monomanias so common to the West.

* * *

The civilized nations of the East knew practically no form of government other than autocratic monarchy. It is of little significance that, as Indian authors like to point out, benevolent Indian kings used to rely on the advice of their self-appointed counsellors. Such a revocable procedure imposed no limitation on the sovereign's power and it did not compare with the tradition in patriarchal kingship by which the ruler was bound to consult the assembly of the people or the council of elders. Nor were the so-called republics in ancient India, cited by Indian, Greek, and Roman authors, exceptions to the rule of absolute monarchy in the East. They were merely relics of tribal times, each with an autonomous council of elders as governing body. Nowhere and at no time did the East produce institutions founded on vested rights, which would have effectively limited the power of the monarch.

While the distinction between the feudal and the monarchical period may hold good for Chinese history, it must never be forgotten that the most important feature of Western feudalism is lacking in China. True, in China as in Europe by receiving their fiefs from the king the feudal lords became his vassals and owed him allegiance consisting in military aid, taxes in kind and the like. But there the comparison ends. For in Europe in exchange for their allegiance the feudal lords had a claim to protection by the king, thus making the feudal system look like the product of a free act of mutual fidelity. Characteristically enough, in China, or wherever the feudal system emerged in the East, it remained a one-sided institution leaving the king as the impersonation of all rights but without any obligations.

From our point of view which emphasizes the practically undisputed predominance of the monarchical, if not autocratic form of government in the East, there is no essential difference between the feudal and the monarchical period. Although there occurred occasionally actual restrictions of the sovereign's power and even the annulling of his real authority in public affairs—as for instance during the long rule of the Shoguns in Japan—the position of the absolute monarchy as the unique form of government in the East has never, prior to Western influence, been seriously contested.

A particularly illuminating example is to be found in Waley's analysis of what is called the Realists' school of Chinese philosophy, under the headline 'Classes to be eliminated'. Enumerating the classes the Realists think should be eliminated, viz., the aristocrats, the artisans, the hermits, the innkeepers, the merchants, the moralists, the philanthropists, the scholars, the soothsayers, and the swashbucklers, Waley makes the pertinent remark that 'it never seems to have struck the Realists that hereditary kingship was a very odd anomaly to leave untouched in a system that purported to abolish hereditary privileges and prided itself upon ruthless logic'.[1]

---

[1] Arthur Waley, *Three Ways of Thought in Ancient China*, New York, The Macmillan Company, 1940, p. 228.

This is not surprising after what has been expounded. For the power element belongs to the natural, whether there be assumed the existence of a power instinct in the proper sense of the term, or an elementary will to power. In either case, monarchy is its clearest and mightiest expression. Power and its adequate realization through autocracy were therefore recognized by the East as the inevitable bases of political life and its abandonment would have resulted in chaos.

Eastern theories of state and society reflect the real conditions. In India from Vedic times kingship found its support in an all-determining religion which, watching over the order of society, exalted the importance of the *kshatriya*, the military caste and the king as its head, yet attaching to the king a priest as guardian and adviser. Under these circumstances the theory of the state had to choose between two possibilities. Either it had to glorify the position of the monarch as it found it, or free the state from the tutelage of religion and explain its nature, task and privilege in its own right. The latter alternative is represented most distinctly by Kautiliya who vindicated the autonomy of the state and the limitless rights of the ruler with a fervour as unscrupulous as that of Machiavelli. Only Buddhism, which was entirely apolitical, showed any interest in the republican form of state. Whatever be the merits of Indian political theory it cannot compare either in scope or method with the Western. The observation of U. N. Ghoshal[1] stressing the gulf between Eastern and Western political thinking limited as it is to a specific problem, encompasses the fundamental difference. On the one hand, there is concept-based theoretical thought moving within a changing reality of political problems—on the other a mind faithful to the original conditions and neglecting pure theory, which prefers to concentrate on the description and analysis of empirical circumstances and human attitudes.

To this there is a single remarkable exception represented by the great Persian philosopher al-Ghazali (1058–1113). In a book called *The Advice to the Kings* which he wrote with the counsel of

---

[1] U. N. Ghoshal, *A History of Hindu Political Theories*, Oxford University Press, 1927, p. 240. '. . . The truth is that there is such a gulf fixed between the whole habit of thinking of Bodin and Grotius and that of the Hindu writers on rajadharma (politics) that to expect in the latter the parallel of the precise and coherent political thought of the former is to expect the impossible.'

the famous grand vizier Nezam ol Molk, he submitted to the king
an idea of representative government based upon his conviction
that only the various groups constituting the people could know
what is good for them. This assembly of representatives should be
responsible at the same time to the people and to the king. This
instance is in the realm of political theory rather than in reality
for needless to say nothing came of the idea.

In view of the conditions in China, the community-spirit prevailing in the Chinese family should logically have fostered a
republican form of government. So likewise, the religious mind in
India should with equal logic have led to a priestly kingship as it
did in Tibet. The natural, however, does not follow logic, or rather
it possesses a logic of its own. Thus it was natural for the East
to maintain an eminently simple form of government which by its
efficiency was directly connected with the instinctive and original
sources of life.

Contrast this monumental simplicity with the incessantly
changing forms of government and political life in the West—
changing not only chronologically but also within the same periods.
Moreover, reflect that since the days of ancient Greece and Rome
all the potentialities inherent in the different forms of government
have been explored. Again, consider the work involved in the
elaboration of political theories and the delimitation of the respective rights of ruler and ruled. And finally one observes that still no
end to this process is in sight. These considerations give us reason
to wonder that these two worlds of so antagonistic a nature not
only could, but have, coexisted over so long a time.

Obviously along with the differentiation in structure, a different
psychological and intellectual life-stream runs through these two
socio-political worlds. Western man believes in man-made, that
is reason-made institutions. Not content, as the Easterner is, to
receive from nature the forms of political life in the hope of filling
them with a richer meaning, he puts his confidence in the forms
he has himself created. Western institutions are therefore essentially the realizations of ideas—indeed they are residues of ideas
in so far as ideas materialize but never fulfil the ideas thought. In
other words institutions are promises never quite kept.

Thus it is that Western man faced with the discrepancy between the institution he has created and the idea from which it sprang, again and again is thrown back on his own mind in search of another idea which promises to succeed where its predecessor failed. Yet his confidence in institutions remains unshaken throughout history. Indeed it had to remain so, institutions being the equivalent of conceptual thought, that Western form of objective reason. Western man, therefore, almost since the beginning of civilized history, has for twenty-five centuries sought with untiring zeal to discover the perfect form of society and state.

Eastern man, on the other hand, has never shared this faith in institutions, but has put his trust, without too many illusions, in man himself. Guided by an intuitive knowledge, he hesitated to entrust his fate to so questionable an instrument as the autonomous concept, anticipating perhaps the dangers inherent in that device. By what appears an act of moderation, he resigned himself to his heritage from nature not wishing to challenge forces difficult to control. He accepted natural, elementary social forms evincing little inclination to change them, and acquiesced in absolute monarchy as the only form of state and government which despite perversion and abuse would not uproot him from his natural ground. This seemingly negative attitude, however, is not all renunciation. It contains an insight into the futility of exchanging one form of government for another, and a belief that it is better to retain monarchy in the hope of raising the standard of rulers. Here, the basic idea is that it is man himself which must be improved, not his institutions. Every form of society and government is good if man be good. And since it is vain to expect improvement through institutions, one must be content with the natural and traditional forms, man himself being the sole worthy object of reform.

The wisdom of this philosophy requires no proof. All Chinese ethics and political philosophies insist that until rulers personify the virtues becoming their rank and task, there is no hope for good government or the public welfare. Again and again the Chinese have stated that a just administration depends on the example set by the ruler. Unless people see the good represented in action they cannot be expected to obey the law and lead a moral life. In India, too, legend, literature and philosophy never tire of pre-

senting a picture of the perfect ruler. However dubious the degree
of success of the East in moulding its rulers to its heart's desire,
the wisdom of its fundamental position remains incontestable.

We in the West cannot be too often reminded that the accumulation of institutions, organizations and regulations distracts
attention from man himself and that to live in a world dominated
by institutions must in the long run degrade him to the state of an
unfree and irresponsible being. This is a dangerous process as with
the growth of institutions man tends to lose sight of what is
actually happening to him. It is wisdom to set up truth as a
monument and not to compromise though such action may seem
inexpedient and impractical. One need not be a pessimist to defend
the view that in the West institutions have changed while man
has remained the same. Yet if this be true, the amount of energy
spent on the building of institutions appears as a monstrous waste.

All that the East has produced in the way of human values,
values created and values lived, was achieved not in spite of the
lack of institutions, but because of that very lack. An accumulation of intensive energy existed there which, but for the interference of the West, might have enabled the East to continue its
creative life in its own tradition. In any case, it was no more naïve
to appeal directly to man in order to lead him on the path to
perfection, than it was to expect him to improve by the mere fact
of changing his social and political institutions.

In the same way, it is no less dignified to base the life of a
civilization on non-conceptual forms of knowledge, than to rely
solely on reason, in the Western sense of that term, as the West
has done. If the East is accused of being unrealistic, the same
accusation may be levelled at the West, in that institutions which
are certainly easier to change than man himself, may be little
more than our means of avoiding the real issue. At all events it
must be recognized that here are two entirely different ways of
dealing with brittle and refractory human material, each of them
rooted in and determined by its own particular mind-structure.

* * *

The unique exclusiveness of absolute monarchy in the East is so
momentous a phenomenon that viewed in its true light it cannot

but confirm the difference in structure between the two civilizations. The fact that aside from the West the only sphere of high civilization where deviations from absolute monarchy occurred is the Near East gives further emphasis to the singularity of this phenomenon. There—and it would seem only in Semitic countries—political forms emerged which might be called republican. Such was the rule of the judges in Israel before the introduction of kingship.[1] Such were the Republics established by the Phoenicians under a single magistrate in Tyrus after the death of Baal II, and their colony, Carthage, governed by two suffetes or magistrates.

In this respect as in so many others the Near East constitutes an intermediate zone between East and West without the strictly determined position of either. This statement, however, in no way impugns the Near East's creative originality, nor does it reduce its importance to that of a mere mediator between East and West. For the sake of our argument only any reference to the Near East must be limited to phenomena prevailing there which might throw into clearer relief the distinctive conditions of Eastern and Western civilization.

In the Near East there is a singular and significant form of government or, to be more precise, a singular and significant variety of absolute monarchy, known as divine kingship. Among high civilizations this institution is to all appearances indigenous to the Near East. It is a form which is difficult to deal with since its criterions are far from univocal. The excessively flattering titles conferred on the king, the quasi-religious ceremonial surrounding him, even the belief attributing his derivation to the gods—none of these necessarily signifies that the king himself claimed divinity or that he was considered a god by his subjects. However, dubious cases aside, there were examples of genuine divine kingship in the Near East which met all the legitimate requirements. They were not numerous, and were perhaps best represented by some of the rulers of Sumer, Accad, and Assyria.[2]

With regard to the origin of divine kingship, it must be remem-

---

[1] I Samuel VIII.
[2] Cf. Calvin W. McEwan, *The Oriental Origin of Hellenistic Kingship*, Chicago, 1935.

bered that from immemorial times the Near East has been the region of flowering magic, and its magic ideas have been inseparably fused with religion as well as with early science. Whether or not the institution of magic kingship dominated the Near East in early times is uncertain. But if it did, this legacy too would have to be taken into account. In any case, it is clear that this institution of divine kingship was in harmony with powerful trends in the Near East and that the atmosphere there prevailing favoured its rise.

It is of great importance that this divine kingship found no place in Eastern civilization and that the East's "mysterious" and "irrational" mind kept free of what might be termed an aberration. On the contrary, it was the West that took up the idea and developed it to a size hardly ever attained in its homeland. Alexander was the first to claim divinity and to accept the veneration due to a god, but it is a strange fact that by express command he limited his cult to Greece. In his time divine kingship had long disappeared from the lands of the Near East. Perhaps Alexander's pride as a world conqueror made him a half involuntary half wilful victim to the illusion that the kings of Persia were revered as gods and that he as their heir should be invested with the same dignity.

The ceremonial surrounding the Persian king culminating in prostration may have encouraged him in this illusion. Such an unwonted and to the Greeks ignominious behaviour on the part of the Persians may have led them to believe that the Persians considered their rulers divine. Actually, however, there is no reason to think that the kings of Persia ever claimed anything of the sort. Not even the great Darius goes beyond the solemn announcement on his inscriptions—an announcement sounding a legitimate pride but also an unmistakable humility—that Ahura Mazdao had entrusted him with the rule of the earth and of men in order to spread the good. Whatever led Alexander to this attitude, it is well known that some of his successors pushed their claim to divinity and worship to the extreme, the first to do so being Demetrius Poliorketes.

The Romans, strangely enough and even before imperial times, adopted a similar attitude toward Caesar, acting perhaps under the influence of examples in the Near East. Augustus established the cult of the Divus Caesar and had temples erected everywhere, particularly in the oriental parts of the empire dedicated to his cult. The fact that later Roman generals, particularly those of oriental origin, who were raised to imperial rank by their legions on Near Eastern soil, claimed divine prerogative is less astounding. The highly elaborate court ceremonial of the Sassanian kings in Persia which in time became the paragon of the Byzantine court ceremonial, may also have fostered the erroneous impression of divine kingship in Persia and contributed to its Roman development. Yet the cult of the genius of the emperor, the worship of his bust and the erection of temples dedicated exclusively to his worship, became a regular feature in the religious life of the imperium. This is significantly illustrated by the fact that the Jews alone won exemption from emperor worship having proved after long and painful negotiations that not even a picture or a statue of their own God was to be found in their temples.

Another less conspicuous source of divine kingship in the West came strangely enough from Greece. There, the ancient, and in popular religion, highly important cult of the heroes—historical figures whose beneficent deeds were rewarded after their death with a local cult—degenerated in the last centuries B.C. to the point where rulers, in recognition of their merits or out of mere servility, were raised even during their lifetime to the rank of heroes and awarded a cult. This custom of hero-worship, developing and degenerating into the deification of living rulers, may easily have disposed the successors of Alexander to indulge in the same privilege.

Although divine kingship is not an important component of Western civilization and history, it is of interest since it demonstrates that unexpectedly extravagant attitudes are by no means the monopoly of the East. On the contrary, the East kept the institution of absolute monarchy remarkably free from any such aberration. There it remained an essentially secular institution which was accepted with all the finality of resignation required by the uncontested form of political authority.

The Persian king considered himself the proxy of the great god Ahura Mazdao who had bestowed on him rule over the nations in order to assemble all good men in the fight against the power of evil. But this mission did not entitle him to more than the reverence which would naturally fall to the sovereign and to the leader of humanity in the fulfilment of humanity's goal. The monuments show the king surrounded with all the splendour of Eastern ceremonial, but in his relation to the great god he is represented as receiving the badge symbolizing his investiture with authority on earth. Persia exalted the mission of kingship to a greater extent than almost any other country, and to a degree which might have suggested deification of the king. Yet nowhere is there a hint of his divine descent or nature.

The kings of India, beyond any other Eastern kings and irrespective of their historical, mythical or legendary reality, preserved a secular character. They could attain saintliness as well as any man. But divine kingship was incompatible with Indian ideas, if only because it would have interfered with the sacred rights of the Brahmin caste which had priority in all things concerning the divine. Only on the foreign soil of Tibet did some of the various incarnations of the Buddha assume with their spiritual supremacy the tasks and position of worldly rulers.

To the sober mind of the Chinese nothing could have been more remote than the idea of divine kingship. Of all highly civilized peoples, the Chinese were the last to create and recognize a cleavage between the natural and the divine. They used the natural to humanize the divine, that is to familiarize man with it and to bring it nearer to him and his needs. They also used the divine to confer a higher dignity on man and his doings. The position and function of the emperor in China must be considered in this light. The comparison of the role of emperor with that of the patriarch in the family shows at least how the farmer fitted emotionally into the whole of Chinese life.

The title 'son of heaven' suggests a specific relation to the powers beyond. This was the emperor's relation to the spirits of his ancestors, in particular to those ancestral spirits who alone enjoyed unconditional immortality. This close connection with the supernatural—if this term can be used for powers so intimately connected with the natural—conferred on the emperor exclusive responsibility for the welfare of the state and people. Just as when at the time of sowing the emperor ploughed the ground with a golden plough, this ceremony had a magic meaning before it became a merely symbolic act, so the emperor maintained a magic relation with heaven and with his ancestors. As long as the emperor enjoyed the favour of the powers beyond, state affairs and the welfare of the people could not but prosper. On the other hand, disorder and misfortune in the empire revealed clearly that the emperor could no longer claim heavenly support.

Then at least in Confucius' political philosophy, which corresponded to popular feeling, it was not only permissible, it became a duty to depose the holder of imperial office and to replace him with a man believed to possess the necessary qualification. This view though not always put into practice, provided an extremely realistic solution to the problem involving the right to revolution, a problem which at one time was the subject of much controversy in Western political theory. Whereas in the West the right to revolution ended in the abolition of the institution that was the object of revolt, the monarchy in China remained unassailable, the revolutionary act being limited to the supplanting of one monarch by another.

As to Japan it is now generally agreed that the divinity of the emperor is a dogma of recent origin—the product of a political and military group for nationalistic purposes. Its doctrinal basis is Hegelian. As a political philosophy it confers on the state the dignity of a metaphysical substance. Thereby the emperor by his identification with the state participates in the state's divine nature. The long period of the Shogunate when the emperor was deprived of all real power, could hardly have favoured a belief in his divine nature, though it might have been to the Shoguns' interest to rule in the name of a divine sovereign. However, there are no indications that such a doctrine was ever proclaimed. On the other hand, it would seem that before the rise of the Shogunate the belief in the magic power of the emperor far exceeded that attained at any time in China. At one time a complex ceremony, the ceremonial taboo, destined to preserve this magic power, seems to have existed. However, in high civilizations, magic kingship neither involved, nor can it be identified with deification of the king.

Thus, absolute monarchy in the East remained remarkably free from those influences which in the Near East and in the West deprived it of its secular character. Though surrounded by a more or less elaborate ceremonial the king was not raised above his subjects as a being of divine order and origin. However, another kind of isolation, sociological and psychological in character, fell to kingship in the East. In the West, the king of medieval and modern times has always been the peak of the social hierarchical pyramid, the first of the nobility. Coming from the aristocracy, he relied on his class for support. From this solidarity of king and aristocracy rose a mighty hereditary class which, rooted in landed property, almost monopolized the high posts in the administration, the army, and sometimes even the ecclesiastical hierarchy. In any event, the king appeared to grow out of the society and he adhered to it as the first among noblemen.

In the East, no such hereditary aristocracy with vested rights ever developed. It is needless to go into the historical reasons for this phenomenon. It merely shows that Eastern autocracy did not risk the threat to it implicit in the existence of a hereditary aristocracy with vested rights and interests. From his isolated position the Eastern ruler faced all his subjects *en masse*. Eastern society is, so to speak, a truncated pyramid without any connection to its royal apex.

CHAPTER V

The Magic World

The aim of the earlier chapters has been to present a picture of the structures of Western and Eastern civilizations and some of their characteristic institutions. And the intention has been not alone to stress the differences, but in addition to investigate the opposed structural principles that determined these differences. A comprehensive description of these civilizations is beyond the scope of this book where we are concerned only with these structural differences and their significance for the understanding of the civilizations they support. Our plan is now to show how the ground for these contrasted structures of Eastern and Western civilizations was laid in earlier stages of human history—how these structures deriving from the magic world emerged—and finally how their respective civilizations appeared on the scene. A thorough examination of this dramatic process should lead to a full comprehension and appreciation both of the structures and the civilizations themselves.

* * *

The magic world is by all odds man's most astounding and decisive conception. Eastern and Western civilizations descend from this common ancestor—the magic world. Their derivation and even their separation from it, can be traced with minute precision. Not only did it contain in potential form the two highest civilizations so far achieved. It marked man's departure from a primitive way of life. This detachment from the primitive and entrance into a new and higher sphere did not entail the abandonment of the instinctive world. For nothing is ever lost in the mental history of mankind. Just as this conception of the magic world lived on in some way in all consecutive civilizations—and by no means merely as a dead relic—so did the compound of animal drives live on. It is the position, the influence, and the value attributed to this magic inheritance that alone have changed.

In every respect the fundamentals in our world are contradicted in this magic world. At first, one encounters the startling fact that its phenomena lack identity with themselves. In our world a thing is strictly identical with itself, and only within certain well-established limits is it allowed to change. Not so in the magic conception. Depending on the level of its development, its unstable phenomena assume crude or refined forms. Among primitives a man may change into an animal, an animal assume human form, a dead object may suddenly be endowed with life and quasi-personal qualities so that it becomes a fetish. An occurrence such as death—though its natural cause be demonstrated—may be attributed to magic influence, to witchcraft. The image of a thing is considered to be the thing itself. Appearance counts for nothing and ocular proof carries no conviction. Here phenomena are not what they seem. Independent of sense perception, they branch out to other visible or invisible things, to relate with them and form real units.

At a higher level, this view assumes the creative form of alchemy which permeated almost all the civilized countries of Asia and Europe before giving rise to the science of chemistry. The belief that base metals could be transmuted into gold, that a universal solvent could be found to bring this about and that this *elixir vitae* would give man unimpaired health and immortality, rested upon the theory of the uniformity of matter and the possibility of converting one form of matter into another. When on a psychological level the terminology of physical alchemy was applied to the stages of inner transformation through which man had to go on the road to illumination and perfection, this trend of thought reached even greater heights.

This term, the magic world, is often used to mean a primitive mentality and culture. Such an identification is entirely erroneous. The conception of the magic world is primitive only in so far as it exists among primitives, but it is neither their creation nor their monopoly. It was in studying primitives that modern anthropologists discovered the magic world in its primitive and in many cases probably degenerate form. For the comprehension of its phenomena a common denominator—mystic participation—gained some currency among anthropologists. But a deeper analysis of the primitive mentality reveals that the term mystic participation, appropriate as it may seem at first, does not penetrate to the heart of the matter. It constitutes but a sector, in fact a minor part of the magic world—which by itself has a fundamental function in the history of mankind.

Regardless of whether this concept of the magic world was a sovereign influence in, or a paramount component of, the world picture, its existence can be clearly identified in all the civilizations which outgrew the primitive stage. In early China it appears in such ancient documents as the I-Ching and culminates in the Taoist philosophy. In India it centred in the all-important ritual of the sacrifice. It also existed in pre-Zoroastrian Persia, in pre-Buddhist Tibet, and in the Near East, particularly in the ancient cultures of Mesopotamia, where it was intimately connected with astral religion and astral science. In Europe it was represented by the Celts of Brittany, Wales, Ireland and Scotland; by the North Germanic peoples whose greatest literary document, the 'Edda', is filled with magic beliefs, and to all appearances by the Etruscans. In the later Middle Ages and at the beginning of the modern era, the magic world was shaped into more or less elaborate systems of philosophy, such as those of Agrippa von Nettesheim, Paracelsus, Cardanus, and of philosophers of various nations during the Romantic period. Beyond these sharply defined systematizations, its lasting influence may be traced to many other places and phenomena.

This could not have been otherwise. The magic world is closely related to the subconscious life of man. Dreams, psychoneuroses and psychoses as well as the normal subconscious, in many respects behave in accordance with magic conceptions. Thus, whatever the spontaneous and creative merit of the magic world in its higher forms, there is a dynamic relation between it and the subconscious. Since human groups of similar racial or mental parentage, and indeed mankind as a whole, have a subconscious life just as the individual does, it follows that the conception of the magic world lives either peripherally or in the deeper regions of the mind of a civilization and is ever ready to reveal itself in tortuous ways when denied immediate influence.

The Magic World

All great world conceptions are the work of the conscious mind. However, the ties which link them to the subconscious cannot be severed. Civilizations differ widely in the acceptance and the recognition of these ties. Western civilization offers the highest degree of resistance to the subconscious, whereas the East has found a way of coming to terms with it. The magic world however, lives in perfect harmony with the subconscious. Indeed this conception is rooted in and feeds upon that eternal subconscious which within limits can be processed and sublimated, but can neither be overcome, nor ignored with impunity.

* * *

This magic world is pre-eminently a world of transmutations. In its preparatory stage and at its lower level things were not yet crystallized. They had no clear and definite shape. This applied not only to physical objects but to phenomena of the mind. Of the sharp distinctions between the animate and the inanimate, the physical and the psychological, the natural and the supernatural which are peculiar to our world, none existed. Nor were phenomena ruled by unbreakable laws. At any moment in the course of events extra-human forces and beings might intervene. Moreover, man himself might acquire the power to control events by immediate action without recourse to normal means. In this, witchcraft was the dominant factor.

Thus, convincing as appearances may seem to us, they carried no conviction. For example, to some African negroes natural death is not natural at all. Rather is it the work of an enemy who has availed himself of the foul services of a witch doctor. The belief in the transmutation of animals into men, of men into animals, of gods and spirits assuming the shape of men and the like, has occupied a central place in the legends and myths of peoples all over the earth. One should bear this in mind in order to understand the magic power which men's faith in the transformation of one form of being into another has at all times exerted on their imagination and belief.

Such a world appears ill-determined and accidental. Psychological forces overwhelm objective and external reality. The world of the psyche is still unclarified. Emotional reactions are immoder-

ate and associations of ideas vague and expansive. The violence
of psychological life penetrates the outside world and overflows it,
as it were, and this overflow results in indistinctness and falsifica-
tion, a state which is not unknown to highly emotional and
imaginative types today. If this world picture lacks structure and
clear contours, it at least contained potentially all the elements of
the later well-developed concept of the magic world.

In the mature conception, physical things as well as the
phenomena of the mind attained a high degree of solidity and
clarity without affecting the principle of transmutation. Though
clearly outlined and shaped, these things remained equivocal. Not
only they themselves. They were more than themselves—other
things. They were iridescent in that, not being identical with
themselves, they played, so to speak, in various colours. And their
transparency permitted other things to be discerned through
them. The separation of the living and the non-living, of the
physical and the psychological was not recognized. And relations
between man and the various kinds of infra- and super-human
beings were simple, and their forms were interchangeable.

All these qualities concurred to make the magic world one of
symbolism. Things were not what they seemed, but represented
other non-apprehensible things. The symbol here was not a con-
ventional emblem as it is in mathematics, physics, music, and the
like. On the contrary, the relation between the symbol and the
thing symbolized was a lively, a dynamic relation. Somehow, the
thing symbolized was really present in the symbol and not merely
intellectually recalled by it. In the same way the symbol was
Janus-faced—ambiguous because it was never only what it
seemed to be.

The meaning of the symbol and the vision of the thing symbolized, was disclosed only to those who could read the symbolic
language of the universe. Everything had what was called in the
occult nature-philosophy of the Middle Ages a sign or seal, and
only the knowledge of this sign—chiefly the knowledge of its
secret name—revealed the symbol's innermost meaning. Magic
thinking, therefore, is the most fitting approach to and expression
of those religious systems in which the Godhead and other positive
or negative spiritual beings are unwilling to manifest themselves

to men in their original shape, and where man is supposed to ascend to his final goal through stages. The systems of Gnosticism are outstanding examples.

Besides being a world of transmutations the magic world was thus a world of significations. This signification however, was not in the weak sense of a subjective quality existing by virtue of thought alone. Rather it was an objective quality—the life of a thing consisting in its power to signify. This was of far-reaching importance. As has been stated, there were no solids in the magic world, no sharply circumscribed things such as compose our world. All things transcended themselves because they were not what they appeared to be, and it is in this way that they were experienced. The concept of the magic world therefore was essentially a dynamic and experienced one.

Things of that world might best be compared to fields of energy. Whatever served as a symbol for something higher might itself be symbolized by something lower. And since the relation between the symbol and the thing symbolized was a dynamic one, the magic world vibrated with a life-stream running in two directions. Thus each thing was simultaneously the receiver and the sender. This magic world with its network of forces running to and fro is suggestive of the universe of modern physics. But there is this momentous difference. The forces in physics are measurable quantities, whereas those in the magic world were strictly qualitative influences dependent on the sources from which they emanated.

These abstract deductions immediately come to life if we consider the basic ideas of astrology. Indeed, there is more than an intimate connection between astrology and the magic world. Wherever that conception reached a peak, whether as the recognized view of the world or the philosophy of an individual thinker, wherever it became a component of religious or pre-scientific knowledge, then astrology occupied a distinctive if not sovereign place. As long as magic thinking confined itself to the earth, it never went beyond the primitive or half-primitive. Only when it turned to the sky to determine the relations between the stars and their influence on terrestrial events did it gain cosmic significance and rise to the rank of a universal world conception.

The extent to which the views and methods of astrology continued to influence the evolution of the mind long after the belief in astrology was undermined is never sufficiently recognized. The word influence, for example, which originally signified the ethereal fluid that emanated from the sidereal bodies and determined events on earth and the fates of men, indicates the nature of the forces at work in the magic world. The qualities of these forces changed according to the nature of the astral bodies from which they emanated. Thus astrology speaks of them as Jovial, Martial, Venereal, and the like. The planets and their movements hold the interest only when they are viewed as dynamic centres exercising a determining influence on human circumstances. Astrology, therefore, is not only the most lucid expression, but the very paragon of magic thinking.

Everywhere in the magic world, material, psychological and spiritual things, in so far as these distinctions existed at all, were equivalent to their significations. And signification meant a qualitative influence. Thus the magic world was permeated by influences that criss-crossed and interlaced. To be, was primarily to influence and to be influenced. Although no one thing was entirely refractory to the influence of other things, and although equally, no one thing was entirely incapable of influencing others, there were certain things and groups of things among which this exchange was particularly intensive. This quality of intense exchange was called affinity, and in turn the dynamic relation founded on affinity, was known as correspondence. In all magic philosophy correspondences between things played a prominent part as, for instance, in the writings of Paracelsus, particularly those on medicine, and in Swedenborg's religious universe.[1] In principle, of course, there had to be a correspondence between all things. This great rhythm pervading the magic world was never more dramatically expressed than by that phrase of Hippocrates —"one confluence of all existing, one breath of life, one strain of sympathy".

* * *

The categories which support our world obviously do not apply in this magic world. The most conspicuous example of this is the

[1] Emanuel Swedenborg, *Heaven and its Wonders and Hell*, Ch. XII. 'There is a correspondence between all things, and between all things and men.'

law of causality. Where everything was based on correspondences
and affinities the relation of cause and effect had no place. It was
too crude an instrument to reveal anything about the deeper
connections between things. Moreover, the relation of cause and
effect has a time element—the temporal priority of cause and this
is foreign to magic thinking. Referring again to astrology, it should
be noted that the sidereal constellation is not the cause of the
character and fate of those born under its influence. Rather the
two realms are connected by a correspondence in keeping with the
principle—as above, so below—and in this the corresponding
phenomena constitute a whole in which causality has no part.

This follows from the nature of the magic world and its atmosphere. The forces there at work were inherent forces operating
between things, whereas the relation of cause and effect is not a
force at all and is exterior to the entities linked by it. More in
harmony with the spirit of the magic world is the teleological view.
This is the conception that everything in existence and man in
particular is directed to an end and lives for the sake of realizing
that end—an idea that is inherent in the Gnostic systems.

The dynamic context in which all things were suspended was
projected in the magic conception of reality. In a universe where
all components were so powerfully interwoven, there had to be an
irresistible urge toward strengthening and extending reality. In
this respect the magic world bordered on the mentality of the
primitive where the borderline between imagination and reality is
so often ignored. Indeed, both the primitive mentality and magic
thinking have a sovereign disregard of the objective world. Their
universe was based upon inner experience. The life of the psyche
overruled the material world and threw over it a network of its
own. The attributing of reality to creations of the mind and to
figments of the imagination however fantastic, was consistent with
this. And so likewise was the fact that objective reality was conferred on the host of psychological and spiritual beings with which
the magic world populated its universe.

The ingenious notion of degrees of reality was likewise intimately connected with this extension of reality and with the
aversion to considering anything unreal. If nothing which appeared was ever regarded as entirely unreal, it is easy to understand

that in such a psychologically determined framework, impressiveness and reality were proportionate to each other. Then at higher levels of magic thinking, greater permanence, influence and value came to be implicit in a higher degree of reality. This idea of differing degrees of reality led in turn to a universe graded according to those differences, and from there into a unique hierarchical order based upon them. Such a hierarchy was distinct from all others, which are based on the idea of value and dignity.

To speak of degrees of reality strikes a strange note in the ears of those who live in a scientifically determined world. However, we find this idea in Greek philosophical schools, and by no means only in the neo-Platonic atmosphere, and likewise in the philosophy of the Christian Middle Ages. Wherever there existed the concept of an *ens realissimum* and *perfectissimum*—of a most supreme being possessing the highest degree of reality and perfection—there too, the theory of an hierarchy of grades of reality found its appropriate place. For it was but natural to assume that the nearer the place of a creature to the Absolute, the more did it participate in its reality. Thus angels being superior to man in their god-like qualities, possessed a higher degree of reality than he did. Ranks or degrees of reality might be discerned both above and below the one held by man.

In the magic world such sharp separation of grades of existence is ignored. Its dynamic idea recognizes but one life-stream in which all beings possess the potential power to transmute themselves in an upward and downward movement. In so doing they share in a plus or minus of reality. So man too may descend or evolve in value and dignity and thereby lose or gain in reality. And he may realize himself—this term being taken in the full sense of its meaningful etymology.

Equally different from ours was the idea of knowledge which is implicit in magic thought. The magic world was one of inherence. The strict separation of the knower from the known was foreign to magic thinking. The intellect never isolated, nor did it confront or dissect the object, for the act of magic knowing necessitated no such cleavage between subject and object. On the contrary, the subject merged as it were with the object in order to become acquainted with it. This idea of inherent knowledge will be more understandable if we recall that in the magic universe all things maintained correspondence with each other. In this way man in particular mirrored and somehow contained the universe. He was the universe on a minute scale—the classic microcosm. In order to grasp the nature of magic knowledge one must dispense with the common idea where some physical or non-physical object opposes the knower. This idea prevailed in Western thought until a recent conception in physics arrived at an intimate interdependence of phenomenon and observer—an evolution which in a measure may be interpreted as a certain approximation to magic thinking.

Until this latest development in physics it was the natural and universal conviction that, in contra-distinction to the object in psychology, the object of physics remains identically the same whilst it is being observed. All eventual changes of the object were due to the inaccuracy of the instruments used or to deficiencies of the observation. This seemingly self-evident idea, which corresponds to the crude experience of daily life, has been preserved in classic physics. But modern physics speaks of the 'non-objective character of the atomic world' and stresses the fact that 'every experiment is an act of violence which we impose on nature'.[1] Thus the idea that in scientific observation subject and object face each other as entirely separated entities has to be dismissed. It can no longer be admitted 'that a description of any selected part of the universe could be prepared which would be entirely independent of the observer as well as of the special circumstances surrounding him'.[2]

All knowledge in a broad sense, therefore, was self-knowledge. Far from dealing with the thing to be known as an object, the magic idea of knowledge was a participation in the thing to be known. The knower insinuated himself into the knowable, and it was this non-conceptual awareness that alone warranted the term knowledge. To know then involved a particular kind of partial identification with the knowable. Here, the idea of knowledge corresponds with what has already been said regarding the signs and seals of things. Knowing is in itself influencing. There

[1] C. F. v. Weizsaecker, *The World View of Physics*, The University of Chicago Press, Chicago, 1952, p. 57.
[2] Sir James Jeans, *Physics and Philosophy*, Cambridge: At the University Press, 1946, p. 143.

was no theoretical knowledge—there was no knowledge which was not by its very nature operative knowledge. Unlike pragmatism, where knowledge exerts power over things though ignoring their nature, magic knowledge derived its influence from the immediate awareness of the essence of things. To surrender to whatever exists in order to live its life involved an insight which had no relationship to our idea of objective knowledge. Such unegotistic empathy into all that exists guaranteed an understanding and an influence which was both unlike and superior to our conceptual knowledge and the power we derive from it.

The profound difference between the two forms of knowledge becomes evident at this point. In the magic process of knowing, whatever the object of knowledge, it was the subject which was ultimately transformed. Our act of knowledge, on the other hand, starts with disconnecting the object from its natural surroundings and isolating it for the purpose of investigation. Inevitably this ends in affecting and altering the object itself. The culmination is scientific knowledge and the creation of a new objective world.

The magic world defies strict definition and description. To comprehend it as the common ancestor of the Eastern and the Western mind and their civilizations, one must grasp its greater contours and feel its strange life and dynamic rhythm. This picture of the magic universe is drawn from its most representative realizations. Though the essential elements are contained in it, it must not be supposed that they were present everywhere, or that they were all expressed with the same clarity.

The most conspicuous general characteristic of the magic universe was its state of equipoise in which all things were suspended—in short, its balance. This was achieved by conferring reality upon all things in existence and by the dynamic correspondence operating between them. Indeed, these correspondences constituted the reality of the magic universe since all things were nothing but emitters and receivers of specific influences. For this reason, the distinctions which the mind later established between the animate and the inanimate, the physical and the psychological, conscious and unconscious, were of little interest. The indifference to such discriminations is more understandable when we remember that the life of things was comprised in their significations, and

106

further that these significations were identical with influences and correspondences. The magic universe is a work of art in which primitive divinations and instincts were coupled in action with deep intuitions and intellectual aspirations. And thus was there constructed one of the great creations of the human mind, a magical conception whose tremendous power is felt even in our own day. With its interplay of forces the magic universe shared the delicate and sensitive character of all balance-based systems. And like them it was exposed to dangers which threatened, if not its existence at least its integration. This explains why in its mature and perfect form it did not spread uninterruptedly over huge connected spaces for thousands of years as did the Western and Eastern worlds. At one time in primitive forms it was disseminated all over the globe, and in quite a few regions it rose to remarkable heights. This was the case among the Celts where it was expressed in a religion, cult, and literature of strange beauty and significance. There it might have unfolded still more had not these cults been overthrown by the Romans and the peoples of the Germanic race, thus arresting and corrupting the Celtic civilization.

However, even without the impact of such violent events, a steady evolution to the higher forms of the magic world conception was not possible by reason of the strain to which they were subjected by their very essence. The superabundance of aspects, the profusion of intersecting and seemingly contradictory trends of thought, the demands upon the imagination, upon thinking power and above all upon the will to and the force of inner experience, are all a sufficient explanation of why the higher forms of the magic world were unfit to reign over many peoples and long periods. In our day Tibet remains the only living example. The magic world could not withstand the impact of the rising Eastern and Western civilizations. It remained to become the privilege of individuals and closed societies who have handed it down as a secret lore from generation to generation.

Again in contrast to the Eastern and Western worlds the consequence of this subtlety of equilibrium among the higher forms of the magic world was a comparatively limited life-span. In a world where phenomena of neither the outer nor the inner realm pos-

sessed clear contours; where reality consisted in the dynamic interplay of influences and correspondences; where instead of conceptual thinking visualization in symbols reigned; and where only an
inherent and subtle equilibrium guaranteed the order maintained
by causality in our universe—in such a world a tension existed
which inevitably brought it to the bursting point. Regardless of
the truth divined, the connections intuitively perceived, and the
degrees of reality immediately experienced in the magic world, it
was in human nature to long for a universe consisting of things
whose appearances could be trusted, of things clearly distinct
from the relations connecting them with other things—a universe
scaled down, as it were, to a more concrete aspect and order.

In the human mind there is an almost irresistible tendency to
create self-sufficient entities. This bias, supported by the structure
of the majority of languages, led increasingly to the breaking up of
influences and correspondences. Reality had previously centred in
the influences and correspondences which contained what was
later to become the substances. It now became objectified and
transformed into those substances, whose qualities and effects
were subsequently considered mere attributes and accidents.
Referring again to astrology, at first the astral body was nothing
but a correspondence—an influence operating between celestial
and terrestrial phenomena. Then as thought evolved, this dynamic
unit split into an entity from which an influence emanated, and
the influence itself. Still later, this awe-inspiring something
assumed personality. It became, for instance, the god Jupiter to
whom the planet stood in the same relation as did the symbolic
eagle and the thunder.

Thus a host of major and minor deities arose within the conception of the magic world and shattered it. Much of its atmosphere
and many of its elements lived on however—a process which can
be traced in the Assyrian and Babylonian religions. It was at this
stage that this conception of the magic world ceased to be the
official creed of nations and regions. Henceforth, it is to be found
as a consummate whole only among dissenting spiritual com-
munities such as the Gnostics, and as an original creation only
among great individuals like Proclus and Plotinus. Otherwhere, it
survived at the periphery of civilization beyond the field of view.

And thus hidden, it continued to accompany and influence in many ways the march of men.

* * *

Among other things most disruptive of the equilibrium of the magic world was the fixing of man's position in the universe. In this world where the distinctions between animate and inanimate, conscious and unconscious, personal and impersonal, were almost non-existent, man could never claim a distinctive, much less the central, place. Caught up in a network of correspondences, he was both an active and a receiving centre. In the same sense and by the same right as himself, all other beings were simultaneously subjects and objects. The opposition of subject and object—the antithesis which is the very backbone of our world—was absent from the magic world conception. And it was precisely this absence which gave to it its balance, its homogeneity, and its harmony.

Those qualities, which were later considered prerogatives of the human subject alone, were distributed in the magic world among all existing things, and for that matter, among all creatures created by the imagination. This is testified to by the convictions of primitives, and as well by myth, legend, and epic, where inanimate things live and animals behave like and are in many respects superior to men, acting as their friends and teachers. The idea that all that exists possesses in some form and to some degree what was later attributed only to the human subject, must have filled man with a deep sense of affinity to his visible and invisible surroundings. However, this affinity was only achieved at the price of the clarity and distinctness of the human subject and his relation to himself. Whether the emphasis be laid on the easy shifting of the subject's centre, or on his readiness to abandon his psychological qualities for others—the important thing was the belief in the transformation of personality and the ensuing experience.

This phenomenon is well known among primitives. They believe that changes in personality are brought about by the use of intoxicants and stupefiants, dancing practices, the wearing of masks and by all kinds of witchcraft or possession by spirits. This easy exchange of personality which was the expression of a vacillating self-experience—was always within the reach of all members of the community. However, the actual belief in transformation and in an alteration of physical appearance and character, has come down to and been preserved by maturer civilizations. But its scope has been drastically reduced. As an assured reality it became the prerogative of gods or other superhuman beings. Elsewhere it survived as an indispensable element in myths and legends. It appeared at the height of the concept of the magic world.

This is of the utmost importance. In Gnosis, in related doctrines, in not a few mystery cults, and in alchemical philosophy, man was not the comparatively homogeneous unit that he is to our civilization. Rather he was a microcosm, related to everything in existence—a potential citizen of those realms which constituted the hierarchical universe of those respective doctrines. On his wanderings, he could fall or rise from the sphere of coarse matter to that of the spirit. He did not, however, assume as an independent entity the qualities characterizing those spheres. Rather these spheres fulfilled the many independent impersonations which he carried with him. He faced within himself and experienced these impersonations as objective personalities whatever they were called—the material, the demoniac, the angelic, or the spiritual man. According to the impersonation he put on, other impersonations then appeared to him. Some of these were in material bodies while others were superior to terrestrial man, having ethereal bodies. Thus man was composed of many sheaths so to speak. In true magic thinking at one and the same time he was and he was not these sheaths, or impersonations, since obviously but one impersonation could be realized at a time. Once he had reached the highest impersonation, a man was considered to have attained his true fulfilment and destination.

In groping our way through this strange world, the psychopathic phenomenon of the split personality comes readily to mind. However, to regard the magic world's idea of the transformation of personality and its ensuing experience as a disintegrative process would be a grave error. Not only do this idea and experience fit into a great archetypal image of the universe. They also serve to interpret existence as a momentous peregrination through various worlds of which the terrestrial is but one. If one conceives a decentralized personality—an entity consisting of a plurality of impersonations with a shifting centre—this comes closer to the magic concept.

As a picture of man, this certainly differs much from our own. Yet there are schools in modern psychology such as that of Jung, which approach this magic concept though expressing their ideas in other terms. Moreover, this concept might well be considered by philosophy and religion as a dramatization of man's spiritual adventure designed to rid him of all impersonations for the sake of his final salvation. But such considerations are not within the scope of the argument. Our exclusive aim is to demonstrate that in the magic world subject and object were not separated by any distinct line of demarcation. They shared those qualities which in subsequent evolution were increasingly monopolized by the subject. Moreover, the subject confronted and experienced the impersonations of which he was composed, not specifically as his own—not as himself—but as related to him along with all other objects.

In this delicately poised equilibrium of correspondences between components of essentially the same nature, the equalization of subject and object was obviously the most sensitive point. In the course of evolving consciousness, man displayed a growing tendency to orient and to assert himself. With the widening of this breach in the structure, evolution then pressed on to the clear separation of subject and object. Thus the whole edifice of the magic world begins to reel. As man, the subject, asserts himself, his unity and identity with himself become firmly established. His contours and contents begin to be determined. No longer does he tolerate the coexistence with and within himself of quasi-independent impersonations, and he wants to be able to say *I* and *mine* in an unmistakable way.

With this crystallization of the ego-subject the disintegration of the magic world commences. The subject, severing itself from the equilibrium of the magic universe, rises above the network of dynamic correspondences. He forms a centre of his own. In shaping and stabilizing himself he becomes the catalyser of the world. For with the isolation of the subject the formation of the object

111

as an independent entity is necessarily connected. Things begin to assume aspects that are clear and permanent, the dynamic influences give way to neutral forces, and the ubiquitous transmutability of all things existing ceases to exist. And so the way is open to new world conceptions.

These new concepts had to start from a new relation between subject and object. Having disrupted the magic world which had held him spellbound on the same level as the rest of beings, man now faced the world as the object. At the same time he aspired to a supremacy unknown to the magic conception. The relation between subject and object became problematic. It had to be determined anew. This task was all the more significant as in the magic world the emphasis lay on the dynamic correspondences— the relations. The poles, that is subjects and objects, occupied a place of secondary importance and were in a way absorbed by those quasi-autonomous relations. Now these poles emerge from their unpretentious position. They come to the foreground and prepare to rise above the connecting correspondences.

What now unfolds is the dramatic evolution of man's consciousness. The magic unit which had embraced the subject-object poles under the spell of the dynamic correspondences embodied a peculiar form of consciousness. Because of the subject's lack of unity, and in consequence of the participation of the objects in conscious life, consciousness soared above both subject and object and absorbed them. From this curious form of consciousness which is exceedingly difficult for us to reconstruct and must ever seem vague and ambiguous, the way led toward consciousness concentrated on the separate appearance of subject and object. Once this process was firmly established the new conception obviously would evolve into two great types. Emphasis could be laid either on the subject or on the object.

For this impersonal statement another may be formulated expressing the same fact in the light of the subject. The evolving autonomous subject positing itself may continue to accentuate itself in the face of the evolving object. On the other hand it may immediately turn to the object in order to find its specific self-consciousness tinged and strengthened through the confrontation with that object. The first side of the alternative is the point of view assumed by the East, making due allowance for variations of minor importance in the individual Eastern civilizations. The second is the main line of thought and action in the West.

The Western mind fixes the object as the *ob-jectum*,—that which is thrown against the subject—in a word, the opposite. The world surrounding the subject is an objective world. It is independent of the subject. This applies in the first place, but by no means exclusively, to the material world. The immaterial realm of the mind and the spirit obey the same bias, though to varying degrees. The objects of religious thought and worship we conceive to exist independent of man. And so it is with the absolute in most philosophic systems just as we succumb easily to the temptation to deal with the host of "isms" as if they were distinct substances. So from its beginning Western civilization has persisted in enriching both the visible and the invisible world by the uninterrupted discovery and creation of new objects. Nothing could better illustrate what the positing of or fixing the object as the decisive act means to the Western mind than the productive occupation with the world of objects and its recognition as a reality. Such is the main trend of Western experience and thought.

Not so the East's. The East did not so entirely cut the umbilical cord between subject and object. Unlike the West, the East did not permit the object to evolve into a realm arising independently in front of the subject. Clearly this means that the East despite its severance from the magic world has remained closer to it than the West. To give full precision to this fact it would be preferable in relation to the East not to speak of object at all. For the term object necessarily implies, and with perfect reason in Western use, the connotation of the opposite *vis-à-vis* the subject. What corresponds to the object in the West, in the East is better named—the other. This term indicates that whatever be the distance between the subject and the *other* it can never turn into the distinct cleavage which separates subject and object in the West. A certain bond and affinity thus persists between the two embracing equally the grim and the friendlier aspects of world and nature. Hence the calm and the serenity which despite the vicissitudes of fate and the violence of passions—both certainly not inferior to those of the West—permeate the East and tinge the creations of its art and its thought. The closeness of the non-subject to the subject—as we might say in avoidance of all misleading connotations—seems to be a residue of the magic world. The result is that the East, severed from the magic world with the same determination as the West, retains some vivid reminiscences of its ancestor. However, the decisive act which constitutes Eastern mind and civilization—the positing or the fixing of the subject—implies the idea that an existence entirely separated from and independent of the subject cannot be conceived. So what becomes in Western mind and civilization the autonomous object, is paralleled in the East by the other which is coherent with and held in existence by the subject. Stemming as it does from the magic world this relation between the subject and the other does not lend itself to exact description. Yet this impossibility of exact definition does not diminish the distinctive reality of the phenomenon itself.

*   *   *

Such are the basic differences of the two civilizations which emerged from the magic world. The West emphasizes the object as the pivot—the East, the subject. Before elaborating on the manifold implications of this distinction a widespread, yet very instructive error must be eliminated. It is a common opprobrium exhibited by Asiatics against the West that Western civilization, with the possible exception of its medieval period, has sought its fulfilment in the physical world. This allegation of a gross materialistic attitude has affected the conscience of many Westerners and has certainly increased the number of those who in the face of our technical evolution have arrived at the same conclusion. This charge, however, is no better founded than the assertion of an all-out spirituality with which Asiatic civilization is so often credited by its own judgment and that of its admirers.

The truth is not as simple. Although the recent stage of Western civilization easily lends itself to such an interpretation, the identification of the object with the material world is an erroneous simplification. Such an identification in Western civilization altogether ignores the idea of its mind-structure. The object must

not be identified with any particular kind of objects be they
varieties of the material or immaterial realms. For the object
embraces them all, and even transcends them since it also includes
all potential realms. The reason why the object is beyond any
specific determination resides in the fact that it is a structure
of the mind. This was clearly indicated when it was demonstrated
how the Western mind building one realm after the other arrived
at the scientific organization of nature only after having organized
its spiritual realm during the Middle Ages.

The term object must not therefore be taken in a material, and
still less in a materialistic significance. It indicates the form of the
mind which deals with any kind of data in an objective way, and
attempts to determine them by concepts which are the expression
of reflective thought, and then to organize the various spheres of
existence according to the principle of unity in variety. Thus, if the
physical world should vanish from sight, the Western mind could
and would still continue to express itself adequately in the
formation of the immaterial world. This is precisely what it did in
the days when theology shaped the transcendental realm as an
objective world on which man depended but which in no way depended on man. The same thing is true of the main metaphysical
systems of Western philosophy where the absolute, whatever be its
determination and its relation to the human mind, does not depend
upon the latter.

By the same token the statement referring to the spirituality
of the East must be amended. True, the Eastern mind finds its
most tangible expression in the spiritual realm just as science and
the technical age may be considered the most tangible manifestation of the Western mind. But the Eastern mind cannot be linked
up and identified with any specific realm. This resides in the
Eastern mind structure. Now the Eastern mind starts with the
affirmation of the subject, and this dominating act implies that
the object and the objective attitude are barred from obtaining
the impact accruing to them in the West.

Whereas Western man moves between two extremes—one
where he asserts his supremacy over the object and the other
where he submits to it—the man of the East neutralizes this
violent agitation caused by the Western relation to the object.

He does not recognize the non-subject as that independent entity the object, but assigns to it the place of the other. Thereby he neither humiliates it to a position inferior to himself nor raises it to one of mastery. So the other, that is to say, all that which is not the subject, appears in a relation of juxtaposition to the subject and is granted the same degree and right of reality as the subject itself.

This is not all. The structure of the Eastern mind being juxtaposition and identity, it follows that the Eastern mind establishes a close relationship with the other so far as it is compatible with the other being the non-subject. The coordination of the other can only subsist because in the Eastern mind there is no such thing as the object facing the subject in its own right. This bent toward drawing and keeping the other near to the subject may be called the subjectifying or subjective attitude of the East in contradistinction to the objectifying or objective attitude of the West.

Obviously we scent here the magical atmosphere. The magic world itself, of course, is left far behind. Gone are the easy personifications of all existence, the transmutability of the human personality and many other of its characteristics. But there lives on in the world concept and philosophy of the East a definite aversion to those pairs of opposites which dominate the history of Western thought—the living and the inanimate, mind and matter, soul and body, the conscious and the unconscious. And the absence of these antitheses is the expression of the closeness in which the other despite its otherness is held to the subject. What characterizes the Eastern mind is not spirituality—it is not its devotion to the spiritual realm. Being a form of the mind the subjective attitude is not restricted to any field of existence. It is active everywhere although not with the same efficiency and in the same mode. Its most penetrating consequence is its denial to the external world of an existence in its own right. Such an objective existence, independent of the perception of the subject, seems to the Asiatic mind absurd and paradoxical—a monstrous idea.

And, be it emphasized, it is not the particular aspect of the world as determined by our senses which is declared subjective. This tenet is a well known trend in Western philosophy. The representative thinkers of Asia agree that whatever lies behind the phenomena shares the subjectivity of the world. Indeed any other view would undermine the predominant place of the subject and its moral responsibility. On the other hand, radical idealism with its theory of the illusionary character of the external world is not innate in, let alone characteristic of, Asia. It belongs as do so many other extremist theories to the West.

If it would be self-contradictory of the equipoise of the Asiatic mind to attribute to the world a reality superior to the mind for which it exists, it need not, however, possess less. And it is in full accordance with the primacy of the subject in the structure of the Asiatic mind that the subject determines the reality of its world. Determination does not mean creation. It means—and here again we are referred to the orbit of the magic world—that a strict correspondence exists between certain fundamental forms of subject and their worlds. But there is this momentous difference from the magic notion. In the Eastern orbit the subject is the instigating and decisive force.

If it is the pivotal idea that the world is held and suspended by the mind, the subjectifying attitude will realize this principle in art, thought and the working out of human destiny. Asiatic thought tries to relate the phenomena nearer to the subject by demonstrating in many ways that they are conditioned by and linked up with the subject. Thus the art of Asia introduces the subject into its creations in quite another sense than the West, and in order to shield them from acquiring an objective character. And the supreme goal of man is kept free from imagery of any kind to the utmost possible degree. Accordingly, the subjectifying attitude fulfils itself with greater perfection by the extent to which the phenomena are divested of their character as the other. A thorough exposition of this would disrupt our argument.

In the end, the ideal situation would be created when the subject meets and experiences itself, freed from the interference of otherness altogether. This would constitute the approximation of the pure and absolute subject. All this is in strict analogy and contradistinction to the ideal situation of the Western mind which insists that the approximation of the pure and absolute object has been achieved when all data including those belonging to the subject have been objectified.

117

This subjective attitude is the outcome of the basic act of the Eastern mind in which the subject posits itself. This act impresses upon the great manifestations of Eastern civilizations their character. Also it is sensed in the whole atmosphere and psychology of the East. At all times, at least until our days, the West sensed in the East a calmness and serenity whose subsistence was unaffected by the vicissitudes which fell to the East no less than to the West. Secret lore and superior wisdom were believed to be hidden behind this façade. Also the bearing of reserve and dignity with which the man of the East has traditionally been credited was admiringly appreciated before the technical age started to belittle these values.

At the bottom is the fact that the man of the East dwells and reposes in himself in quite another mode than the Westerner. In keeping with the evolution and the depth of the self, this inner imperturbability imparts to man a fundamental remoteness which has no relation to asceticism. In the East passions, good or bad, have often exceeded in violence those of the West. But there existed an inner voice warning that all things, fascinating though they may be, are not the real, and that however vehemently they may affect the soul they remain the other.[1] This remoteness has never failed to impress the West in its dealings with Asiatics and has evoked the feelings of timelessness and reverential wonder.

The characteristics of the Eastern mind derive from that ontological act whereby the subject fixes itself in its own consciousness prior to the object. Hence there follow two seemingly contradictory aspects of the Eastern mind which significantly complete each other. The basic facet presented the subject separated from the other and was expressed psychologically in the experience of remoteness. The other facet showed the subject in its subjective attitude whereby it tried to draw the other nearer to itself—an effort which came to fruition only when the other became identified with the subject. With this insight into the functioning of the structure of the Eastern mind the "spiritual" East appears as much an undue simplification as the "materialistic" West.

Neither East nor West is committed to exclusive spheres of

---

[1] Cf. the chapter 'Psychology' in my book *Iran*, New York, Columbia University Press, 1945.

existence. Their mind-structures, though expressible in concise formulas, operate as orientations indifferent to any kind of material. However, it remains true that to each of these structures there corresponds a specific sphere which exemplifies its clearest manifestation. So while the objective attitude of the West is applied with momentous results to art, psychology, philosophy and even religion, when it deals with nature it reveals most clearly its virtue and power.

The Eastern mind attracts and penetrates the non-subject in manifold ways so as to divest it of as much of its otherness as possible. But it reaches its clearest expression when the subject returns to and is alone with itself. Thus the central problem of the East consists in the relation of the subject to itself. And inseparable from this relation, is its discovery of the real subject. It can thus be seen how identification is operative in the subjective attitude and how it triumphs in the subject's coincidence with the absolute subject. The West, on the contrary, aims at the discovery of the absolute object as its main target and revolves around the problems of the relation between subject and object. Uniting the variety of things which its objective attitude creates in every field of existence, is the method it employs to achieve its final purpose.

A structure of civilization is a principle expressible in categorical form. In operation it can be considered an entelechy that is to say an unfolding realization which tries to mould everything according to its pattern. And in so doing it determines the very essence and aspect of civilization. The herald that announces the creation of these structures—or in non-poetical language, the prerequisite fact that precedes their appearance—is that decisive mental act whereby the object or the subject is posited. It is this act that marks the break with the magic world. And to a certain extent this act contains or hides the structure.

When as in the East the subject is posited first, it becomes the central unit. Correspondingly the non-subject—the other—will then appear as multiplicity, as the indifferent, unorganized juxtaposition of the phenomenon. And the appropriate way of dealing with and disposing of this multiplicity will be to reduce as much as possible the number of its components and to bring

119

the rest closer to the subject for potential ultimate identification with the subject. This then is the structure of the Eastern mind—juxtaposition and identity.

On the other hand, in the West it is the object that is posited first. And in this case the world facing the subject constitutes the great unit. Despite its multifariousness it does not fall apart. Man enters the cosmos as a part and his effort to organize the phenomena assumes quite consistently the form unity in variety. In the end we see therefore that these two structures are composed of two parts. The base consists of variety in the West as against juxtaposition in the East. The operative device is unification as contrasted with identification.

CHAPTER VI

Wonder versus Awe

Our argument now requires an elucidation of the manner in which these two structures appeared, and how their appearance illumined, as if by magic, the atmospheres of the civilizations of the East and of the West. This we have termed the inburst of the structures on the magic world.

Civilizations that rest upon structures represent the mature types of the civilized mind. From this it must not be deduced that the Western and Eastern civilizations monopolize the highest achievements. (For example the Near East has been the torchbearer of civilization, yet it seems impossible to discover a structural base of Near Eastern civilization.) What it does mean is that they alone stand upon a systematic foundation which confers upon them incomparable stability.

These structures started the civilizations of the East and of the West with a sudden impulse. They announced their entrance with such portentous phenomena as pre-Socratic philosophy and the most ancient of the Upanishads. These were truly inspired creations which unmistakably bore the mark of these structures. Once the latter became immersed in the life of the civilization they operated as entelechies. In this manner in their unfolding they shaped everything and thus in the course of time realized themselves. This development may assume the form of evolution as it does in the West albeit that term cannot be properly applied in the East.

In any event it is not the structure which undergoes the evolutionary process. The reason for this lies in the fact that evolution cannot apply to the Mind in the sense which is under discussion here. For these structures belong to a sphere beyond that of the intellect or reason. They are in the realm of pure forms of the Mind which transcend the ordinary mental processes.

121

Hence, they do not evolve on lines parallel with our psychological and mental endowment. It is an inburst or irruption that characterizes the appearance of anything belonging to the Mind. This can easily be illustrated by well known phenomena.

All original and creative ideas occur in a shock-like inspiration. And this is regardless of whether they belong to the religious, the philosophical, the artistic or the scientific sphere. Their appearance resembles a sudden burst of light even though they may be the result of a long preparatory process of thought, experimentation or contemplation. The sensation of the individual is a feeling of being lifted above the regular flow of the psychological and intellectual stream. One touches for that illumined moment another realm. Such an experience constitutes a profound stir of the whole being.

Often there is no deliberate preparation directly related to the actual revelation. This idea, this intuition or even better this inspiration—this last term being etymologically the most suggestive—may come at a moment or from an angle least expected. It may ignore all preceding preparation and direction and thus the philosophical or scientific proof may have to be constructed afterwards. The psychology of great inventions and discoveries, of artistic and philosophical conceptions and of religious revelations amply illustrates this inburst of the Mind. So momentous an experience makes man feel less a spontaneous creator than the chosen instrument of a higher power, or perhaps the mere scene where a pregnant event is taking place.

In the history of civilization the inburst of the structures is of precisely the same character. And the human agents in whose minds the structures first manifest their original creations are surrounded by an aura characteristic of a prophet. And how could this be otherwise? For they personify the devices of the two outstanding civilizations and they anticipate the potentialities of the millennia to come.

In order fully to grasp the inburst of the structures on the magic world, and thus to recognize the hour of birth of the two civilizations, we must retrace those centuries which are unique in importance in the history of mankind. These are the fifth and sixth centuries B.C. in Greece and Persia, and the two or three preceding centuries in India and China. In the pre-Socratic philosophers, in Zoroaster's conception, in the Indian metaphysics of Oneness and the teachings of the Buddha, in the Chinese metaphysics of Yin-Yang, the Tao and the doctrine of Confucius—the Western and the Eastern mind reached out into a higher form of consciousness. This was not primarily because of the greatness of these ideas. Rather it was that in them the structures of West and East emerged with unmistakable clarity, conferring an awareness and conclusiveness not elsewhere to be found.

In one mighty thrust Western and Eastern civilizations transcended myth and belief. As a result, men inquired not only into the essence of mind and nature, but were equally concerned with the scope and validity of cognition or knowledge. Free of divine commandments they tried to determine the supreme goal of man and to establish the nature of good and evil. Western and Eastern civilizations owe not only this penetrating lucidity but a pointedness of means and purpose to this fact of structuralization.

The respective structures were not the result of evolution. Neither can they be explained by nor are they derived from preceding stages. However, they did not drop out of the sky. When the conditions were ripe they burst from the ontological sphere. Just what these conditions were it is impossible to determine even approximately as the peoples in question have been shaped by these structures for as long as we have known them. Probably what was needed was a concurrence of external factors and particular human material. But no definite conclusions can be drawn as to those particulars. The psychological atmosphere which heralded the emergence of the structures is, however, clearly recognizable. This atmosphere is the clear radiation of those structures, just as the false dawn is the light of the unseen sun.

This atmosphere necessarily differed in the West and in the East. When Plato declared wonder to be the beginning of philosophy, he voiced a psychological fact pertaining not only to the Greek mind but to that of the West as a whole. In the psychology of wonder not only is there a clear separation between man in his act of wondering and the object of his wonder but his state of wonder lacks the elements of fear and dread. He also retains his freedom of movement in the face of the object. He does not hesitate to investigate it. Philosophical wonder is evoked first by the very fact of existence and second by the nature and variety of that which exists. In this state of wonder there is then an intellectual element which takes precedence over others and grows rapidly in importance.

This psychological fact gains in significance when compared with the attitude of the East. There it was the experience of awe which roused men from myth and traditional religious belief to the adventure of a great civilization. Awe—a state of solemn dread and arrestive veneration—unites man with the cause of his awe. And while the depth of the experience and thereby the awareness of the awe-inspiring entity may vary, the state of awe is sufficient unto itself. This is evident from the restraining influence that awe exerts on the Eastern mind. In the attitude of awe, even when its components such as the intellectual and the volitional begin to assert themselves, the basic experience prevents their developing into independently functioning activities. And thus it maintains a wholeness rarely found in the West.

In pre-Socratic philosophy, it is true, the experience of awe is not entirely lacking. But where it does exist it is emasculated and it lacks the unfathomable, arresting character it possesses in the East. More important, it is expurgated of its constituent element —fear. This reverential fear, of a sublime nature, lives on as a key-note in tragedy and as an essential motif in the mystery cults. The divestment by Greek philosophical thought of reverential fear was a momentous achievement. By this act, it determined the secular character of Western thought and philosophy. Not even during the Middle Ages did Western thought belie this attitude. For no sooner did theology establish dominion than philosophy opened a campaign to wrest back its lost ground. And when modern philosophy upheld the existence of God, it was not permitted to interfere with the process of secular thought.

To quote a few major examples—even to philosophers of orthodox faith like Descartes and the Cartesians, God was but a *deus ex machina* called upon to solve otherwise insoluble problems such as the connection between mind and matter. To Kant, God was an ethical postulate. And in the systems of Spinoza and Hegel the idea of the Godhead bears no resemblance to the God of orthodox

124

religion. This independence the secular mind of the West owes to that state of wonder which, never sufficient unto itself, drove man on to investigate the object of his wonder.

The basic separation of subject and object in the Western mind now becomes manifest as well as the emphasis on the object. This act of marvelling, this state of wonder transcends and points beyond itself. The state of awe, on the contrary, encompasses subject and object, not of course in the totality of their being, but in a species of partial and mutual absorption. In this primordial experience the awe-inspiring entity is at once near and remote, known and unknown, desired and feared. The link between subject and object is therefore strangely effective. Contrary to the state of philosophical wonder, the state of awe need not transcend itself to reach its object. The awe-inspiring thing is in some indefinable way anchored in the experience of awe—so to speak, in the awe-inspired subject.

The experience of awe considered here does not of course coincide with that of the primitive who stands spell-bound before his fetish any more than philosophical wonder concerned with the Isness and Thusness of existence corresponds to a curiosity that stands agape. Man feels unmistakably though dimly that the awe inspiring entity is essentially of the same nature as himself despite its difference and further that he is called upon to descend into himself to discover it. What makes this state of awe so prodigious a phenomenon is the immanent homogeneousness of man with the cause of awe, combined with that solicitation to follow it to the end.

While nowhere as clearly defined as in the identity of the individual soul with the absolute Brahman, yet the presence of the ultimate reality, veiled as it is in other experiences of awe, cannot be ignored. It is inherent in the conception of Tao. It is not lacking in Confucius. True, in the West and in modern China the doctrine of Confucius assumes the character of a sober and dryly realistic system of ethics. Yet in classic Confucianism the idea of human society and man himself, far from being rationalistic, was permeated with that sense of awe which, though less concentrated than in India, is distinctly to be felt. The same thing holds good for Iran. In the sacred scripts of Zoroastrianism the powers of good and evil were far from being as distinctly personified as the gods of the polytheistic pantheon. For this very reason it was easier for man to feel himself linked with the supernatural in the experience of awe.

Such were the contrasting atmospheres which heralded the emergence of the structures in West and East. The structures themselves made their appearance in phenomena of the highest spiritual and intellectual order.

* * *

Three key-words could well be written over the entrance into Western civilization. All three were coined by Greek philosophy— θαυμάζειν, wonder or marvel—ἀρχή, *arche*, vaguely rendered as principle—and διασώξειν τὰ φαινόμενα, which means, when literally translated, the phrase 'to save the phenomena through'. Together these terms, encompassing as they do the psychological incentive and the methodological problem, constitute the soul of Western philosophy. We have already dealt with the phenomenon of wonder. That of *arche* or principle must now be investigated. This is an idea within which the Western structure of unity in variety unfolds, just as it contains the lasting dynamic impulse of the Western mind.[1] The term *arche* which was introduced probably by Anaximander who died in 546 B.C. appears in pre-Socratic philosophy in various forms. It was used to designate origin, the beginning in general, primordial matter or whatever the substance was from which everything was supposed to derive, principle or essence, real cause or the principle of knowing. What united all these divergent solutions rooted in the manifold meaning of *arche* was an ardent desire to find a fulcrum from which everything in existence could be understood. It did not matter whether they stressed the humid element of Thales, the aerial element of Anaximenes, the atoms of Leucippus and Democritus, the infinite of Anaximander, the pure Isness of Parmenides, Heraclitus' idea of a dialectic principle as the ruler of the world-process; Anaxagoras' idea of reason as principle; or the Pythagorean intuition of numbers, that is mathematical relations as the essence of things.

These individual solutions are unimportant. So likewise is their plurality. What is vital is the difference and the originality of these

---

[1] The 'saving of the phenomena' will be taken up in Chapter VIII.

variant approaches to the problem of *arche*. For this is the form in which the Western mind structure, unity in variety, burst into being—in this conception of *arche* teeming with views and methods that converge to the same end, and driven by its inherent tension to unfold, to clarify and to evolve its potentialities.

In Western civilization, questions are as important as answers. Genuine evolution proceeds according to unity in variety creating ever differently, ever anew. And thus there is a continual need of breaking up old units in favour of others better fitted to meet new requirements. The pre-Socratic philosophers initiated this process and gave it its lasting model. The naïve nature philosophers simply asked 'What is primordial matter?' Then their crude materialistic view was superseded by the scientific thought of the atomistic school, and this idea was never lost. But Anaximander, and, with infinitely greater intuition, Parmenides, questioned whether reality could be found at all within the scope of sense-determined data. Thus was created the paragon of pure idealism to be taken up by Plato and all those who for two thousand years claimed to be Platonists. In the next step Heraclitus asked himself whether pure being was even thinkable. Then he decided that becoming must be the only reality as it united being and non-being in an endless dialectic process. His lasting influence culminated in Hegel's system.

If the simple causal thinking of the nature philosophers was thus replaced by the view of idealism and the dialectical method of Heraclitus, Anaxagoras introduced the teleological principle when he declared that the order of the universe could not but spring from reason. To the Pythagoreans, the essence of things lay in their corresponding numerical proportions. In contradistinction to these efforts toward comprehending the world on the basis of intelligent and intelligible principles, Empedocles tried to explain all existence as the result of a blind antagonism between a positive and a negative force. And anticipating the theory of natural selection and the survival of the fittest, he regarded living organisms as the products of a mechanically operating chance which eliminated all unsuitable forms of life. At the end of this process came the Sophists whose subjective relativism was a logical conclusion to this overwhelming variety of propositions.

The Western form of objective thinking is obvious in pre-Socratic philosophy. It started with an attempt to cognize or comprehend the universe. At first this was chiefly nature, but it soon comprised man and his place in the universe. It was the world at large however, the cosmos, which retained the primary interest. Indeed, the main reason why man himself became the object of philosophical preoccupation was the failure of nature philosophy to produce satisfactory results. Man had to admit that sense data did not communicate reliable information and hence that knowledge based on sense perception was doomed to frustration. Thus was the mind which had set out to conquer the world thrown back on itself. And then it was, in a flash of insight, that thought alone, independent of the senses, was considered the only trustworthy source of knowledge. This discovery with a full awareness of its importance was first proclaimed by Parmenides in the words— 'Thought is its own object.'

This basic proposition of Parmenides further implied that being and thinking are identical. The conviction that thought could find within itself the essential truth led on the one hand to the Platonic doctrine of ideas, and on the other, to the critical investigation of reason by reason itself. Be that as it may, nothing could distract the pre-Socratic philosophers from their innate interest in nature. Parmenides himself wrote a book on physics accompanied by the pertinent warning that what he had to say on this subject was but a mortal's opinion and made no pretensions to truth. Equally significant was the sophist Gorgias' book which was entitled: *On that which does not really exist, or on nature.*

The history of the human mind, in so far as the harassing problems of the origin and meaning of the world and of man are concerned, does not begin with questions. It commences with answers. The most primitive tribes possess explanatory myths which grow and are still with them. This is likewise true of prehistoric man whose beliefs can be reconstructed from his burial rites and symbolic designs. The origin of these myths is as impenetrable as is that of man himself. They are as natural and indispensable to man as his basic instincts and his capacity to adjust to environment. Were this not so, his awakening consciousness, lost in a world of riddles, would be crushed by its helplessness and loneliness. As it is, his psyche stands in need of immediate and reassuring solutions, just as his body depends for its subsistence on the bulk of its instincts. The mytho-magic world—for all myth is essentially magic—answers questions before they are asked. Its tales satisfy the intellect, they canalize the emotions and direct vague spiritual feelings. Thus, myth constitutes a great wall of defence behind which the life of the mind may grow in safety and fathom the depths of existence.[1]

Twice, however, in the history of civilization, the mytho-magic world which so cautiously and with such efficiency contained the unknown forces along with the cryptic meaning of existence, burst under the pressure to which it was continually exposed and had to cede hegemony to other powers which had matured under its aegis. This was the situation which characterized the inburst of the structures marking the birth of the Western and Eastern civilizations. The traditional answers had ceased to satisfy the mind. So had the forms that evoked them. The fundamental problems disclosed themselves undisguised and with inexorable clarity. Other capacities and instruments of knowing—conceptual and intuitive reason—assumed the leadership and claimed the power to find the true solutions.

The break with the mytho-magic world was incomparably more radical in the West than in the East. The Greek philosophical wonder, that secular and implicitly scientific attitude, drew the subject mercilessly from itself, pointing to and recognizing the object as an independent entity outside of the subject. This view treated the numberless phenomena of the objective universe as a variety of things to be explained by the *arche*. Thus this Aristotelian wonder was and remains the West's ever-renewed incentive to confront nature as a totality of objects, or, to be more precise, to expose all data to the utmost possible degree of objectivity.

* * *

The nature of awe on the other hand produced entirely different results. Nonetheless both wonder and awe have one all-important characteristic in common. This is the freedom from primitive fear

[1] The most impressive example of this is presented by India where until our days the disguise of mythological symbolism permitted imagination, thought and experience to probe the dimensions of human existence.

which paralyses the capacities of the mind. The psychological attitudes which characterize the awakening of consciousness and its release from the protective bonds of myth and magic, are utterly devoid of this primitive anxiety. They herald the epiphany of new worlds. Holding out promise and hope, they are the sources of a vast creativity.

In a state of awe, man is not tempted to recognize the object as his antagonist and the objective world as existing independently of himself. This fundamental experience of the Eastern mind involves the placing of the subject, not as a self-contained entity, but simultaneously with the other. This means that otherness contains nothing foreign to, nor independent of the subject. Therefore it must be recognized that the non-subject presents itself to the Western and to the Eastern mind in two fundamentally different modes. This has a vital bearing on the significance of the phenomena and particularly on their relation to the subject. Nor does the distinction stop there. It extends into the imagery itself, that is, into the qualities and aspects of the phenomena. While this may apply in lesser degree to material phenomena, in general it holds true of psychological phenomena.

Since the Eastern mind does not see the object as opposed to the subject, it does not look for reality in the objective and least of all in the physical world. The structure of the Eastern mind leads it to regard reality as somehow co-ordinated and akin to the subject. The innate tendency is to bridge and diminish the distance between reality and the subject. Not only is the objective world here deprived of sovereignty, but the urge to objectify data is replaced by an opposite urge which is no less powerful in its way than is the Western. The East avoids what must seem to it deviation and a detour. Choosing a direct path, the man of the East arrives almost immediately at answers which to all intents and purposes are for him binding and definitive.

Here then is a remarkable difference between East and West. Whereas in each civilization the inburst of the structures is equally clear and magnificent, the first creations which proclaim that inburst and bear the mark of the structures, play very different roles in the mental history of the two civilizations.

The fascination of the few fragments left of the writings of the

pre-Socratics derives from the fact that they fathomed the depths
and established the dimensions of the Western mind with imagination and intuition as well as intellectual awareness and methodical
clarity. They threw open the doors revealing a new land. They
invented the means of exploring it. And they arrived at a variety
of solutions. As is amply demonstrated by the evolution of Western
thought, their decisive function and perennial significance consists
more than anything else in what their thought generated. What
is unique is that their originality, far from endangering the work
of their successors, proved a permanent incentive to independent
creative thought. Their views and solutions became fundaments
and principles, hypotheses and orientations. Their supreme glory
perhaps was that they suggested thoughts and systems greater
than their own. Be that as it may, the variety of the beginning was
in harmony with objective thinking. This was based on the structural principle, unity in variety, and the monopoly of a mind to
to which reality appears in objective form and which at its start
turned to the outside world as the most conspicuous presentation
of objectiveness.

To the East reality is somehow intimately connected with the
subject, whatever the meaning of the term subject may become in
the course of the mind's unfolding. This is what is felt in that state
of awe where man stands in the presence of something touching
his very essence. The coexistence of man and that which inspires
awe in his awful experience finds its consummation in the identity
of both regardless of the interpretation of the terms subject and
identity given by sages and schools. In this way, the Eastern
structure is indicated by the East's ontological experience.
Ignoring the objectifying process of thought, the East dismisses
the outer world as the all-important object of speculation. Instead
it stresses the necessary relationship of the Real with the subject.

This, of course, radically changes the position and meaning of
the term subject. As the subject, to the Easterner, is relative not
to the object, that is to an objective world as the essence of reality,
but to an entity close to him, the word *self* will hereafter be used
wherever precision requires it to indicate the subject in Eastern
thought. This immediacy of the Real enables the East to reach
at an early moment supreme answers to basic problems. These

answers in the depth and fullness of their significance have never been seriously questioned and, despite varying interpretations, they have remained the guiding lights of the East. From the East's standpoint, it has reached with astounding clarity and by dint of its own unique effort what the West is eternally searching under ever-changing forms. The Westerner, caught in his own net, would declare that where the Eastern mind stopped the Western mind started. Furthermore, considering the East's basic creations as parallel to its own, it would accuse the East of having taken as an end what was only an hypothesis.

Those creations which mark the inburst of the Eastern structure constitute at the same time the peak of the East's creative power. There are few if any subsequent philosophical ideas and systems in the East which can claim true originality. The divergent ones often testify to their dependence on the originals by their hostile character. The fascination of these original creations has resulted in their being continually modified and reinterpreted.

There is no parallel in any nation to the influence of Confucius on China, his teaching having been that nation's paramount formative power as well as its noblest expression. In its main lines and apart from Taoism and Buddhism, Chinese philosophy is heavily marked by Confucian thinking, the successors of Confucius having either followed and modified, or opposed and criticized his doctrine. The metaphysics of Taoism have not undergone any remarkable change since their emergence from the magic period. As to India, the idea of the One and the path to salvation connected with it, which is the gospel of the most grandiose Upanishads, has retained its sovereign position to this day. Even the great Shankara of the ninth Century A.D., the central figure of the Vedanta philosophy, while fully recognizing the absolute reality of the one Brahman, did no more than secure a relative reality for this world, and corresponding to it, a lower kind of knowledge subordinate to supreme truth. In Iran, the rise of Sufism and its penetration of life and poetry is traceable not so much to the influence of Islamic monotheism as to the fact that Sufism constituted a definite triumph over Zoroastrian dualism.

The monumental insularity and representativeness of these original creations belongs exclusively to the East.

CHAPTER VII

Distinctions in Philosophic Thought

Upon a first open-minded approach to Eastern philosophy immediately the notion arises that there is a basic distinction between it and Western philosophy. On deeper investigation this notion is intensified. And then comes the realization that the term philosophy is actually inapplicable—that it serves to obscure and to falsify the spirit of Eastern thought. Neither the origin, the purpose, nor the intellectual means and methods are the same in the East as in the West. No universal term exists that is sufficiently suggestive to embrace the approach of both West and East.

The etymology of the word philosophy hints unmistakably at the point of difference. As conceived by the Greeks, this love of wisdom included everything worth knowing, not as merely accumulated material, but organized according to value and significance. Thus philosophy, all-encompassing and relying on metaphysics— the first philosophy—assigned to each field of knowledge its place, the categories constituting its object and likewise its method of procedure. In principle this was and it still is the idea of Western philosophy, albeit for obvious reasons its realization has become increasingly difficult. The main characteristic resulting from this idea is the deep conviction that all wisdom, from the supreme to a lesser order, is, and it must be, expressible in concepts. Wisdom at any level is based on and is contained in conceptual thought, and its existence depends on the clarity of its formulations.

The East does not share this conviction. Discarding the multiplicity of objects and the fields of knowledge, ignoring to the utmost possible degree the concept as the vehicle of philosophic thought, the East attempts to establish immediate contact with the Real. This communion and what derives from it is, to the man of the East—wisdom. Thus the Eastern mind is not concerned with love of wisdom in the Western sense, but with love of reality or essence. If we adopt the Greek word for essence, *ousia*, the difference between the Eastern and Western ventures is cast into clear relief by the coining of a new word—philousia—the desire for essence or Isness—and by opposing philosophy to it. In thus by-passing whatever stood in the way of an immediate relation to the Real, the East emerged in that spiritual fulfilment which is evidenced by its early yet determining creations. The majesty of these creations not only depreciated all divergent conceptions but made them appear superfluous—almost paradoxical.

The objectifying mind of Greek philosophy, on the other hand, evolved a creativity of its own with its unique conception of the *arche* as the dynamic principle of creation, evolution and organization. Posing the problem of the *arche* in ever different ways and relating it to the various aspects of the material and the non-material world, the Greeks early began to define with increasing clarity the spheres of human experience as semi-independent sciences. Philosophy in the narrower sense unfolded in metaphysics, logic, psychology, and the like, whereas sciences such as physics, biology, medicine, and the humanities—history and political science—were ever ready to draw from the leading ideas of metaphysics even when established in their own right. The apotheosis of philosophy as the all-embracing doctrine of human knowledge was the system of Aristotle. Mathematics alone, let it be said, developed in its own right but it did not escape the jurisdiction of philosophy. Pythagoras and Plato in their respective ways made it the pillar of metaphysics. And this was a conception unparalleled in the East.

This process has been repeated in modern philosophy. The nature-philosophy of the late Middle Ages and the Renaissance, which derived its universality from theology and was represented by men like Agrippa and Cardanus, broke up under the impact of the new science of nature. This was the signal for that extraordinary revolutionary movement in the course of which science split away from the humanities, unfolding with demonic fertility into ever new fields with no end in sight. The striking difference between this later process and the first lies in the unconditioned independence of the scientific fields that had emerged and their interrelation without recognition of a supreme authority. The great philosophical systems of the period, however, tried to restore the original state by synthesizing the sum total of the knowledge of their time under the guiding light of a central idea. In our day philosophy—the Great Mother—is weakened by this resolute defection of her offspring. Her genius languishes in proportion to the growth of the science of nature.

Though it be a significant phenomenon it is no consolation that not a few leading physicists have become philosophers and have sought to evaluate their work in terms of philosophy and to apply the results to such problems as free will, the destiny of man and his place in the universe. Legitimate and desirable as these efforts are, they cannot compensate for the lack of an independent, spontaneous creativity on the part of philosophy itself. For it is unlikely that any philosophical thought that is based on a specialized branch of scientific knowledge can ever reach that freedom and universality which is the life-breath of philosophy. This brings to mind the biological theory of evolution which a hundred years ago entered the realm of philosophy. But while a stimulant there as it was everywhere, it did not produce anything comparable to the great systems which had been created by philosophy in its own right.

The extension of these individual sciences into the philosophic field is highly indicative of the Western mind. It constitutes a testimonial to the fact that all our scientific knowledge derives originally from philosophy and that the spirit of philosophy as conceived by the Greeks is still the inspiring force. When eminent physicists, biologists and historians—to mention only the three most comprehensive fields—find it necessary to crown their work with philosophical considerations, Aristotle's word appears to hold true—that what is prior in nature is perceived by us as the posterior. Applied to our statement this means that even though the need for philosophical conclusions appears at the end of a work, it is the hidden incentive for the whole undertaking.

The process of Western thought can be understood only if we see it as a stream, the source of which is in the dynamism of the Greek conception of philosophy. Originating in philosophy and growing within its precincts, the variegated branches of knowledge inherited from philosophy their most precious legacy. This was the spirit of disinterestedness in everything but knowledge itself. This dispassionate spirit, disinterested only in so far as it was determined by the motive of systematic knowledge for its own sake, was inherent in the state of wonder. And it was possessed by Greece alone.

In the East, scientific knowledge no less than general knowledge grew out of the interaction of natural curiosity with the drive of needs and desires. Of course such motivating forces as these were active in the West too. But with the advent of philosophy they were superseded by a far greater power. By themselves, the limitations of these forces are obvious, though they can go a long way in producing useful knowledge. Important as were the achievements of Indian mathematics, they came to an early stand-still. If China did not expand most of her many inventions, it was because she lacked the original impetus which leads from the universal to the particular and gives a significance to such discoveries. Thus, the invention of printing was applied only in a very limited way to the printing of books—the discovery of gunpowder was limited almost entirely to fireworks—the construction of the compass never made of the Chinese a great seafaring people.

True, the Near East and the West are indebted to the East for an indeterminate number of ideas and inventions. However, if the importance of the East is to be judged by this kind of creativity, it would not be what it is. This would likewise be true of the West were it judged solely by what it accepted from the East. The important thing to consider is whether the acceptance of ideas led merely to imitation or whether it stimulated a process of creative assimilation. Western knowledge stems from the spirit of its philosophy, from that first philosophical question with regard to the universe, and from the impulse born of the attitude which was implicit in that question. This purely theoretical attitude augured and it still augurs unforeseeable results. When not directed toward magic and myth the East's drive for knowledge remained as a whole determined by natural needs, the scope of which was limited by tradition. Thus everything connected with such needs shared their conservative character.

136

Distinctions in Philosophic Thought

★ ★ ★

This conservative attitude ensues necessarily from the uncompromising philousia of the East. Philosophy, on the other hand, which is the science of first principles, lays the foundations of all that merits the name of knowledge in the Western sense. This conception of philosophy is made ever more difficult by the growing independence of the branches of knowledge. Compared to philosophy, philousia appears at the same time more pretentious and more modest. Its aim is limited—if a limitation it is—to their immediate attainment of Reality as apart from all other knowledge. Such an ambition precludes any desire to trespass upon other territories. Neither favouring nor actively hostile to either secular or priestly knowledge, philousia pursues its own way with supreme indifference.

Most illustrative of this is the scene in the Chandogya Upanishad.[1] Here the young Brahmin, very proud after his instruction in Vedic lore, returns to his father, to whom he enumerates his studies which are comparable to ours in the academic field. Thereupon, he is shown by his father that he has not been taught the one thing worth knowing. On the part of the father there is no contempt for these studies. They are simply to be replaced by a new teaching. In a similar way, Buddha waves aside all knowledge which is not strictly indispensable to salvation. In Confucianism, too, knowledge which is not concerned with the doctrinal core— the golden mean—is merely auxiliary, and provides a formative acquaintance with the ancients, with ritual, music and poetry. What there is of scientific knowledge in the East originated not because but independent of philousia. Thus again is illustrated the structural principle of juxtaposition in contradistinction to the relation of Western philosophy to scientific knowledge.

From its beginning philosophy was pure *theoria*—a movement of the mind toward investigating the data of existence in order to visualize the truth. This had no purpose save the attainment of knowledge, and it was therefore entirely disinterested. And from that disinterestedness there derived its boundless expansion, its continuity and its restlessness. Between this knowledge for knowledge's sake and the Greek's aim of forming man there is no contradiction. To the Greeks this disinterested pursuit of scientific

---

[1] VII, 1 *et seq.*

137

knowledge contained a formative value which would have deteriorated had the knowledge been put to a practical use. This movement of the mind toward investigation and this spirit of disinterestedness science inherited from philosophy.

Such an attitude is not shared by the East. To the Eastern mind, nature may lack purpose and meaning, but what man can know at any level must have purpose and meaning and be oriented towards demonstrable ends. This applies to secular, scientific knowledge no less than to the pursuits of common life. Thus, far from lacking an intelligible purpose, philousia fulfils its end undisturbed by theoretical interpretation. Indeed, theoretical philosophy cannot be compared to this conception of supreme knowledge and its importance for spiritual life in the East.

Eastern philousia however, is not only the counterpart of Western philosophy. It also sets itself off from religion, which merely provides its environment and atmosphere. Both marking the inburst of the structures of East and West, philousia and philosophy are independent and original creations of the mind. The fact that neither the one nor the other was derived from the then prevailing religions does not mean that the ground for their appearance was not laid by the evolution of religious thought. In fact this is what happened.

In Greece there can be traced an evolution in the course of which a distinctly monotheistic trend arose which separated itself from popular religion and was given expression by poets like Hesiod. In it Zeus, losing his mythological character and overshadowing if not extinguishing all other deities, became the Godhead, the creator and the ruler of the universe. In the decisive hour this idea was supplanted by the conception of the *arche*—a conception of quite another order, that of a powerful beginning— not an end. In conceiving the idea of *arche* the Greek mind secularized the godhead. Taking over all the power and potentialities contained in the notion of the godhead, the idea of *arche* started the West on its way to rule the universe in thought and to a more modest degree in action.

In its way the East followed the same pattern. In some respects the ground was laid for Confucianism by the ritualistic trends in Chinese life and some of the thoughts in the Book of History and the various annals. Yet neither the personality of Confucius nor what he taught and represented can be compared to these fore-runners. Similarly, Taoism was rooted in the magic world, but the depth of its dialectic thought and its application to man were entirely its own. The outstanding example of the severance of philousia from religion occurs in India. Two ways led up to the inburst of the structure on its civilization. First there was the growth of the idea of sacrifice—from a primitive ritual to that sublime form where sacrificer and receiver are fused in the act of sacrificing. The other, and the more important, was announced by the Verdic verse—'That which is one, the sages call by various names, Agni, Yama, Matarisvan.' This desire for unity, this feeling that there can be but one cause, but one essence, haunted the Indian mind and was expressed over and over again in the Brahmana texts until it rose to a peak of clarity in that scene from the Chandogya Upanishad:[1]

'Fetch me from thence a fruit of the nyagrodha tree.'

'Here is one, Sir.'

'Break it.'

'It is broken, Sir.'

'What do you see there?'

'These seeds, almost infinitesimal.'

'Break one of them.'

'It is broken, Sir.'

'What do you see there?'

'Not anything, Sir.'

The father said:

'My son, that subtile essence which you do not perceive there, of that very essence this great nyagrodha tree exists. Believe it, my son. That which is the subtile essence, in it all that exists has its self. It is the True. It is the Self, and thou, O Svetaketu, art it.'

From a Western point of view the Indian mind should have been arrested by this recognition of Oneness, or it should have embarked upon a systematic development of metaphysical speculation. Certainly there followed a variety of philosophical systems. All of them magically attracted by this first great intuition, circle around it, assenting, elaborating and interpreting, or criticizing and con-

[1] VI, 12.

tradicting. But the decisive step had been taken. What happened was this. A *volte-face* was made into the self with the words—*Tat tvam asi*. That thou art—these words are among the greatest ever spoken by man. India was convinced that the One could not be the Real if man's self could not enter into the closest possible relationship with it. This is identity. But further, this phrase—That thou art—raises intuitional knowledge above the level of purely theoretical insight, and it does so by virtue of the implication in it—Become what thou art. The *that* cannot be equated with thou—man's self—so long as that self remains unchanged and in its actual present state.

In this way, the Eastern mind achieved at its peak that part of its structure which is identity. At the same time the deeply teleological and in this sense pragmatic character of the East becomes evident. Whatever its designation, the Real concerns the East only in so far as it enters into the closest possible relationship with man's true being. This is identity. The idea of a Godhead which exists in and for itself and is essentially independent from man's self, as conceived in the West and the Near East, exists in the popular religions of the East but not in philousia at its peak. In the East, Isness or the Real cannot be said simply to determine the end and the purpose of man. The Real is man's consummation and it must therefore be one with him. The oft-quoted phrase of Confucius—'It is not truth which makes man great, but man that makes truth great'—suggests the same fundamental idea with a slight paradoxical overstatement.

If the clearest expression of the structure of the Eastern mind is in Indian philousia and pre-eminently in the Oneness of the Upanishads and in Buddhism that structure is also easily discernible in China. Confucianism is always presented as a system of ethics, intentionally secular and practical. But such an interpretation disregards the subtlety of the mind of Confucius and of his follower Mencius. True, there is no metaphysics in it. The recurrent terms of 'heaven, its order and laws', remain vague. This cannot be otherwise for the order of heaven is not a transcendental substance but is inherent in the conditions of human existence. This is the regulative principle to be recognized and realized. It raises the affairs of man above crude materialism and it imbues them with that evasive and indefinable essence which characterizes the best in Chinese personality, life and art. The way in which Confucius presents his teaching is in itself illustrative. There are no moral commandments, nor are there comprehensive philosophical arguments and proofs. The perfect man acts in such and such a way. His distinct qualities are these. As in Chinese paintings, the picture is done with few brush strokes. It is infinitely subtle, powerful and always struggling with the essence of things.

The picture thereby presented is effective by and of itself. At most there are hints of the disastrous consequences of missing the right path. The perfect man conditions the perfect family, society, government and state. This seems a mundane outlook on the world. It is—yet it is not. Again the Absolute functions for man's sake only if man is willing to recognize and to introduce it into his heart. There again is the identity of the essence of man with heaven, an identity which, when realized in man and in human conditions, is termed by Confucius, balance or harmony. With a simple grandeur, Taoism also demonstrates the identity of the Absolute with the essence of man and things. In the negation of the pairs of opposites which constitute our world-image, and in existing where those opposites meet, Tao acts by not acting and rules by non-rule. This derides our exertions and truisms. But once this way is followed, paradoxical though it may be to our way of thinking, everything enters and re-enters the perfect state.

OPPOSITES VERSUS POLARITIES

Of all the trenchant distinctions which sprang from the structure of Western mind, none was more fateful than that between form and matter. Indeed, this separation of form from content became in many respects the decisive theme of Western thought, whether through the investigation of its significance and consequences, or through attempts to bridge the gulf. The overwhelming majority of the great philosophical problems of the West arose from this separation, or at least gathered weight from it. This is true of such pairs of opposites as the animate and the inanimate; body and soul; thought and existence; freedom and necessity; and, particularly, mind and matter.

From solution to provisional solution these problems have

haunted the Western mind. None has proved conclusive—neither the absorption of one part by another; the assertion of their essential identity; nor the appeal to a higher unit of which they were considered the aspects or attributes. Nor are we in any better case today when, disregarding metaphysics, we seek by a pragmatic attitude to silence these disquieting voices which still brood within us over these apparently inevitable questions. Thus, the body-soul unity has been made a working hypothesis in psychology and psychosomatic medicine. Atomic physics is coming to grips with the problem of life and attacking in its own right such questions as free will and teleology.[1] But neither psychology nor physics has reached any fundamentally new solution, or even deeper insight into the reason for the persistence of these pairs of opposites.

The division of all experience into form and matter, which was clearly established in pre-Socratic thought, constitutes the core of Plato's philosophy with the limitless on the one hand, and on the other the limiting function of the ideas. The Western Christian world conception and theology were decidedly influenced by this idea. And thereby, strangely enough, they helped to determine the intellectual prerequisites of modern science in its isolation of matter and its opposition of matter to life, the soul and the mind. The extraordinary productivity engendered by these pairs of opposites in metaphysics and theology, in philosophy and science, and later in political and social theory, was paralleled by the spiritual and intellectual controversies arising from it which were all too often resolved at the price of fanatical intolerance and continual bloodshed.

The secret of the productivity stemming from these rifts in the Western world and the futility of trying to resolve them conclusively, lies hidden in a single basic fact. And that fact is that the one pair of opposites which underlies all others and yields them significance and power, is not derived from experience. For this fundamental distinction between form and matter cannot be traced to an empirical origin. On the contrary, it is the free creation of autonomous reason—in the proper sense of the word a *theoria*—an intuitive conception of the *logos*. In the totality

---

[1] This is exemplified in the publications of the physicists Schroedinger, Plank, and Weil.

of our experience nothing resembles a pure form, any more than there is an entirely formless matter. By its inherent authority reason alone distinguishes these categories which co-operate in the building and the evolution of the inner and the outer world.

Form has been considered the spontaneous formative element, be it termed God, essence, soul, idea, entelechy, mind or thought. And the search for this form—its definition on the one hand and the investigation of its possible co-operation with matter on the other—constitutes the main problem of Western philosophy. Rooted in this conception of form is its intrinsic relation to mathematics. For in mathematics, geometrical figures as well as arithmetical numbers represent the matrices underlying the world as it extends in space and time, and express symbolically metaphysical ideas and relations. Whereas idealistic philosophy faced the problem of the existence and purport of matter, the empiricist and sensualistic doctrines dealt with the still more crucial problem of explaining form. Thus, whatever the position and influence of these doctrines, the superiority of the realm of form over matter has seldom been seriously questioned, even when materialistic pursuits have prevented higher values from being realized.

* * *

The significance of these pairs of opposites and the greatness of this conception as well as its limitation come into clear focus at once when it is recognized as peculiar to the Western mind. The East too has its pairs of opposites. But there, due to the structure, they are polarities. Unlike the antagonistic opposites of the West, these polarities complete and balance each other, and no one pole is irreconcilable with its corresponding pole. The classic examples of this are in Yin-Yang philosophy and in Taoism, where heaven and earth, light and darkness, male and female, father and son, great and small, reason and instinct coexist with all their mythophilosophical connotations. They condition and correspond to each other unproblematically, in a great preordained harmony of the universe. These polarities are elemental, familiar, and concrete in character. In fact they are properties of nature, and can be experienced as such.

To the East, nature at least does not admit of genuine antagonism. While hostility and contrast exist, they are at the empirical level, and in the phenomenal world. They are irrelevant to essence. For the Eastern structure with its subject-other relation is refractory to those splits which spring from the initial antagonism between form and matter and cut through the Western world-image. Such an antagonism is rooted in the subject-object relation and is basic to the Western mind.

In the East, then, nature is one whole, a single violent and irrepressible life-stream which is not entirely without an inherent regulative order. Never have the Chinese faltered in their conviction that such a natural order exists, simple and demonstrable. Whether this order be the balance and harmony of the polarities reigning above and below as in Yin-Yang philosophy, or their coincidence and identity as in Taoism, or the golden mean of Confucius, the basic concept of contrasting rather than contradictory poles is the same. While the Indian mind did not succeed in thus harmonizing the universe, the experience of existence as a single, incessant and irresistible stream bearing away the numberless worlds and creatures seems to have been implanted in it since Vedic times with the conception of the one Godhead—the Lord of creation and destruction. Apart from this main line of Indian thought, a further insight into the Chaotic pantheon reveals the ambiguous character of the sovereign deities who in uniting in themselves so many divergent qualities and functions seem to symbolize the structure of nature itself.

On the other hand, ancient Persia conceived the world as based on the antagonism of Good and Evil. Such a distinction split the universe into two opposing parts. And in this, though not in the idea itself but rather in the mode of thought behind it, Persia approached the West. With its original opposition of Good and Evil it stood isolated and was comparable in this respect to the equally rigid Hebrew monotheism. True, it was considered that Good would eventually triumph over Evil, but that victory would be qualified. It did not involve the destruction of the principle of Evil which as a principle was eternal, but the end of the rule of Angru Mainyu—the Evil One. Though this view satisfied religious needs, it was scarcely a philosophic solution to the prob lem of the opposites.

Thus contrary to the West, to India, and to China, ancient Persia left the problem of the pairs of opposites untouched. Either it was stunned by its weight or unwilling to face its philosophical implications. This may explain why, during the Achaemenian, Parthian, and Sassanian periods, Persia, while abounding in artistic creations, was sterile in speculative thought. Not till the advent of Islam was the spell broken. Then the Persian genius launched an astounding variety of creations in mystical speculation and experience, in philosophy and religious poetry which neutralized the opposites and thus overcame not only the dualism of Zoroastrianism, but also the opposition of God and man in Islam itself.

The East takes opposites as they are immediately experienced from life and nature. Thus while the principle of the contraries is recognized, they are left in their original context and to the original operation. For this reason they have been interpreted by contemplative thought as polarities whose contrariety, which is more apparent that real, conceals the deeper meaning of balance and harmony. But the Western mind rooted in Greek philosophy projects the pairs of opposites into the comprehension of life and nature. Thus they are regarded as ontological—as inherent in existence itself. Due to this origin in the *logos* the Western pairs of opposites, starting with the split between form and matter, have resulted in boundless creativity. Were these opposites, as the term ontological suggests, really contained in the nature of things the West would have been obliged to accept them with the same finality as the East accepted its polarities. There would have been an effort on the part of the West, parallel to that of the East, to penetrate their meaning, but nothing resembling Western thought and civilization would have been possible.

Nonetheless among the variety of the Western philosophies, the concrete opposites of the East are not entirely lacking. The world conception of Heraclitus interprets the dialectical interplay of the opposites as the moving force of a universe revolving in an endless process of creation and destruction. This conception, while seemingly in accord with the Indian, differs basically from it in that Heraclitus presents a purely natural, almost scientifically conceived process from which there is no escape and expounds it in philosophic terms.

Distinctions in Philosophic Thought

The trend which was destined to dominate Western thought started with the distinction made by Pythagoras and Parmenides between form and matter. This distinction was not derived from experience. It was the creation of creative reason, the *logos*, which therefore retains dominion in the realm of form. Yet it likewise deals with matter, first as an actual force in the shaping, penetrating, and thereby raising of matter to ever higher levels, and then theoretically, as the supreme endowment of man. And it is the comprehension of this process which leads man to self-knowledge. The fact of matter has been cause for grave perplexity in Greek as in modern philosophy. For the failure to solve the problem of matter's coexistence and co-operation with the *logos* has led the Western mind to a somewhat desperate consideration of matter as the only reality. This is just as if a blind submission to a blind master were a safer way to enlightenment than coping with the dilemma.

* * *

The history of the idea of the *logos* is also the history of the schism between Mind—*esprit*, *Geist*—and matter. This drama, certainly one of the most fateful in the evolution of mankind, was initiated by Parmenides. Severing reality from the sense-perceived world, he identified it with thought and stigmatized empirical knowledge as misleading. Pythagoras and Plato, each in his own way, conceived this split to be between form and matter. They admitted the close coexistence of the two, while maintaining at the same time a fundamental separation of the *logos* and empirical knowledge. Then their problem became to determine what these forms were, how they connected with matter and what was their final purpose.

In this first flight of the Western mind there exist two facts of equal importance. First, the *logos*—the sovereign creative reason —was conceived as totally distinct from the psycho-physical nature of man including his intellect which is always oriented toward practicality. Second, the nature of the *logos* was considered ascertainable. In the Middle Ages, Christ the revelation incarnate. superseded and at the same time carried on this philosophical view of the Greeks. Modern—Cartesian—philosophy, in opposition to the medieval, has stressed clarity and distinctiveness as the criterion of all *logos*-born truths. Thereby it established an *a priori* rationalism capable of producing incontestable truths from a few principles, and in this way it came closer and closer to mathematics which then became its paragon and support. Despite its interruption by the systems of the Romantic period, this ascendancy of mathematical thinking over philosophy characterized the march of Western philosophy. But while the model of mathematics proved for some time a stimulating power that inspired men like Descartes, Leibniz and Kant, it eventually paralysed the self-confidence and the creativity of philosophy. Philosophy, which had been during the Middle Ages the *ancilla theologiae*, the handmaiden of theology, now became the *ancilla mathematicae*. Such was the main trend.

Kant represents the great line of demarcation. For while Fichte, Schelling and above all Hegel, were still exalting the *logos* as absolute and supreme, Kant had already denied to it the capacity of arriving independently at unquestionable metaphysical truths. Confining the power of *pure reason* to the analysis of the formal conditions of experience, he maintained that mathematics and logic were the only sources of *a priori* knowledge. Theoretical philosophy was adjudged incapable of revealing substantial and fundamental truth. The idea of the *logos*, as it had formed and accompanied the Western mind from its awakening, was thus dethroned. This split between the *logos* on the one hand and the psyche and intellect on the other became meaningless and degenerated into the problem of the relation between psychological and somatic phenomena. Important and intriguing as this opposition may be it occurs at quite another level, and is of an entirely different order. If a symptom of and a cause for the end of Western civilization as it has been handed down is sought, no better one could be found than this defection from the *logos* idea. More striking and more profound than any other adducible argument, this denial of the great classic split announces the end of an era.

According to philosophy all fundamental antagonism—the dualism of the West—stems from the great cleavage between form and matter. This split is predicated upon that peculiarly Western relation between the subject and the non-subject, in which the

147

two stand in opposition to each other. This is true both chronologically and ontologically. For in establishing this opposition,
the mind detached itself from the magic world and initiated the
theme of Western thought and civilization. The phenomena of the
physical world are the chief representatives of the object. And
their objectivation in science is the most striking and tangible
result of objectivation.

The ultimate aim of science and the manifold uses to which it
lends itself are but accidental effects of this process of objectivation inherent in the Western mind structure. This bent to objectivation is without limit. It extends to all data of the outer and the
inner experience, trying to bring them under its sway. We must
beware, however, of identifying it with objectivation by means of
science and its methods. It does not necessarily imply that
phenomena of a non-physical nature such as those of our inner
experience must be expressed as being basically physical in nature.
They possess an objectivation of their own. Since classic times in
the West the phenomena of inner experience have arrested attention and study. This interest differed from that in the East. There
they were valued as the material for moral and religious training
and adventure. Such an interest was certainly not absent in the
West, not even at the start. However, they were valued also for
their own sake as a part of the study of man and his relation to
the world and of his spontaneity in the world of the mind. The
result of this attitude is to be seen not only in philosophy and
psychology but also in literature where the Greeks and the Romans
developed an analytic and descriptive interest in the phenomena
of the soul quite distinct from that in the East. This process has
gone on with increasing vigour until our own day when literature
and scientific study compete in unveiling the variety, the intricacies and the potentialities of mind and soul.

Thus psychology and psychiatry, biography and autobiography,
history, the novel and dramatic literature—all of these bear wit-
ness to the West's increasing urge to objectify mental phenomena
to a point where they could be dealt with as objects. This subject-
object relation does not subsist in the rigid antagonism of mind
and matter in terms of physical matter alone. It consists in the
capacity of the West to confer on anything that presents itself,

regardless of its nature, the shape and existence of an object. By this incessant urge—this will to posit objects, the subject itself creates its own antagonists. Yet it is this same will which also constitutes the means of mastering them. Thus the West moves on, ever discovering and ever creating new objects. This is an endless process since the investigation and explanation of those objects already established requires the positing of new ones. Thus modern science and our profound interest in the physical world in general, are but the most outstanding examples of this mind-structure and attitude of the West.

*　　*　　*

All this is alien to the East—the entire construction with its schism between the *logos* and the empirical world and the ensuing pairs of irreconcilable opposites. The Eastern mind is not interested in shaping the non-subject into an independent object. It simply ranks that non-subject as the other. From the very beginning, the main problem was to secure an unassailable position for man in the face of all that exists within and around him. Against this uncompromising standpoint, it is easy to see how to the East the attitude of the West might seem ambiguous, even contradictory.

Opposed to the pairs of opposites in the West there stands in the East the sovereignty of the polarities. The difference is fundamental. The opposites contain a hostile antagonism. To overcome this hostility and its consequent sterility it is necessary to raise up a principle which on a higher plane neutralizes the opposites. This from Plato to Hegel is the idea of dialectics in Western philosophy. The Eastern mind operates differently. The place of the antagonistic opposites is taken by the polarities. The polarities too face each other as radically different. However, they resemble more the forces of a magnet which work in opposite directions, but not against each other. At a determined point they neutralize each other. This point of neutralization symbolizes the Real. In Eastern philousia the Real so to speak absorbs the polarities whereas the Western Absolute conciliates the opposites on a higher plane in a new creation of the mind. One has only to read and compare the Platonic dialogues with those of Indian or Chinese philosophers to grasp the difference of the two mind structures. There is on the one hand, the juxtaposition of the polarities, contraries indeed, but not fighting each other, and their absorption into the identity of the Real. On the other there are the dynamic antagonisms of the West and their transcendence by a higher principle which functions to the end of their unification.

What has been and has had to be expressed in abstract terms is reflected in concrete disparities. Two of the most important call for mention. The history of the Western mind in general and of its philosophical thought in particular is characterized by two great conceptions. Neither assumed a prominent role in the East. The one is mathematics—the other the idea of evolution.

Important as the invention and knowledge of mathematics are in China and particularly in India, the East cannot claim anything comparable to the systematic development of mathematical theory and applied mathematics in the West. The idea of an organic evolution from the unicellular to the most complex organism and the general application of this idea to all living processes as well as to the history of mankind in general and to that of the mind in particular—all this is in complete harmony with the structural principle of the Western mind—unity in variety. In fact, it constitutes its most imposing expression. For the idea of organic evolution is but the expression in time of the Western structure. For any organism in the proper or figurative sense of the term constitutes a unity which wants to unfold its potentialities in time.

The Eastern structure—juxtaposition and identity—lacks inner relation to evolution and to evolutionary time. Instead it knows succession and gradual progression. The worlds emanate from Brahman in unimaginable but finite aeons and to Brahman they return in endless repetition. Regarded as they must be against this background evolution, realization and progress lose their meaning. In applying the idea of evolution to historical periods as distinct from those of deterioration, the Chinese are far from conceiving their own history as an evolution—a genuine unfolding like that of an organism. They regard time as the endless succession of time units. Yet their grandiose seclusion and their self-centredness in the past made them feel the endlessly flowing time as duration. And what endured was the Chinese people themselves and their civilization. Thus by a psychologically understandable process they could live the endless time as duration and experience duration as an almost timeless presence.

What is the secret of the triumphal march of the idea of evolution in Western civilization? In conformity with what has been said the answer is this. The belief in evolution hides the hope that evolution is the 'open sesame'—that it is the magical key which will achieve the conciliation of the pairs of opposites. For this is the fundamental problem which has haunted Western thought from its beginning. Was it too much to expect that this idea of evolution, particularly since it could rely upon the rapidly developing sciences of nature, biology, comparative anatomy, zoology and the like, might with the aid of chemistry be able to explain the origin of life from matter, that of consciousness from life, and the unfolding of consciousness from its most elementary manifestations to its supreme creations. And at the end could it not give us the solution of the eternal problem of the relation between mind and body?

Today, in spite of an unforeseen progress in all these fields, we can hardly claim that one of those eternal problems has been solved. Perhaps they have not even been brought nearer to solution. The Western pairs of opposites still stand unconquered. In fact the theory of evolution could do no more for their conquest than did the equally vain attempts of radical idealism and materialism. In fairness to the idea of evolution it must also be recognized that the mathematically based science of nature was no more successful in coping with the pairs of opposites. In the history of Western philosophy the importance of mathematical thought on the one hand, and of the idea of evolution on the other, is vividly illustrated by the fact that with few exceptions the most important philosophers can be grouped as those who were inspired by mathematical thinking and those who followed the line of the idea of evolution. The first group is represented by men like Pythagoras, Plato, Descartes, Leibniz and Kant while the other can claim the names of Heraclitus, Aristotle and Hegel.

If philosophical mysticism is credited with having vaulted this chasm, it did so at the price of ignoring the structure of the Western mind as well as its premises and aspirations. In this fashion it succeeded in avoiding the issue. It is no mere coincidence that the two outstanding representatives of this are to be found at the periphery of Western civilization—Plotinus, who was born in Egypt and inspired by the currents of Eastern thought, and Spinoza, of Jewish descent. Both men demonstrate their unorthodox doctrines with all the implements of classic Greek and Cartesian philosophy. Undoubtedly, Plotinus and Spinoza represent the closest approach of Western philosophy to Eastern philousia. It is futile to speculate how far this affinity really goes. No quotations from these two, no comparisons or interpretations regarding so subtle and elusive a matter, could be conclusive. One point, though, may be stressed. There is no mysticism in Eastern philousia. What is called by this name is the natural outcome of the Eastern mind, the clear expression of its philousia. None of its creations which are pertinent to this contain anything 'hidden, unknowable and unfathomable'. On the contrary they reveal a general delimitation of a definitive experience attainable under well-determined conditions. And this, once attained, leaves nothing more to know or desire.

Whatever shape the Absolute may assume in Western philosophy, it retains the more or less pronounced characteristic of objectiveness which corresponds to the West's ceaseless urge to its expression and definition, an urge which is equally present in Western theology. This objectiveness the Absolute must retain because its function consists in guaranteeing and explaining the unity of all that exists despite its diversity. Science, which is the clearest expression of Western objective thinking, is unable to offer a solution compatible with the demands of the structure. True, science also proceeds according to the principle unity in variety and it aspires logically at a universal formula from which the variety of all phenomena could be derived. But it does so only after having established the omnipotence of the physical realm. This means above all the dissolution and absorption by science of the subject and its inner world.

*　*　*

In our day, however, a momentous change has been taking place. With the recognition that no scientific fact can exist abstractly and apart from the observer, or his position and his means of observation, the subject has had to be admitted as constituting the scientific fact itself. It cannot be foreseen whether this conception will influence philosophical thought. But this change is momentous. Thus in the structure of the scientific fact itself, the subject, the observer is no longer an unwelcome *additum* which should be eliminated. He is now recognized as a constituent element. Imagining a situation where the mind has finally discovered the universal mathematical formula, Eddington lays it down that at that moment the mind will face and recognize itself in the formula —'In the end, mind faces itself.'

This vision, though not entirely unambiguous, reveals clearly enough the structure of the Western mind. Thus in the course of coming to know nature, the mind would have been led from one conception to another only to find at the end of its journey that it was not nature which it had discovered, comprehended, or even sought after, but mind itself. In the light of this knowledge the position of nature becomes problematic. Now that the mind has found itself does it continue to exist though deprived of value? Does it disappear, its seeming reality dissolved? Or is the recognized identity of mind and nature the ultimate result? Whatever might have been Eddington's answer to these questions, they do not bear on our argument. What is important is the fact that the mind faces and recognizes itself in this formula as in a mirror. And more than that, although the formula is not an object in the current sense of the term, yet it retains a kind of objectiveness. For it is a product of the mind, not the mind itself. Thus, what the mind learns at the end is that it can know only itself—that it has been misled, lured on by a spectre.

Whatever the Western mind will gain by the possession of its supreme formula, the knowledge which it attains will have been reached by means of something which still preserves the hallmark of the Western mind, that is, objectivity. This however, is not all. As has been said, in this consummation of the scientific effort nature will be replaced by the mind as the only real object of knowledge. On the other hand, it must be stressed that by avoiding the subject as the receiver of supreme knowledge, the mind is charged with this cognizing function. In other words—just as nature will eventually have to undergo denaturalization, so the subject of knowledge will have ultimately to be depersonalized and supplanted by Mind.

If this interpretation seems to read too much into the statement, it is still in the straight line of scientific thought. Science, when faced with a final conclusion, will have resolved into its formula the sum total of natural phenomena. But the idea of science is such that it does not stop with non-physical phenomena. It will not be satisfied until psychological phenomena are controlled and understood by scientific insight. The moment that this has been achieved, the subjects of knowledge themselves will then be objectified, and their reality will enter and be absorbed by the universal formula. Then it is that Mind will recognize itself, whatever its determination at this final consummation.

This ultimate achievement, of course, is a dream, and perhaps not even a beautiful one. In any case, the vision of the physicist Eddington is remarkably close to that of Aristotle, the metaphysician. Mind, in recognizing itself in a formula which has resulted from its quest for the comprehension of nature, reaches the insight that the Mind itself is its own proper object. This corresponds to Aristotle's definition of the supreme being as *noësis noësëos*,[1] the cognition of cognition. In this pure form of knowledge which is essentially thought it cannot have any other object but itself. Thus does this definition hark back to Parmenides' statement that in the sphere of reality thought and the object of thought are identical.

The impersonality of these definitions is the outcome of the Western structure with its orientation toward objectivization and its emphasis on the object. With the exception of those writing under the influence of Christianity, all Western philosophers have conferred on the Absolute an impersonal character. In a civilization which glories in the discovery of the value of personality and its cultivation in every field of existence this may seem strange, even contradictory. Yet this seeming incompatibility disappears in the face of a psychological explanation. The Western structure psychologically evaluated demands self-forgetting, if not self-

---

[1] *Metaphysics*, XII, 9. Therefore Mind thinks itself, if it is that which is best; and its thinking is a thinking of thinking.

abnegation. It amounts to a theoretical and not only theoretical asceticism, which at times revenges itself on its creator by launching him into a reaction of exaggerated worldliness. Be that as it may, the exalting of personality is a natural psychological antidote against the structure, an attempt to alter its course. Hence, the incomparable array of great personalities in the West may not unduly be interpreted as the human protest against a mind-structure bent on objectification. Objectification is hard to reconcile with the idea and evaluation of personality. However, it should be borne in mind that the majority of great personalities in the West, with the exception of those in the field of art, particularly music and poetry, were the same men of thought and action who, from the beginning of Western history by their achievements, revealed the structure, started it on its way, and continued to give it ever increasing strength.

Paradoxical as this may seem, it is but one of the labyrinthine ways of the human mind and fate. It is highly indicative that even Plato's supreme idea, when he identified the Good with the Deity, did not possess personality-character. Thus, during the succeeding periods when philosophy wanted to shield the value of personality from the assault of scepticism or sensualism, it almost always borrowed from religion, and moreover, from a religion of non-Western origin, for the necessary safeguards in the ideas of a personal God. Then His world-and-man creating act, and His appearance on earth, proved irrefutably the objectifying strain in the Western mind structure.

*　　*　　*

Compared to the West the East presents an unequivocal and a more consistent aspect. The emphasis on the subject inherent in the Eastern mind-structure confers on the Absolute a meaning which makes the term—*absolvere:* to set free, to loosen—inappropriate. Thus it had better be replaced by the Real. And the Real, as has already been stated, maintains a definite closeness to the subject. This proximity is conspicuous in Confucianism and in all schools directly or indirectly connected with it. And so far as there is any transcendency at all, it permeates the only true metaphysics China has produced, Taoism. The Tao, which in itself is indefinable and known only by its ways, is immediately translated into what it means for the transformation of human attitudes and conditions. However, the outstanding proof of this closeness of the Real to the subject is the Upanishads of Indian philousia, for example the Brihadaranyaka-Upanishad.[1] There the Real is revealed as identical with the great Self whose presence must be recognized in all that exists.

Although this formulation, which is chosen for the purpose of introducing the Real, is a long way from hinting at a personalized Deity, it cannot be incidental, any more than is the neuter, impersonal form in which Aristotle expressed his Absolute. The motive behind the Upanishad formulation is the desire to avoid anything which might suggest an objectified Absolute, that is an Absolute existing in and for itself. To achieve this purpose, a form of the unconditioned subject which did not convey the connotation of personality had to be chosen. Thus the Real equally transcended the personified deities as well as any other kind of objectified existence.

However, the structure of the East points to the intrinsic closeness of the Real to man. This proximity reveals itself, once it is understood that what we call personality is not the essence of the individual. The essence is the real person, discoverable behind the screen of his cherished personality. It is this real person which is guaranteed by the Real, the whole conception implying neither a nebulous pantheism nor the immortality of the apparent personality. Just as every precaution is taken to prevent the Real from deteriorating into an objective Absolute, Eastern philousia does not permit it to assume even a vestige of personality. But the subject-character is conferred on the Real and in fact the Real is the Subject. If an atmosphere of ambiguity seems to hover about this conception, this is due not only to the matter itself, but also and perhaps even more to the sharp differentiation of our Western concepts. There remains what cannot be determined. And this is true not only in philousia, but even as we learn today in physics. Yet this does not mean that it is mysterious or absurd.

Eastern philousia prefers to lead us to the threshold of the right room rather than to cause us to enter the wrong one. This act of

[1] II, 4.

entering defies conception, and so does the experience connected with it. What can be said is that the orientation points to identity, albeit what this means is not open to theoretical determination. However, it must be kept in mind that the Eastern structure rests upon the subject as the constituent element. This fact alone implies a more tangible assurance against a complete disintegration or absorption of the real person in man than does Western philosophy. For conditioned by its object-directed structure, the philosophy of the West is unable to equal this position without borrowing from religion.

Plato, Aristotle, and the other outstanding representatives of the Western mind including their most significant predecessors, withheld from their definition of the Absolute anything that might suggest any character of personality. At the same time they avoided the concomitant dangerous temptation inherent in the objectifying structure. This is the risk of identifying the Absolute with a material object, be it in ever so elusive an image as the atom. Consequently these philosophers considered the Absolute as the objective Mind, as cosmic reason, the highest idea, the Good. Or they tried to conciliate matter with spirit, for example by resolving it as Hegel did into spirit, or co-ordinating matter with other modes as manifestations of the Absolute.

A parallel though not an inner relation exists between the Eastern and the Western structure. The Subject which is the consummation of the Eastern mind is not linked with personality. And the Absolute which constitutes the conclusion of the Western mind has no relation to any concrete physical object. Nevertheless, the Absolute not only retains its objectiveness, but it is objectiveness itself—*the* Object. That momentous expression of the Western mind, science, inevitably bears the mark of this structure and hence of this philosophy. Nature, the object of science, having been represented until modern times under more or less concrete images, is now changing its form. For to the equation between matter and energy there is now a corresponding picture of the atomic structure where matter, its structure becoming ever more subtle and unseizable, seems to dissolve. Not so, however, objectiveness. The universal formula detaches itself so to speak from matter, but it still continues to point to the Object, be that Object called Nature or Mind or both, and whatever may be the imagery connected with it.

The meaning of objectiveness, as represented by the idea of the Absolute in philosophy, has thus been established. It is knowable in principle, however uncertain and variegated the solutions and definitions may seem. The idea of objectiveness in science—a derivative of philosophy that is neither identical nor merging with it—is an ideal which will be reached at an infinitely remote future. Both of these conceptions, the philosophical and the scientific, stand out in unmistakable contrast to the Real in philousia. For under certain prescribed conditions the latter is at all times accessible to realization.

It has been repeatedly stressed that in transcending the physical the Western idea of objectiveness implies all possible modes of pictorial concreteness. Despite the fact that this objectiveness constitutes the decisive characteristic of the Western mind, it is not the final word. Not until its intrinsic and unique connection with the Western concept has been recognized is its significance fully appreciated. Indeed it is the concept which renders the object in the Western sense possible, just as the concept itself rests on the objectifying structure of the Western mind.

Thus is the idea and the means of knowledge in West and East presented as the next topic.

CHAPTER VIII

Knowledge East and Knowledge West

Nurtured by and existing in the realm of concepts Western knowledge has severed every close tie with the magic world. But Eastern knowledge, albeit it has undergone deep changes and conquered new lands, points clearly back to its magic origin. True, in the structure of the Eastern mind the magic essence lost much of its aura and has allowed within wide limits the evolution of conceptual thinking. However, at the higher levels of knowledge the magic impact returns purified and exalted.

There, the Eastern mind structure, although it is strong enough to wrest the magic name designating its object from the magic atmosphere, does not want it to develop into the autonomy of the Western concept. For that will have the effect of radically separating the designation from the thing designated and the thing designated from the mind applying the designation. In Eastern philousia one can still feel that those words which designate supreme and essential entities transcend the function of a mere verbal sign. The legitimate heirs to magic thinking, when fully understood they lead immediately into the entities designated. Thus they do not produce intellectual understanding. Rather do they permit real participation and thereby a change of mind and soul. Such is the sacred word which from times earlier than the Upanishads carries not only a meaning but also a form of being down to the living sages of India. When Confucius insists on the necessity of rectifying the names as the condition of well-being in the affairs of man and the state his meaning is not only and not in the first place, the self evident truth that wrong ideas lead to wrong action. To Confucius the right name is more than a name. It is more than an intellectual concept. It evokes and realizes by

159

its own inherent power what it means. The distant echo of the magic world is clearly to be heard.

An examination of the functioning of Eastern philousia gives rise to a vivid impression. In its scrutiny of the outer and the inner world, the Eastern mind becomes closely bound to designations once they are established. The freedom to modify the meanings and still more to dismiss designations in order to create new ones with new meanings is limited. These characterizations should be understood as relative to the Western attitude. What stands out is that once the designation is adopted, it is connected both with the designed entity itself and the subject. Here then is a tie closer than tradition and authority which points back to the connection between man and thing in the magic world. This tenacity, coexistent and consistent with inner weight and dynamics, has from its very beginning distinguished the Eastern designation from the Western concept.

Whatever the degree of ambiguity of Eastern designations in their original context as compared to the concepts of Western philosophy, there can be little doubt that the difficulties of translating Eastern philosophical terms into Western languages do not derive entirely from purely linguistic intricacies. Rather they stem from this suggested difference in thinking. And as has repeatedly been emphasized, this difference decreases as thought descends from its highest objects to those of a more common nature. The close cohesion of Eastern designations with the entity designated confers on the designation a more definitive character than the Western idea which although meant by its inventor to be final, cannot escape the intrinsic urge to evolve, change, produce and decay, which is to say that it is for ever *arche* that is simultaneously principle and beginning.

Western knowledge is acquired and preserved by conceptual thought. But Eastern knowledge proceeds through other means and it treasures its achievements in other depositories, that is to say in states of consciousness. To comprehend the significance of the term—state of consciousness—one should recall the magic world. There the knowledge of the secret name which was believed to confer power over the thing was the fruit of great effort and trial. Of equal importance with this is the conviction that true knowledge consists in the reception into the knower of the entity to be known. This means a more or less complete transmutation of the knower into that entity. These powerful conceptions were by their very nature restricted in the magic world to symbolical expression. They were taken over by the Eastern mind to be clarified, transformed and raised to new heights.

Philousia is also permeated by this idea. All insight, whatever be its character, high or low, is conditioned by the state of the subject as a whole. Yet it should not be thought that this conditioning refers to the psycho-physiological status of the subject, such as spontaneity or fatigue, attention or distraction, interest or indifference. Nor does it even apply to intellectual capacity, or education. These are incidental conditions which do not fundamentally impair the spontaneity of the act of reason. It was the conviction of Socrates that it needed nothing more than the removal of erroneous belief caused by intellectual indolence to make everybody see the truth and thereby induce him to right action. Without this conviction Socrates could not have exercised his famous method, nor could Plato have required mathematical training as the only entrance condition to his academy.

Thus, according to Western tradition philosophic wisdom is attainable by any clear and desiring mind, whereas the East believes in an ontological relationship between the knowledge of which a man is capable and his general condition. This knowledge in the East has a double aspect. On the one hand, it is a state of consciousness dependent on and relative to the condition of the whole subject. On the other, once it is acquired it implies a change in the whole condition of the subject, and indeed this kind of knowledge only exists in so far as it effectuates this change.

The clear separation between man as a sentient being and as a reasoning being is one of the many distinctions of Western philosophy. While not unknown in Eastern philousia this differentiation has never been allowed to occupy a central place. Doubtless, man felt that his deep consciousness of himself as a whole would be threatened by admitting the antagonism of reason and will. Hence the transformation from one level of consciousness to another appears to be as much a condition as a result of this new cognition. If the import of this philosophical concept is as significant in the East as it is in the West, the reason is precisely this. In contradistinction to conceptual knowledge Eastern cognition involved not alone the thinking power and thought of man but his whole being.

One must forgo' asking questions about the mutual relationship of cognition and will—whether knowledge or will holds the primacy in the mind, and then the resulting question—how if knowledge and will counterbalance each other, can there be any progress of cognition? The only significance which attaches to this kind of questioning is that it illustrates the particularity of the Eastern mind. States which embrace the whole of man, not acts of thought or of will, move on. This at least is the Eastern idea. It matters little whether this apparent inflation of the idea of cognition is regarded as an exaltation or qualification. It can in fact be viewed from either angle. For if it requires cognition to embrace the whole of man, at the same time it makes cognition dependent upon the whole man. As a man is, so is his cognition, and as a man's cognition is so is he.

In all important Indian doctrines the image and cognition of the world is a function of the subject's level. An applicable metaphysics demonstrates that not only does the significance of the world change according to the state of knowledge, but other circumstances may appear on the path of the seeker of truth. Chinese thought moves in a similar direction with only a psychological difference. Here the metaphysical realism occupies a more modest place and the world of phenomena remains more or less untouched, while its order and meaning undergo radical revolutions, so that to all intent and purpose the world is no longer the same. In order to create a state of knowledge which alone will enable a man to see the world and himself as they really are Confucius sets in motion a thoroughly planned apparatus. The emulation of the exemplary figures of the past, the performance of a ritual adapted to all situations of life, the cultivation of music and poetry, the study of classic texts are in his book all means intended to foster the cognition of the Golden Mean. Similarly the Taoist school, not to speak of Zen Buddhism, abounds in techniques to transform the whole state of the ego, which transformation is considered indispensable for the attainment of cognition. Thus does the inseparable connection of being and knowing become evident.

That which in philousia seems sometimes to be like spontaneous theoretical thought is suspended between the preparatory state constituting the condition for the acquisition of knowledge and the final state for the attainment of which knowledge exists. Certain modern Eastern philosophers who are anxious to prove that theirs is a theoretical philosophy comparable to that of the West, present us with a mutilated image. They sever ideas which possess more or less superficial similarity with those to be found in Western philosophy from the life-stream which gave them birth, and then present us with artificial creations which nobody versed in Western philosophy can regard as truly analogous.

It need not be emphasized that similar ideas are here and there to be found. Were it otherwise, man, the thinking being, would not be what he is, nor the number of ideas be limited as they are. But such comparisons of Eastern with Western philosophies lead only to superficial analogies. They ignore what is essential in West and East. It may not be entirely impossible to divorce Eastern philosophy from the two supports which hold it, in order to present it as an autonomous and theoretical philosophy and to develop it in the light and according to the pattern of Western philosophy.

But if this is done—and to the degree that it is done—philousia will divorce itself from its past. And it will cease to be what it has thus far been. An imitation of Western philosophy with an Eastern flavour may arise, or—what is more unlikely—something new may originate. In any case this unknown magnitude would not be the East with which we can and must deal. Indeed, historically among all the schools of Western philosophy the Pythagoreans alone it would seem took a view akin to that of the East. Not that the East requires monastic life as indispensable for the cognition and realization of truth, but the Pythagoreans, in pursuing their goal within the regulated life of a strictly esoteric community, adopted an idea of cognition similar to that of the East.

*　　*　　*

The more we weigh the Eastern notion of cognition, the stranger and more devious must our Western conception of it appear. The idea that man has the power of leaving his finite state behind in order to reach the realm of the Real by virtue of his reason alone seems to approach the highest degree of arrogance. While, in magic belief, knowledge and power over an object require a species of psychological absorption of the object, the high forms of spiritual alchemy and magic-based religions introduce the idea of a gradual transmutation as the means of attaining truth and the path to perfection. The East raises this conviction to the idea that cognition is a state—or more precisely a state of being or consciousness. This means that at each successive level all the capacities of the subject are affected according to the nature of the respective levels. It means further that consciousness, in the sense of waking consciousness, is not necessarily a characteristic of that state. Thus, it follows that Western thought is distinguished by an act-character, which is not inherent in the Eastern state of being. Western conceptual thought aims at an object, in the last resort at an idea.

All these determinations result clearly from the Eastern mind-structure. In positing the subject and linking with it the non-subject as the other, this structure renders impossible a form of knowledge which proceeds by concept. For that form of knowledge separates the non-subject from the subject as an antagonist. By a parity of reasoning Eastern cognition cannot include a conceptual knowledge of the subject itself because manifestly this presupposes that the subject becomes the object. Hence, in the East there is no psychological science comparable to that in the West. What may appear as such are merely pragmatic constructions—contrived patterns of the parts of the soul and their correlations for the sake of orientation, the definite purpose of which is to give direction to higher development.

From whatever angle we approach Eastern cognition it is not concept which contains knowledge or which is itself knowledge. The reason for this is that the all-important insights cannot be reached by reasoning power alone. They require, moreover, as a condition of their attainment a state of mind other than an intellectual act. The higher we ascend the scale of insight, the more that state of mind loses the character of condition and merges with a means of knowledge. Finally, at the summits of philousia, this state is itself knowledge. '*Being equals knowing*' and '*no knowing without the corresponding adequate being*'.

Albeit the divergent structures permeate the civilizations in the entirety of their historical appearance they are most lucidly expressed in philosophy and in philousia. For there the mind is exclusively occupied with itself. And there the forms of knowledge may be seized in full clarity. Then as we descend through the manifold transitions to common life, though they are still at work, they lose their purity and their power.

In all the preceding argumentation the main topic has been the subject-*other* relation discussed as the opposite of the subject-*object* relation. It has not been emphasized—though it has been tacitly implied—that this term subject cannot carry the same significance in both structures. The subject which faces the object is not the same subject as that which holds the other close to itself. Indeed, the subject-other relation tends to exert on the subject the same mitigating influence that it has on the non-subject. Then the subject, though it maintains its undisputed predominance, does not stand in opposition to the other. It maintains its supremacy by admitting into its sphere the non-subject as a more or less remote relation. All these comparisons the reader should realize are nothing but imagery utilized to illustrate a particular ontological fact.

This subtle relation decidedly points back to the magic world. By a wise insight the subject not only definitely secures its position, but it safeguards the possibility of its unhampered development. The history of Eastern philousia shows that the subject is far from being exposed to the uprootals and negations which fall to his fate, not alone in Western philosophy and psychology, but indeed in the very life of the West. Nor does there exist the unrestricted, perhaps the exaggerated evaluation of the subject which is inseparable from the history of the Western mind.

Western man is characterized by an unwillingness to comply with his outer and inner environment. He is an inherent rebel. Therefore, his evolution assumes the form of more or less revolutionary changes with corresponding alterations of self-experience. Of this philosophy is both motor and expression. To a degree Eastern man is spared these theoretical and factual perturbations.

And the reason is that a conservative character pervades his conceptions as well as his life and actions. While this includes resilience it finds its strongest support in the following qualities. His endowment, which is the clear consequence of the closeness to the subject of the other, tends to prevent and if need be, to absorb the shock of changes in the outer and inner environment. The subject acquires this protection at the price of discounting the value he places upon the singularity and immutability of personality a notion which is so dear to our world. This deficiency, however, is balanced by what is achieved in the East's proper realm, that is the subject itself. Shielded by this endowment Eastern man proceeds in the realm of consciousness to adventures which are different from those of the West.

For the experiences of Western man are almost always aimed at or at least they are inseparably linked with transformation of the outer and psychological environment. To adduce but one important evidence. From early times the philosophy of the West appears in close theoretical and practical connection with attempts to influence existing conditions. By assuming the government of city-states the Pythagoreans set the example for Plato's attempt to materialize his political ideal. And from thenceforth, there were but few leading philosophers who did not take a creative interest in political and social problems. Even religion had to submit to the strain of objectivation. The Catholic Church, Protestantism and Calvinism all became militant *ecclesiae* and competed with secular power in constructing their own political and social theories. Omitting the strange picture of bishops fighting as war-lords in the Middle Ages, the Church's great spiritual figures and even monks and saints, took a leading part in political life as ministers, counsellors. Or they instigated in their own right politico-religious movements such as the Crusades, thus creating a tradition which has been followed by the other denominations.

When one considers the effort of the West to realize the political and social ideas of its philosophies and religions, the instances of active interest taken by Eastern philousia in trying to reform actual conditions are like isles in an ocean. There the entire trend was toward the factual acceptance of traditional forms of social

and political life. Mazdak's elaborate idea about A.D. 500 of a
religion-based communist society is one of the very few instances
when at least a short-lived attempt was made to put a politico-
social theory into practice. And significantly enough this was with
the consent of the Persian king who apparently had not realized
the consequences of his decision. Almost all the other theories are
satisfied either by vindicating monarchy in its absolutistic form or
by investigating the virtues and duties of the ideal ruler and the
corresponding qualities of the people. This is even true of the
Chinese thinkers who were so deeply concerned with political and
social problems. Indeed, how could a philosophy which identified
king and state engender the idea of any drastic reform.

This emphasis on the subject does not mean that the East is
alienated from the realities of the world. It is the approach only
which differs. Whereas in the West experience and actions are
connected with the objectifying concept, in the East experience
lies in an immediate relation between world and subject, and
hence in the immediate influence to be exercised by the subject
on the non-subject. Therefore, the foremost task of philousia is to
investigate the subject and its potentialities. Since for the East
the subject is essentially consciousness, the task of philousia is
better defined when it is termed an exploration of the realm of
consciousness and its possibilities. Now returning to the problem
of cognition the conclusion imposes itself. *Eastern cognition is
interested in consciousness itself. Western cognition is interested
in the objects of consciousness.*

* * *

The distinction is by no means one of mere aspects and view-
points. It does not mean simply that the East emphasizes consciousness whereas the West invests more in the objects of consciousness. What is to be emphasized in the contrasting statement
are the two opposing conceptions of consciousness. But even this
formulation does not reach the depth of the distinction. What
must be recognized is that the two conceptions are rooted in two
kinds of consciousness each functioning in a different way.

From the position held by the object in the Western mind-
structure it results that there cannot be consciousness without a

content. In other words with the disappearance of an object consciousness fades and fails. Consciousness and consciousness of something are inseparably linked. Consciousness can seize itself only through the intermediary of a content of consciousness, be it sensation, feeling, thought or whatever. Without asserting that the absence of stimuli means the absence of consciousness it is the necessary thesis of the West that consciousness without content is inconceivable. This is confirmed by the idea of metaphysics and the analogous idea of science that consciousness eventually must become its own object.

In the Eastern mind-structure consciousness by its very essence is independent of its contents. Whatever it may contain, otherness is linked to the subject. It depends upon it and though at times it may empirically overpower and draw the subject to itself, the basic dependence upon consciousness can never be annihilated. Indeed, the East in its quest for the elimination of otherness has developed techniques to dismantle otherness. Eastern consciousness, though of course normally appearing no less connected with content and objects than is the West, is essentially self-sufficient. Objects are to be considered contingent. Pure consciousness is not only possible. The very essence of consciousness is to be free from any object. And it is the attainment of this state which is the goal of philousia. Thus the absence of content does not equal absence of consciousness. As consciousness learns to withdraw from object to limit the scope of objects and to draw nearer to itself the equation absence-of-content=absence-of-consciousness loses its validity.

The fact that lack of content does not imply lack of consciousness throws new light on the teaching of the Upanishads.[1] There,

---

[1] Brihadaranyaka Upanishad 4, 3, 9: And there are two states for that person, the one here in this world, the other in the other world, and as a third intermediate state, the state of sleep. ib. And when he falls asleep, then after having taken away with him the material from the whole world, destroying and building it up again, he dreams by his own light.

ib. 2, 1, 19: when he is in profound sleep and knows nothing . . . as a young man, or a great king or a great Brahmana, having reached the summit of happiness, might rest, so does he then rest.

ib. 4, 3, 15: That person having enjoyed himself in that sleep (dream) having moved about and seen both good and evil, hastens back again as he came, to the place from which he started, to be awake. And whatever he may have seen there, he is not followed (affected) by it, for that person is not attached to anything. ib. 4, 3, 19–23.

deep dreamless sleep is considered a state of highest light and bliss, the union with Brahman. To interpret deep sleep as a privileged state and parallel to if not identical with pure consciousness and awareness, is to be perfectly consistent provided only that consciousness is not intrinsically linked up with objects. The faint resonance—hardly to be called remembrance—that deep sleep leaves behind, is a sufficient urge to reproduce at will this all too transient experience, and thus to attain with full consciousness this unmerited gift. The science of Yoga is called upon to fulfil this purpose.

However, what must attract attention is the daring perspicacity of the Indian mind in recognizing the deep relationship between the two so seemingly disparate states as pure consciousness and deep sleep. This intuition could only happen because the Eastern idea of consciousness does not basically connect it with an object. We of the West ordinarily oppose sleeping and dreaming to the wakeful state. Only recently has psycho-analysis taught us to bring the dream state and waking consciousness closer together. Indian wisdom has resolutely severed the normal waking state from pure consciousness or awareness. Moreover, without ignoring the dream state as a possible transition to deep sleep it has clearly emphasized the common nature of the waking and the dream state thus laying bare the identity of material and the underlying motives in both.

In stressing the resemblance of the waking and the dream state Indian wisdom sharply deprecates the arrogance and pretension of waking consciousness and knowledge. But having once established this relationship they are even more closely linked by the recognition that each is imperfect since neither singly nor together are they self-sufficient. Each of them, and here they seem to separate, points in another direction—the dream to deep sleep— the wakeful state to pure consciousness, awareness. However, the states of deep sleep and pure consciousness are held to be identical though differing as to finality. There is the insight that the relation of the dream state to deep sleep is contingent, that is the dream state may or it may not pass into deep sleep. And there is the other insight that a deliberate effort to transfer the waking state into pure consciousness, or awareness, guarantees the result of its lasting presence. Therefore, the willed transmutation of the waking state into pure consciousness is what commands the dignity and the destiny of man.

And so the circle is closed. On its upper and visible half the waking and the dream states part company in seemingly divergent directions. The one leads naturally from the waking state to the sleep and dream state and from there into deep sleep. The other deliberately and systematically transforms the waking state into pure consciousness. Yet these two ultimate states—deep sleep and pure consciousness—contrarious and irreconcilable though they be at the surface, are identical in essence and meaning.

Whether the analogy and finally the identity of meaning between deep sleep and consciousness is accepted or rejected as the play of imagination, in no wise reflects upon the Indian conception of pure consciousness. What is assumed to happen in deep sleep is contingent, fleeting and entirely forgotten, yet its interpretation as the strict analogy of, or even identity with pure consciousness is not mere speculation. For we must keep in mind that the Indian position necessarily proceeds from the Eastern form of consciousness as independent of the existence of an object. In its other aspect, however, the superiority of an essentially identical state of mind when attained with full consciousness as the result of unyielding toil, need not be stressed.

To describe or even to imagine this experience of pure consciousness or awareness is an impossibility. The important point to grasp, however, is that it hinges on the Eastern mind-structure. It is the final result of the Eastern process of divestment or dismantling. At the same time we must not forget that we of the West are in no better case as regards the aim of the objectifying process. The conceptions which philosophy and science successively present are strict parallels to the Eastern states of consciousness which normally develop in the course of transmutation of normal to pure consciousness. It should be borne in mind that our scientific objectivation of the realm of the soul is in its very beginnings. This of course is not identical with the physiological or physical explanation of the psyche. But how and where all these semi-independent objectivation-processes are going to converge cannot be anticipated any better than the real meaning of the supposed goal, which is to say the knowledge of knowledge or the thinking of thought.

In exploring the potential states of consciousness the East disregards to the utmost possible degree contents and objectives. Moreover, this exploration is not achieved by theoretical speculation on their nature, but by realizing them. Or to express the same fact in another way, the East uses speculation mainly as a means to realization. Because of the intrinsic relation between being and cognition this cannot be otherwise. Western cognition on the contrary is preoccupied with the objects of consciousness, be they physical or non-physical, and it is intent on building them into conceptual systems. In Plato's realm of ideas all the ideas which constitute the human soul are to be found, such as unity, the good, the just, or the ideas pertinent to reason as the true and the like. This should be stressed because one looks in vain for the idea of the subject, the self, the personality. So likewise when Aristotle defines the supreme being, the absolute, in the impersonal term of the knowing of knowing, this definition is open to misinterpretation if translated by self-knowledge. Nowhere is there an immediate relationship between knowledge and the objects of knowledge on the one hand, and the subject on the other. Still less is there any inherent dependence on the subject of knowledge and the contents of knowledge.

Thus Western knowledge, by virtue of its structure, quite logically includes the objectivation of itself. The clear result of the West's philosophical act of positing the object is that the existence of the object is independent of consciousness. Correspondingly consciousness, without something which presents itself to consciousness, is unthinkable. The nature of the contents of consciousness is, of course, of no avail. On one of the heights of Western metaphysical speculation—and perhaps the most revealing height for the recognition of the structure that is in Aristotelian and Hegelian philosophy—the Absolute is conceived as the consciousness which has no other object than itself. It therefore is pure thinking because it has itself as its object. Thus are there demonstrated with the utmost clarity three propositions. First, thinking is considered the highest form of consciousness. Second, for this very reason even the highest form of consciousness must be conscious of something. Third, pure thought can only have itself as its object. In this way the hidden meaning of the term objective finds its fulfilment. The objectifying mind has itself undergone objectivation.

That this happens at the peak of idealistic philosophy is inevitable because the objectifying mind must submit itself to its own law. When in the philosophy of idealism, terms suggesting a subject are used to designate the Absolute, almost everywhere they are nothing but metaphors, the residues of and the relapses into religious ideas. And as regards science, it is nowadays bent on evaluating the disturbances introduced into the phenomenon by the observer. The direction to the pure object, however, remains unshaken. Thus, wherever one looks in the Western world the subject is on the retreat. This is the logical consequence of a structure which absorbs all data in its objectifying process. The absorbing entity and power is the conceptual thought.

THE PRESERVATION OF THE PHENOMENA

To characterize Western knowledge as constructive, and Eastern as dismantling, does not imply any evaluation. Nor can these terms be used without warning against possible misunderstanding. All great civilizations and structured civilizations in particular, testify to their greatness by abundant creativity. Construction is always predicated upon the elimination of something existing, and there can be no annihilation which does not directly or indirectly give birth to creation. Finally, civilizations of divergent structure will be easily tempted to impose their own standard of evaluation on each others' ways of life. However, even after accounting for these considerations there remains sufficient reason to uphold the terminology.

The constructive aspect of Western knowledge illuminates the working of the objectifying mind. The urge to objectify the data of consciousness implies an ever increasing expansion of conceptual constructions. Of this the changing variety of creations in classic antiquity alone is an adequate illustration, and the history of Western thought shows again and again that when its creativeness comes to an end in one field it turns to another, there to continue its irrepressible effort. Although the path is littered with the cadavers of abandoned conceptions, many of these are resuscitated under new forms and prove creative in new combinations. The objectifying construction of religious belief and experience has been followed by those of science. Modern medicine and its auxiliary sciences have achieved an objective picture of the functioning organism in a close connection with the new conception of the elementary structure of matter. Eventually psychology made a decisive step in the same direction. Then transcending the psychology of the schools, psycho-analysis created a concrete psychology which operates with defined psychological magnitudes and dynamic laws. In all spheres of life and mind the original data recede to be superseded by constructions. These pretend to be objective reality and if they are not, they are at least a step on the way.

This is a procedure of thought of which science has latterly become the most striking and palpable example. But it was expressed with unequalled precision by the formula of the Greeks *to save the phenomena through*. Regardless of whether this phrase originated in the atomistic school of Democritus, or was later conceived by Hippocrates, it condenses the profound preoccupation of Western knowledge. This preoccupation starts from the knowledge that all phenomena are uncertain with respect to their qualities as well as to their reality. Therefore, the main task of philosophy is to find ways and means of ascertaining the reality of the phenomenal world. This aim can be achieved in various forms. The best known seems to be to conceive an atomic world as the real one underlying that of the sense perceptions. This theory which was known to the Greeks fulfils the purpose of saving the phenomena through, which is to say by means of the legitimate doubt and criticism which philosophical reasoning opposes to the appearance of their reality. There are others destined to the same end. There is Plato's conception which comprehends the reality of our world as derived from the true essence of the Ideas, or there is the less sophisticated view which looks at the world as the creation of God or a god.

The world of phenomena cannot stand by itself. This is the main trend of the Western Mind and it applies as well to the humanities as to science proper. The substructure or superstructure is continually being built up in close connection with the phenomena to explain them and to guarantee their being there. Disagreement exists as to the definition of the phenomena, but despite that uncertainty, construction, conscious as it is of its task to preserve the phenomena, never lets them out of sight.

This intellectual procedure—the preservation of the phenomena —together with the profound metaphysical wonder which we have found to be the basic attitude of the Western mind and the search for the *arche*, constitutes the triad of the components of the Western mind. The wonder at the very existence of phenomena and then their variety suggests the search for their real nature, and thereupon the investigating process moves on endlessly in view of and for the sake of phenomena. Because of the fundamental importance of this saving of the phenomena it cannot come as a surprise that at the entrance door of modern science and the philosophy of nature, Copernicus took up the idea with almost the same words—*apparentias salvare*—to save the appearances. Such is the organic nature of the great process of construction.

The deficiencies and inconsistencies of sense-perception are revealed by the discerning intellect. But if that discerning intellect is perspicacious enough to discover the insufficiency of the phenomenal world it is not competent to save the phenomena from the fateful consequences of its own criticism. Though a great achievement, this criticism is purely negative and it leaves man the despairing victim of his own discriminating perspicacity. The problem is to restore confidence in the world, and its solution is not within the reach of discerning intellect. To *logos*—creative reason—falls the task of preserving the phenomena from this devastating though legitimate criticism of discerning intellect.

Measured by this standard, the phenomenal world is not trustworthy. Nor does it possess objective reality. However, creative reason sees to it that it is not merely illusion and deceptive appearance—that it is not simply non-existent, that is to say the opposite of the really existent, Isness. The phenomenal world occupies a place between Isness and non-existence which Greek philosophy designates by an untranslatable term $\mu\grave{\eta}$ $\check{o}\nu$. This means that existence applies to it only in a conditional way. If when measured by the standard of objective reality the pheno-

menal world lacks truth and reality it is the relation to *logos* alone
which may confer upon it a share in reality. The eternal function
of the genuine concept is to move to and fro between the phenomena and the ideas representing reality. By this process of mediation it produces the uninterrupted chain of constructions which
bring the phenomenal world nearer to reality.

The conviction dominating classic science—that sense-
perception interferes with the knowledge of objective reality—has
found an unexpected application in contemporary physics. Transformed and intensified it emphasizes the interaction between
observer and observed phenomenon which, whatever the instruments of observation, cannot but be influenced by the observer.
The distinction between the position taken by classic physics and
that held by contemporary physics is philosophically most revealing. Classic physics eliminated the deceptive influence of secondary sense qualities and relied on the rational concepts of scientific
reason. Thereby, it felt assurance that observation based on these
free creations of thought, far from interfering with physical
reality, could not but disclose it. However, if this holds good for
the heavenly bodies or other bodies of our experience irrespective
of their size, according to contemporary physics it does not apply
to particles of ultra-microscopic dimensions, which are the real
components of the objective world. There, according to Heisen-
berg's Uncertainty Principle, it is impossible to determine simultaneously the position and velocity of a particle because of the
disturbing effect which the light, necessary for observation, has
upon that position and velocity.

Of the important philosophical consequences two may here be
stressed. First, in classic science the secondary qualities of sense-
perception had to be dismissed because of their misleading character. This source of error was a passive one residing in the nature
of the receptive organ and could easily be eliminated by the withdrawal of scientific reason from the dubious source of sense-
perception. In today's physics observation is proved to be actively
disturbing and further that disturbing effect is inevitable. Second,
since in the assumption of classic physics thought could conceive
the cosmic laws because of the complete harmony between the
constitution of the thinking mind and objective reality, the line

of demarcation did not run between thought and reality but between thought and sense-perception. Today the observer himself is drawn into the phenomena to be observed. And since through his means of observation he is a part of nature, he influences the observed phenomenon and introduces inevitably a moment of uncertainty. Thus, we have on the one hand the antagonism between perception and thought and on the other the harmony of the theoretical mind and its object nature when it is untouched by the perceptive mind. Both disappear. Then the place of this construction which is all too clean and clear is being taken by the conception of the interaction between the observer and his observed object.

Of all the, at times fertile and at other times questionable, foreign influences which have exerted themselves on philosophy after it lost its dominant position, that of mathematics and science continues to be the most powerful. For this reason the clarification of the philosophical problem of constructive knowledge and the saving through of phenomena require that the relation of science and philosophy be not neglected. Since their rise mathematics and science have exerted their influence in many ways, particularly in philosophical rationalism, in critical idealism and in empiricism. Clarity and evidence as recognized by rationalistic interpretation as the distinctive characteristics of mathematics, determined the principle and method of the Cartesian school. In Kant's Critical Philosophy the interpretation of mathematics and particularly of geometry as proofs of the existence of *a priori* forms of all potential experience, served to establish the limitations of our knowledge. The naïve but fertile empiricism of the sensualistic school also looked at the concrete imagery of science as a model for the construction of the world of psychological and mental phenomena. Further, inspired by the atomistic theory, it found in simple sensations the original components of our world picture as well as of our inner life and in the laws of association, the parallel to the laws of science.

* * *

The claim of science to have discovered the definitive answers to basic philosophical problems or at least the safe road to their solution, could not but provoke the challenge of independent philosophy. Thus originated the great metaphysical systems which recognized in their own right first principles from which they derived all existing things. Or following the inverse way they started from individual phenomena to demonstrate how their analysis invariably led to higher entities. However, in all these efforts, the urge to preserve the phenomena by means of the constructions of objectifying concepts remains untouched.

Today the leadership in finding a solution to this perennial task seems again to fall to science. Albeit philosophy can hardly be said to have produced a new answer, it may claim the right to investigate where science is heading as its supreme goal, and to weigh the philosophical significance of this attempt with regard to our main problem of Western and Eastern forms of knowledge. In classical physics which was founded on mechanics, the expectation that one might arrive at a complete knowledge of the object seemed justified. The perceptive subject faced the object as a well-defined entity. Then in order to create the appropriate situation for the right knowledge he had only to divest himself of all ideas deriving from any source other than pure reason. Once this condition was achieved, the knower, armed with the right intellectual instruments, and nature stood opposed to each other as congenial entities destined each for the other.

However, the inevitable idea of a world-mechanics pushed to its end had to arrive at a strange conclusion. Not that it found any logical obstacle to its fulfilment. The objects, whatever their nature, remained what they were and waited, indifferently, to be known. But there was this. As a result of the Western mind-structure the objectifying process could not stop before the knowing subject itself. Thus, at the ideal moment when the knowing subject had been made the object of successful objectifying knowledge it would disappear as a subject. What was left would be the known object comprising all existence. At this moment, though, the term object would likewise lose all significance since its relation to a subject had disappeared. Hence it follows that the absolute object being an impossibility, the goal of the objectifying mind is itself impossible.

But the outlook changes if we adopt the view of contemporary

177

physics. According to this, knowledge is not the sublimely indifferent instrument it was believed to be in classic physics. It is itself or at least it is through the means it uses, a phenomenon of nature. Therefore the object of knowledge cannot remain unchanged by the act of knowledge. Since the interference of the observer with the phenomena observed will never be zero, the distinction between the observer and his observed object will never cease to exist. Hence according to this theory, the object can never be fully known. The object, even though the knowledge be pushed ever so far and as far as it may, will never be the absolute object. This then is the conclusion. In both theories the pure absolute object remains unrealizable. In classic physics this is because the absolute object known would no longer be an object. In contemporary physics the knowable object can never be the absolute object because of the interaction between knowledge and object observed.

This negative conclusion cannot come as a surprise. Nor can it be considered more than seemingly negative. True it is that science, whatever be its idea of knowledge, is unable to save the phenomena through by discovering the absolute object which alone would crown its work. Within its own sphere, however, science approximates to objective reality and thereby it pursues consistently the task prescribed by the structure—that of saving the phenomena by use of the objectifying concept. But pure science is only one branch of the human mind and within its field the effort to save the phenomena through has been highly successful, more so than the parallel endeavours of other scientific branches, such as for example, psychology and historiography. However, the preservation of all phenomena transcends the competence of any specialization.

This task is the eternal liability of philosophy. Its fulfilment may at times be interrupted, but it will never be completely arrested. Philosophy alone can resolve the dilemma left by both classic and contemporary science. And the question transcending science is this. Is it possible—and if it is, under what conditions is it possible—that the absolute object could be identical with the known object? And in like manner, is it possible, despite the interaction between knowing and the object known, that the knowable object can remain the absolute object unimpaired by the act of knowing? Then the answer which metaphysics stands ready to give is this. It is possible—if Isness can be defined as knowledge, so that knowledge is virtually and eventually its own object. Then there would remain to be determined how the Absolute, when thus defined, is compatible with the 'being there of phenomena' and finally how it can comply with the function of 'saving them through'. The consistency of such a result with the Western structure needs no emphasis.

The whole intellectual activity of the West is one and the same endeavour. It is to find an objective substructure capable of preserving the phenomena—for they constitute our world. To them we return during the constructive process again and again and definitely so at the moment of imagined attainment when their existence will have been secured beyond doubt. While this preservation of the phenomena by science is but the most conspicuous expression of the refusal to acquiesce in them, their systematic objectivation remains the only means to make them bearable.

The ingenious answer Eddington has formulated with regard to science, striking as it is, is by no means unambiguous. However, its legitimate meaning seems to be this. In the universal formula the mind faces its objectified self. More particularly the mind recognizes that the formula which it has elaborated is but its own creation and is the result of its having transcended any kind of imagery. No new world has been discovered, since all imagery which has been shaped on the way to the formula is eventually dissolved in it. As compensation the formula will confer unlimited power both for the dominion of the phenomena and to create new ones to an extent surpassing imagination.

This creative activity, however, infinite as it may seem to be, must be limited. For it is intrinsically conditioned by our phenomenal world from which it started and, moreover, it must be assumed to be one among an undefined potential. Since this formula is nothing but pure thought, and the subject recognizes itself in it, there is not yet an exact identity of thinker and thought. There is only the nearest possible approximation. The reason why they cannot be identical is that the mind is still intent on something else. And further while continuing to be the phenomenon it always has been it must learn that this something else coincides as the object of consummated knowledge with the mind itself. The objectivation in science is not the only one. A particular form of objectivation characterizes any clearly defined aspect of the phenomenal world. Thus whatever may be imagined as the final word in psychology and history for example, will be formulated in a system of condensed concepts.

Then once the mind has arrived at this quintessence of psychological or historical knowledge it will again face itself as it did in the world formula of science. And if gradation is possible it will confront itself with greater evidence and intimacy than it did in science. But here too the confrontation will be a qualified objectivation. It will not face itself unconditionally. Only under an assumption that objectivation can happen without qualification and without the interference of intermediaries would the mind face itself. But an assumption such as this is impossible within the range of experience even if the forms of objectivation at our disposal are conceived to have reached their end.

Then metaphysics must come to the fore to assert the reality of a situation where the subject disappears as subject having itself undergone the process of objectivation. Then indeed the mind will face and recognize itself. The mind will be its own object, and there will be nothing through which it cognizes itself. Such is the logical consequence of the Western mind's structure either as descended from or exalted to metaphysics. The men who have penetrated and expressed the structure of Western mind with perfect insight are Parmenides, Aristotle and Hegel.

THE PROCESS OF DISMANTLING

The core of Eastern endeavour is the realization of the pure subject as the equal of pure consciousness. The West comprises the subject among other objects of its investigation, applying to the solution of the subject-problem with few exceptions the same conceptual objectivation it does with other objects. In the mind of the East the subject holds the predominant place occupied by the object in the West. Thus, to penetrate to the real subject the East elaborated a new way of knowledge and a new procedure, which is the strict reverse of the Western. Where the Western mind constructs into objectivation, the East dismantles or divests and discards the other in order to move nearer and finally to reach the pure subject.

Like the Western this method contains both constructive and destructive elements. Therefore, the terminology adopted to characterize the two forms of knowledge would be in themselves exchangeable. They have been chosen only in regard to our Western view. It is the orientation and the evaluation which are decisive. In the West each construction which is left behind predicates a new one. In the East each position which is abandoned, is abandoned for the sake of another which is equally doomed in an eternal progress nearer to the subject—a procedure which may be termed 'de-struction'. Just as in Western knowledge all that is subjective disappears in the process of objectivation, so in the Eastern mind the subject absorbs apparent reality whilst pursuing its way of dismantling what presents itself as non-subject, 'otherness'.

Already it has been stressed that in the subject-other and in the subject-object relation the subject cannot be of the same nature. The way of the Western subject which tries to arrive at self-comprehension through objectifying conceptual thought is matched by the way of the Eastern subject which endeavours to achieve its aim by withdrawing from or shedding what there is of objective constructions. In so doing it turns away from intentional acts to live more and more exclusively in a particular form of consciousness which we have called state of consciousness. This state of consciousness is in contradistinction to intentional consciousness. In principle it is self-sufficient and it embraces the whole subject. It is not, and certainly not primarily, oriented toward the perception of something. And there is nothing in it which is akin to the intentional act of the genuine concept which rises within the general frame of consciousness and then transcending it, reaches forth for its adequate object, the idea.

In the East the subject is not an object of conceptual knowledge. Since it is a pure consciousness it will be reached by a thoroughly planned series of states of consciousness. And these in turn are acquired through an increasingly successful divertment of phenomena. This dismantling embraces psychological as well as physical phenomena. All psychological and mental phenomena show a

181

tendency to becoming entities pretending to a life of their own. But in the East they must not be identified with the subject. They must be discarded—dismantled. Thus the borderline of the subject is receding ever farther from the world of phenomena. This process of recession from otherness earmarked by the rise of ever clearer and more self-sufficient states of consciousness, constitutes both a progress of knowledge and a becoming of realization in the two-fold sense of the term.

Reduced to its essence Eastern knowledge is a form of being, a state of consciousness, that is lucid and self-sufficient. The gist of Eastern knowledge does not of course live up to this idea. Yet it bears its mark distinctly enough to make it clear that eventually it is oriented to pure consciousness there to find its consummation. Thus in the East the subject enjoys a more immediate relation to itself, and to this immediacy corresponds the Eastern form of knowledge in the form of being, that is a state. Only that is comprehended which one becomes and is.

Western knowledge is a form of having. Thus it needs an instrument to seize what it wishes to bring in to its forum. And this instrument is the concept. Going to and fro between subject and object in the process of knowledge it links both together and at the same time it keeps them apart. The concept thus is the great mediator between subject and object and in this mediation the Western mind lives the mature and the essential part of its life. If knowledge is a form of possession it follows that one possesses only what one understands. For what is not understood cannot truly be called a possession. Pragmatism is a disinherited offshoot of the true idea of Western knowledge because it is satisfied with the fruition of what it does not possess by comprehension.

The great religious, political and social forms of the East act as protective measures to permit knowledge to follow its proper course. It is as if Eastern wisdom provided for man certain fundamental indelible forms of life. By keeping to these courses he does not lose the immediate contact with himself by embarking on ventures reserved to the objectifying mind. An analysis of some of these forms will demonstrate that they live up to this function.

In India an abundance of divine and semi-divine beings stemming partly from pre-structural times were admitted into advanced religion and even multiplied there. These have undergone a process of concentration and reinterpretation the result of which has been to transform many of them into mere symbols and the partial aspects of a few domineering deities. These latter came to be conceived as differing aspects of a single impersonated or super-personated principle and thus they are to be reconciled with the creations of philousia.

This unifying tendency is unmistakable. Looking back from the height of philousia it even seems as though the original pantheon served the hidden purpose of rendering absurd the idea of an illimited plurality of personified supra-human beings. Monotheism on the contrary appears as the end of an evolution. In this development qualities, and particularly the positive aspect distributed among various deities, are transferred to and united in the one divine personality. Yet the monotheistic idea lies in the direct line of polytheism. Therefore, it is neither the logical nor the genuine conquest of polytheism. The genuine conquest of polytheism coincides with that of monotheism itself. It is to be found in Eastern philousia which transcends both, being the antagonist of neither polytheism nor monotheism.

A similar dismantling process occurs in the political field. Eastern autocracy lives its life unharassed by the legal restrictions which have curtailed the power of Western rulership from early Greek times not only *de facto*, but *de jure*. In the proper sense of the term, Eastern kingship cannot even be called an institution. Indeed it does not radically differ from the kingship of magic times. It lies in opposition to kingship in the West which soon became an institution, that is to say a form of government recreated by reason, founded upon theory and set off against other forms. This legal character of Western institutions makes them more vulnerable. They have constantly to fulfil obligations entrusted to their care as the guarantee of their right to existence. Legal delimitations and evolution of theories in addition to challenging existence and prerogatives confer upon institutions in general and forms of governments in particular, their objective and intensely living character.

In the East it remains a self-evident truth that there be a ruler. This is a fundamental and natural fact. And on a higher level that the ruler exercise his function guided by justice and concern for the welfare of the people. The deification of a ruler constitutes an aberration of the objectifying mind. It is not at home in the East which keeps state and society as well as rulership within the boundaries of natural phenomena and hence close to the subject. Life moves in men and natural groups, and not in institutions and organizations as it does under the reign of the concept.

If this conception appears simple and abortive compared to the evolution of Western political and social theories, it must be viewed against the proper background of Eastern aspiration which permits nothing to stifle the attainment of the pure subject and consciousness. When to this end the necessity of the evolution and variety of political forms is denied yet the need of effective government is recognized. This is represented by the Vedic ideal and illustrated by legendary and historical examples where the ruler at a certain age like the head of any high caste family hands his place over to his son and retires into solitude to work out his salvation. One has only to recall the fury and the dire consequences of the endless struggle between church and state in the West to understand the radical difference existing between the antagonism of institutions and the comparatively mild conflict between the interests of two social groups such as the upper castes in India.

The position taken by China bears out this argument with even more striking clarity. There a theory of personality, of the emperor and administrative body, took the place of a theory of government and state. The problem of government is reduced to the investigation of the ethical and intellectual attributes supposed to qualify for rulership. The acquisition of these qualities, their distinction and the proof and the belief that through their application and the paragons presented to the people, the welfare of state and people will be attained, is the base of Chinese wisdom in the political field. In any evaluation of this conviction it must be emphasized that Chinese wisdom does not put its trust in the acquisition of individual moral and intellectual qualities. Rather it requires a real transmutation and conversion.

184

CHAPTER IX
Concentration

The discovery of the pure subject is the supreme goal of Eastern knowledge. This is the equivalent of pure consciousness, and it is what remains after all physical and psychological phenomena have undergone the dismantling process. The possibility of attaining this Eastern goal and the comprehension of its significance do not baffle the imagination as does the goal of the West. The significant question is this. In this dismantling process what becomes of the other? It will change as the subject changes and lose both reality and meaning as the subject advances on the way to pure consciousness. This is the result of the other's proximity to and dependence upon the subject. Then once this state of pure awareness is reached, there will be no other. Either that, or it will be reduced to the significance of an empty shell.

The second question as to whether one may be permitted to speak of a subject once the other has been eliminated, is void of sense. In contradistinction to the Western subject which by virtue of the subject-object antagonism is fatally entwined with its object, the Eastern subject maintains its sovereignty with regard to the other. It is free to deal with itself and, if it chooses, to undergo transmutation. Whether a state of pure consciousness is compatible with the continuance of a particular kind of self-consciousness it is impossible to tell, but what is far more important is to recognize that this state is by no means so remote from our experience as that phrase would seem to indicate. If we cannot realize it to any degree of perfection, yet we can attain preliminary states of a fairly analogous character. And these have often been illustrated in literature.

As a guide the psychology of concentration will serve us well. In a normal state of concentration attention is focused on the object with the intention of penetrating deeper into it and acquiring more knowledge about it. Naturally through this interest and the intended purpose attentive concentration is bound to the object. Whether this concentration be the scrutinizing and thoughtful or the contemplative and aesthetic, the subject-object relation remains unimpaired even when the subject forgets about himself throughout the process. Indeed, if the subject remained conscious of himself, the opposition of subject and object which is the condition of the act of concentration would not be possible. To empty the mind entirely and to occupy it with the object in thought or contemplation is a difficult art, if it be not bestowed as a gift of nature. The better the concentration, the more does the object appear as what it is, and the clearer is the thinking or contemplative consciousness of the subject. Thus, whatever be the form of concentration, the subject-object relation remains undisturbed.

The East which at all times excels in the refined enjoyment of the sensual as well as of the higher goods of life, has devoted an equal ingenuity to the creation of techniques designed to sever, both subtly and radically, the ties which bind man to his earthly existence. The vehicle of almost all of these manifold efforts is a technique of concentration. The question which first impresses itself on the mind—concentration on what?—does not carry the importance which might be expected. True, in the various philosophical schools, there is a great variety of objects of concentration beginning with the bodily sensations and processes as in Hatha Yoga and on to the highest deities and the One, just as there is a variety of techniques of concentration. However, what each tries more or less adequately to accomplish, is to collect the mind forces in one point, and in so doing, give the mind back to itself and to the Mind of which it is a manifestation. Thus the objects of concentration, however they may differ in value, are in the last resort but means to the same end. And so the question—concentration on what?—becomes a merely technical problem on which sages and schools may differ, whilst motive and goal remain basically the same. As the thirst for the supreme unifying knowledge which is the motive asserts itself in the mind of the one struggling toward that aim, its innermost meaning becomes mani-

fest beyond doubt. Then does it appear that there is nothing outside of the subject to be known. Rather, the process is one of
becoming—of a transformation of the subject himself. In the
whole process nothing accrues to man. On the contrary, something
is being taken from him. This is the illusion of his own selfhood
and of the reality of the world. Instead, he is restored to what he
really is, before and beyond his individual existence. This is his
Conversion to the Real.

What happens in this process is the systematic dismantling
of the normal ego and therewith of the corresponding phenomenal
world. Consciousness is being emptied. A void is produced. This
expression, adequate though it may be when referring to the
contents of normal consciousness, is far from signifying a negation.
The void which is created at the price of tremendous effort leads
to the state of pure consciousness, or whatever other designation
may be employed by the deficiencies of language, such as light,
bliss, identification with the divine, Nirvana and the like. All
of these attempt in vain to express the state of pure consciousness
for by its very nature it transcends expression. This state is the
necessary consummation of the Eastern mind-structure. It is
impossible to be explicit as to whether anything like our concepts
of a subject emerge in this state of pure consciousness. Bearing in
mind, however, that the structural basis of the subject is different
in the East from that of the West, we may assume that the
equation, pure subject=pure consciousness, carries some significance which can be realized only by experience.

The crucial point is this. Since the Eastern structure posits the
subject first it can never conceive of consciousness as being intrinsically connected with an object. Although consciousness usually
coexists with some sort of contents it can be detached from all
real and potential contents and restored to itself. The word
awareness might be appropriate to this state. It implies that there
can be awareness without anything of which awareness is aware—
hence a state of pure lucidity.

There are reliable testimonies of people who have recounted
such experiences. However transient, these experiences have been
obtained by means of exercises or as the result of a gift of particular circumstances. There even is a state of awareness within the

reach of each of us although by its nature it escapes attention. This is that fleeting, almost imperceptible moment which sometimes comes between sleep and full awakening. Then a sudden flash of lucidity, a full awareness may come before this exquisite state is eclipsed by the inner or outer objects of our surroundings and concerns. The very existence of such a state as this carries a certain guarantee that consciousness without an object can exist. Although this state and the others just described cannot be compared with the state of pure consciousness which marks the peak of the Eastern way, they may be said to be of the same generic character. Thus they serve as an indication, found even within the Western mind, that the state of pure subject or consciousness is possible.

Nonetheless this pure consciousness which transforms the whole being and thus becomes identical with or replaces the subject, remains ever beyond the reach of the Western mind. For according to the Western structure, this state would always be tempted to turn to something the subject possesses, even if the subject-object relation could ever be left behind. Instead of giving itself up to and becoming a state of pure consciousness the Western subject would retain its possessive form of knowledge and would hold the state to itself with a thin but iron band. Thus that which signifies fulfilment for the East would mean annihilation for the West. The Eastern way is only open to the West as an intentional desire which ignores the conditions of pure reality of its own and the East's existence.

* * *

Here—in this almost invisible yet momentous instant—we see both structures at work. And thus do we become aware of the deep chasm which separates them even when they seem to draw ever nearer to each other. When the Western structure seems to approach the state of pure consciousness there will always arise an irresistible temptation to experience this state as a possession. The subject would want to emerge from behind the state to assure itself of its attainment. This constellation is bound to return even in the ecstatic states of the great Christian mystics. For whatever be their experience of God, in the act of supreme knowledge either they possess God or God possesses them.

Concentration

The efforts of Western and particularly Christian mystics to express their experience and render an account of it to themselves and to others are untiring. This reveals an unmistakable insecurity. Indeed this insecurity is inevitable. It derives from the fact that whatever the definition of the *unio mystica*, in some aspect and to some extent, the distinction between divine and human substances must remain. To the Eastern mind in general and the Indian in particular, such an embarrassment not only does not exist. It apparently is meaningless. What to the West is a crucial problem shrouded in insoluble mystery is to the East the unproblematic consummation of a long and clearly ordained path. It would be incompatible with the very idea of the supreme goal even to admit the idea that anything problematic can subsist. There is the simple statement or a figurative description of the final state but any theoretical discussion of its phenomenology and interpretation is lacking. The supreme state is realistically considered the inevitable result of a well directed effort. But there is no exuberance of emotion. The state itself contains nothing mystical although in our terms it is certainly supernatural. In contradistinction to this transcending simplicity, the term *unio mystica* hides in the deepest sense a mystery.

This mystery is the forever incomprehensible fact that despite their unification with the Divine Substance, the individual souls remain distinguished from the Divine as well as from all other souls sharing in the *unio*. That this problem should have aroused the passionate interest not only of the mystics themselves but also of the scholastic philosophers is understandable enough. But it is equally understandable that no satisfactory solution has been offered if we are not ready to accept the idea worthy of the religious genius of Saint Bonaventura (1221–74) who declared that what alone distinguishes those united with God is the remembrance of their past sins. No such problem exists for Eastern philousia. For there the self-sufficient process of transformation aims at pure consciousness which equals pure being. What there is of imagery is recognized as such and it serves as the auxiliary means for contemplation and concentration. Thus is identity—that part of the Eastern mind structure which is destined to overcome the juxtaposition of things—led to victory. It is of passionate interest to state that in Sufi mysticism the Western can be clearly distinguished from the Eastern influence. The first group try to describe their experience of unification with God in all the forms poetical imagery may suggest. The other, far less in number though not in importance, refuse to adopt such ambiguous terminology and substitute for it the truly mystic expression *fana fi'l fana*—the disappearance in disappearance. This is indeed a characterization which puts an end to all questioning about the ineffable.

Closely related with this difference is another of no less importance. This one is of an affective character. It regards the Western idea of love and what corresponds to it in the East. The West has produced two fundamental ideas of love—the Greek one of Eros and the Christian one of *caritas*—both contradicting yet in this way completing each other. The first is represented in Plato's *Symposion*—the banquet—where Socrates in a contest having the praise of Eros as its object, develops the idea of Eros as the sublime drive which gradually rises from the love of beautiful bodies to the love of beautiful souls and eventually to the love of Beauty itself—the Idea of Beauty. Here love is a movement of mind and spirit. Starting from a love of the beautiful which is still connected with erotic desire, it rises to the intuition of the idea of the Beautiful itself.

The counter movement is to be found in Christian love. It has its origin and seat in God and it moves down to the fullness of His creation embracing man, not as a species, but every individual in his own right. By nature and origin this love is selfless and free from desire. It is a love of deep understanding and of compassion for individual man. Man's love of God corresponds to this act of divine love, reaching out from below to above. The duty of man's love for his fellow men is in the last resort not so much a spontaneous movement. Rather is it the result of the belief that every man, being created in the image of God, may claim the other man's love as a God-created immortal soul irrespective of his rank and value. Such is *caritas*—the Christian love.

Thus does it follow that in the West the perfect act of love centres on the individual. This is because the individual is more than a mere phenomenon of nature. For it represents as in Greece the highest idea, that of the beautiful—in Christianity, the immortal image of God. In either its religious or secularized form, love preserves its character of action and is directed toward the personality-centre as its aim.

Both Greek and Christian ideas of love are foreign to the East. The East, not relying on conceptual thinking as the vehicle of reality, presents analogies to those ideas but not affinities. In India the place of Eros is taken by kama—the endless desire for existence and its pleasures. When the recognition of the endlessness of the insatiable desire flares up it awakens in the enlightened mind the thirst for liberation from this bondage, for oneself and for one's fellow-creatures. Thus does an infinite compassion arise which is not limited to men but comprises all that lives. There is then an essential difference between the Indian and the Christian ideas of compassion. The Christian derives directly from God's compassionate love of man and therefore is but a concomitant manifestation of love which aims directly at the immortal soul. As to the Buddha, he recognizes that all-pervading compassion coupled with the right insight into the vanity of the world, constitutes the only power which can lead to final liberation from the sufferings in this world and those of future reincarnations. Even in the Bhagavad Gita, which in many respects comes nearer to our feeling, bhakti cannot be translated by love if love is to retain its true significance. For from its whole context and atmosphere bhakti is fervent devotion. Indeed, the God Krishna says of himself: 'I am indifferent to all born beings; there is none whom I hate, none whom I love. But they that worship me with devotion dwell in me, and I in them.'[1] The God Krishna cannot and does not ask to become the object of love. As to Chinese dispensations, supreme and adequate objects of love are equally deficient. Emphasis is laid on social virtues such as devotion, reverence dutiful respect, friendship and the like. These are exalted in theory as well as in public and even in private life, that is to say in the emotional attitudes offered to the spirits of the ancestors, the emperor, the parents, the scholars and so forth.

It needs no particular emphasis that human nature demands its due everywhere. Thus the exaltation of love between the sexes has its place in Eastern literature as for example, the love between

---

[1] Bhagavadgita, IX, 29.

Radha and Krishna in the Gita Govinda, in the great Indian plays, and the Chinese love-novels and plays. In this fact there is no reason for surprise nor can it be tendered as a disproof of the sovereignty and validity of the structure. For if all phenomena of life and the mind were in unrestricted agreement with the structure there would be nothing left but the straight road to fulfilment and fulfilment itself—a monotonous and inhuman spectacle. On the other hand, through its realizations the structure radiates everywhere. And while determining the atmosphere of the civilization, it leaves ample space for the abortive and the imperfect and touches the all too human but imperceptibly. However, the place conceded in the East to love in general, and to that between the sexes in particular, together with its factual significance, can hardly be compared to the space and appreciation it holds in the West.

The isolation and the self-sufficiency that characterize the perfect sage of the East certainly do not mean that he is not ready for a life of sacrifice and the sacrifice of life. Of this the great example is the Buddha who at the moment of entering Nirvana turns back to the world to start again to toil for the salvation of all beings. However, such a decision and action is not inherently necessary, and the Buddha who chooses to disappear into Nirvana is no less a Buddha. In all the great spiritual figures of the East there is a remoteness not to be found in the greatest of Christian saints. Leaving aside minor points the reason for this is the fact that the relation of the sage to world and to men is determined by universal compassion. Universal compassion turns to the individual case as one among the many but universal love, on the contrary, seizes upon the individual case as unique. And so it maintains between the saint and men a bond inspiring the faith that the saint is there not only for all, but for each man as an individual.

* * *

Such are the conclusions to which our analysis of the state of pure consciousness drives us. It should be stressed that this state and form of Eastern knowledge must not be regarded as static. Since Eastern knowledge is not theoretical it is a relatively self-contained entity. It is a form of being. Like the concept it possesses its own inherent dynamics with this difference: the concept is oriented to the object whereas the state does not point beyond itself. This is in accordance with the now familiar characterization of Eastern and Western knowledge—the East concentrates on consciousness as such, whereas the West is interested in the content of consciousness. In the exploration of consciousness and the penetration of its depths the East proceeds by realizing states. In probing the object of consciousness the West invented the genuine concept. Remembering the ultimate goal of both Eastern and Western efforts, the contradistinction between Eastern and Western knowledge can now be expressed as that of pure awareness as against the pure idea.

Thus these results can join with those reached in our discussion of cognition. In the East the establishment of the absolute subject is synonymous with pure consciousness, although the meaning of subject in this final state remains unknown until the experience is realized. In the West on the other hand, the absolute object is the cognizing mind which takes itself as its only object, but here also one cannot anticipate in what sense the term object will thereafter be justified.

The apprehension of how the course of Western objectivation was directed by its inherent goal presents no difficulty. Objectivation means a concreteness which finds expression in the ever varying abundance of phenomena formed by demonstrable categories. Thus there is no problem in understanding how and why the construction of the pure object bestows its character on Western civilization. Not so easy is it to picture the different aspect of the East together with the atmosphere that pervades it. There the emphasis of the structure on the subject makes it a more subtle task to sense its supreme destination. Thus may it rightly be asked, how is it possible that the attainment of pure consciousness shapes the life of a civilization? The solution must be found in its power of and will to concentration *which is the specific endowment of the East.*

Naturally while the shades and levels of concentration vary, the fact itself remains. What in Eastern history appears as conservatism in all spheres of life is the outcome of this concentrative effort which itself gives expression to the belief that the change of outer and inner environment is a waste of energy. Concentration then is neither the faithful preservation of tradition nor has it a value and an aim in and of itself. It is a means of hoarding power in the individual and the society. The danger and the travesty of conservatism is stagnation, just as the Western process of systematic objectivation is caricatured in undirected change and what passes for progress. We are of course not concerned with these deteriorated forms but with the civilization as a whole and with the manifestations that reveal the principles of their life.

As regards Eastern concentration the Westerner may be tempted to put two questions—Concentration on what? And concentration of what?—Yet both questions miss the mark. In some way it may be just as legitimate to answer—concentration on anything as concentration on nothing. And it will be equally impossible to qualify concentration by defining it as concentration of attention, love and the like. Such questioning ignores the fact that concentration constitutes the Eastern form of existence and gives it its indelible character. Another term for this concentration could be chosen—inner collectedness which would indicate a state of being where the subject experiences itself as a universe in itself. As exemplified by its true representatives the Eastern mind is inclined to receive things, whatever their nature, as a whole. This brings unification with the self and preserves to the utmost the integrity of the things received as well as that of the self. This may be illustrated by a Zen story:[1] A distinguished teacher was once asked,

'Do you ever make any effort to get disciplined in the truth?'

'Yes, I do.'

'How do you exercise yourself?'

'When I am hungry I eat; when tired I sleep.'

'This is what everybody does; can they be said to be exercising themselves in the same way as you do?'

'No.'

'Why not?'

'Because when they eat they do not eat, but are thinking of various other things, thereby allowing themselves to be disturbed;

[1] Quoted from Daisetz T. Suzuki, *Introduction to Zen Buddhism*, New York, 1949.

when they sleep they do not sleep, but dream of a thousand and one things. This is why they are not like myself.'

It is not intense concentration on eating and sleep that is required, and still less an effort to prevent being swept away by these occupations. It is a state of mind where each is *there* as the only content of consciousness, a state which presupposes the preceding emptying of consciousness of all other content. This is the exercise. It is no mean achievement and—be it stressed—it is proof that the element of action is present in Zen though in an extremely subtle form. Yet this is not all and it is not even the most important meaning of the story. The simple presence of the content, unimpaired by others, is the preparation for the presence of the pure subject or self. This is why the whole scenario is called an exercise. In our terminology it shows a remarkable achievement by way of dismantling the other thereby reducing its existence to a mere presence. And thereby it points forward to the realization of pure consciousness.

The great figures of Eastern philousia show in their teaching the unassuming serenity which characterizes their portrayal in sculpture and painting, thus illustrating the difference from most of their Western countertypes. In like manner with the philosophers the saints of the West are guided, though in another way, by an objective orientation which becomes clearer as they approach their goal. The state of rapture[1] as it is described by them and represented in art, demonstrates the openness and the receptiveness which is the condition of the divine vision in one form or the other. Here certainly is an exclusive application and orientation to an object, which differs radically from the state of pure concentration.

To adduce other forms of Eastern concentration, a particular aspect of oriental kingship comes to the fore. In the Orient the institution of kingship in some of its great examples, particularly in China and Japan, still bears the birthmark of its magic ancestor. The ruler sits in state on his throne in rigid majesty surrounded by a strict and elaborate ceremonial. Both posture and ceremonial stem from magic kingship. The motionless attitude is meant to hoard magic power and thereby to guarantee the prosperity of the

[1] 'ecstasis', stepping out of oneself, is the appropriate classic expression.

land. The ceremonial is believed to protect the people from the deadly contact with the king and to preserve his magic power which would be impaired by such contact. There is much to be found in the ceremonial attitudes and the courts of Middle-East, Indian and Far Eastern rulers that derives from the magic world. Moreover, this connection of oriental rulership with the magic world is by no means an isolated phenomenon. On the contrary it is quite evident that the ideal of the state of concentration and the energy accumulated thereby derive from magic ancestry. The shaman of so many primitive and half-primitive peoples who, having acquired his powers, lives a life of his own within or apart from the community, is the initiator not only of a long line of various imposing figures of highest religious, spiritual and intellectual standards but he also epitomizes the cell of a civilization which regards the state of concentration and the accumulation of inner energy as the core of the superior life.

India perhaps offers the clearest example. There the ascetic practice of *tapas*, probably in use among pre-Aryan magicians and hermits, was originally more a physiological than psychological technique of creating increased body heat in order to endure naked the low temperature of the North Indian and Himalayan winter. Soon it began to assume the significance of the inner strain connected with ascetic life in general, developing into an ever deeper conception of self-conquest and culminating in many characteristic figures. What galvanized this whole gamut was the self-seclusion and concentration which started with the objective of magic effects and reaches fulfilment in the search of the true subject.

From whatever angle the East is viewed, it presents itself in the fullness of its achievements, as a system for preserving and increasing potential energy. This is as true of man himself as it is of his creations. Through the eyes of the Western observer it is as if there were some mysterious force continuously at work restraining Eastern man from exteriorizing himself beyond a certain measure. This measure is marked off not by his innate possibilities but by his aim or, more exactly, his destination in life. This mysterious force, however, is nothing but the structure of the Eastern mind thus appearing in one of its inexhaustible concrete manifestations. For the Eastern man, then, this is the inner voice of warning. And it tells him that it is wiser to accumulate vital energy than to waste it in the persistent pursuit of aims of which the value is as uncertain as their number is endless. Such at least is the air which pervades Eastern civilization. Assuming for a moment a didactic and even pastoral attitude, one is tempted to say that Eastern man on his way through history has suffered less injury in his soul than has the man of the West. Against the objection that the West has risked more than the East there is always the pertinent answer that the avoidance of risks need not necessarily have a negative quality. It may well be the outcome of wisdom or the response to that inner voice whatever be its nature.

Returning to the characteristic appearance of the magic ruler we may deduce from it as well as from the comparable figure of the self-concentrating sage, a general psychological observation regarding the Orient's fundamental demeanour. Ever since its first encounter with the East the West has been impressed with a certain dignity marking the bearing of the man of rank and of the common man as well. This impression has been admirably described by a French naval officer who visited China a hundred years ago. 'It is remarkable how with the most distant peoples who differ the most by their moral customs and their physical aspects there exists something perfectly identical which somehow expresses itself in certain gestures and manners, so as to present outwardly the sentiment of personal dignity which ordinarily is inspired by nobility of character and superiority of rank.' This dignity is but another expression of that intensive energy which results from concentration. It is an astounding proof of the impact of this attitude of dignity that it is not necessarily connected with high moral quality and value. For it was strong enough to impose itself as the decorous attitude even when those inner prerequisites were lacking.

Dignity may be said to occupy the place assumed by honour in the West, and its nature becomes apparent by a comparison with the latter. Honour can be assailed and offended. It may even be lost if not properly defended and the assailant called to account. Moreover, honour has always been in the West a class privilege.

But dignity is above attack, it cannot be defiled and nobody in any station of life is excluded from sharing it. Whereas honour has the character of a possession, dignity is one with the person itself. And when honour looks around, so to speak, in order to assert itself and be acknowledged, dignity rests in itself and is self-sufficient. Its inherent power derives from the fact that the subject is its own point of reference. Thus it is self-evident that concentration finds its climax and fulfilment in philousia. There it is at home. And it is appropriate to say that from there it descends and spreads, imbuing all the other strata of life.

CHAPTER X

Art, Artistry and Style

The forms of knowledge are not rooted in the psycho-physiological system. Nonetheless they determine the way that system functions. In the West the external world is primarily relative to sense-perception and more particularly to the higher senses, whereas in the East, it is primarily relative to the instincts. This distinction neither means that the Western individual is any the less subject to the power of the instincts than the Eastern nor that the world perception of the man of the East is in any way inferior in clarity to that of the West. What it really emphasizes is this—the existence of two fundamental forms of cohesion between man and his outer and inner environment and their corresponding evaluation. The adequate expression of these forms is to be seen in art and in the attitude to nature.

The corporeality of things is first established by the tactile sense and this likewise incites the first notion of their varying distance from the observer. The impressions on the tactile organs or the body-surface at first are necessarily sensations of a change in our physical condition. But the experience of resistance points to something beyond the body. The primitive experience of distance and materiality and therewith of an objective reality, gives way to a visual world picture which reveals the lucid abundance of phenomena and goes beyond the limits of the tactile experience. A dark vague impression of reality soars to the perception of unlimited distance and space. A choice is then to be made between a world-experience which preserves a certain fidelity to this primordial preponderance of the tactile sense and the other which, limiting this influence, lives in a world determined essentially by the visual sense. Save in rare cases the resulting difference will not appear in ordinary experience. Rather it finds its expression wherever the deeper undercurrents come to the surface in the reflection of the world picture and in experience in art and philosophical interpretation.

It is the West whose world perception accentuates the visual sense, whereas the East keeps closer to the rule of the tactile. To give a single striking example—one may cite the inherent relationship existent between the form of cognition and the sensorial basis. Distance which characterizes the visual sense, corresponds to the mediate cognition through the concept separating the subject and object, whereas the immediate contact given by the sense of touch is related to the Eastern form of cognition which is to become or to be the object. Thus do we speak of the Western act of seeing in harmony with the act-character of conceptual thinking. But there is no act of touching—only an activity confined to the use of the tactile organ. The sense of touch itself is regarded as mere receptiveness.

The significance of the tactile sense is less conspicuous than that of the visual sense for the aspect of a civilization. The reason is this. The visual sense is homogeneous and it is clearly circumscribed in essence and function. Not so the tactile sense. What we usually mean by the term presents but a small section of its domain—that which is turned outside to make us acquainted with the body-surface and the objects of our immediate surroundings. However, there are widespread ramifications of the tactile sense which reach deeply into the sphere of the instincts and are inseparably connected with instinctive activities. Sex and food drives for example, are intrinsically connected with such tactile sensations as touching, grasping, absorbing and the like which is to say with the most natural connections with the object.

Thus appears the deep relationship of the tactile sense with the instinctive forces of life. The corresponding world-experience must be one which interlaces man with world and nature on the one hand and with the physiological side of his existence on the other. The emotional value of this experience may change. In India the feeling of the massiveness of the instinctive powers dominates the infinite variety of their personifications. And this feeling is all the more pungent if it is assailed by inner revolt. The Chinese finds himself more profoundly intertwined in the network of the vital instinctive currents of life than the denizen of any other civilization. If in his outer and inner world he wisely affirms them it is with an intuitive anticipation that in subtly following up the ways of nature somehow will he find the pivot on which the whole spectacle turns.

In the West where the world and nature as the object opposes the subject, the fundamental conception of the Greeks is preponderantly related physiologically to the optic sense. It is not that the powers of instinct in the individual are necessarily weaker. But their impact on the formation of the world image is less obtrusive, and in that way the clear separation of object and subject is facilitated. Greek art, religion and popular belief mirror with picturesque impressiveness the difference between West and East.

In India and to a large extent in the Far East the portrayal of the powers of instinct as fiendish grandiose monsters, or in sculpture as insinuating tempters continues unimpaired down through the centuries. But in Greece the rise of the mature classic era was marked by a drastic rupture of the mythical belief in these fabulous creatures in the shape of man or brute which are the incarnations of primitive instinct. Greek tragedy triumphs over the irrational and demonic powers of the instincts, and while they subsist as a central problem of ethics and philosophy, henceforth they are faced as the natural endowment of man and are separated from his rational essence.

The liberating, one may even say the redeeming, function of the optic sense as the agent of the structure is most conspicuous in the inherent coupling of Greek sculpture with mathematics. From early times demonstrable mathematical forms and proportions determined the shape of isolated figures as well as of compositional groups. Also it fused in a unique perfection with the organic forms and expressions of the human body. Thereby the work of art was removed from the space and time of our experience and placed in an ideal space. Thus originated the unchanging ideal distance between the spectator and the work of art. This distance confers on the latter a life and truth of its own, independent of any resemblance it may possess with the represented object. Thus also can be explained the sublimation and exaltation which the contemplation of Greek sculpture arouses—a state of mind akin to that produced by Greek tragedy.

The art of the East knows nothing of this ideal distance. There the tactile sense in close relationship with the instincts reflects the nearness of object to subject. This seems all the more strange since the major part of Indian art, and sculpture in particular, is dedicated to religious aims. However, the Indian attitudes of awe and worship with their corresponding emotions are of an entirely different nature from the Greek. They refer not to the work of art as such but to the contents and the significance of the represented object. In almost paradoxical contradistinction this ideal distance of Greek sculpture pertains not alone to the human form which constitutes the almost exclusive object of sculpture and in which the gods fully participate. It pertains also to the nude body, the favourite theme of Greek sculpture. And with this natural appeal to the instincts one would expect this ideal frame to be rejected.

Indian sculpture teeming with gods, monsters and men has a vital corporeality which appeals to the tactile sense, the one sense which is above all connected with the instincts. The forms of Indian sculpture call out to be felt and to be touched. They seem to press forward to the spectator. They live the real life and they are meant to create real states of emotion and thought and, possibly beyond that, to lead to decision and action. So Indian art is essentially illustrative and purposive. Theirs is a world which does not enter into a union with mathematics in order to place its creations in another space and at an ideal distance nor does it possess the deep empathy into organic life in general, and the human body in particular. The movements of the figures in Indian sculpture, expressive as they are, differ in principle from those of the Greeks. For they are essentially changes in the position of a piece of matter just as the human body is primarily intended to be a material and not an organic body.

In harmony with this conception the underlying idea of Indian architecture is that of working, carving and elaborating a mass of matter. Thus it is not essentially different from the sculptured figures which in profusion adorn the exterior of the Indian temple. Just as their number could be increased and diminished without harming the plan of the construction, so the construction itself would not suffer by having its size either enlarged or reduced. In the same way the Chinese pagoda permits the addition or sub-

traction of the stories which are the basis of its construction. All
this indicates that in spite of the grandeur, beauty and impressiveness of Eastern architecture, its inner coherence and unity cannot
be compared to that of the West. At the root of Western architecture—and, it must be added, Islamic architecture—is the
intuition of enclosing space in artistic forms. This visualization
determines the shaping of the material.

The life-stream of great Western architecture not only encompasses the exterior but it fills no less the interior. At the same time
neither the proportion of the parts nor the size of the construction
can be altered without destroying its idea, or significance and
beauty. It is likely that the immutability of this inner law depends
on mathematical relations or on the co-operation of mathematics
with an inherent organic conception. The explanation of this vast
difference is rooted in the instinctive basis of the Eastern relation
to the world as contrasted with the predominantly visual relation
of the West. After important achievements in the field of mathematics this instinctive basis in the East impeded the evolution of
science. The growth of the systematic application of mathematics
to nature as the independent object was stunted as was the
reciprocal and regenerative repercussion which this application
exerted on mathematics itself.

* * *

If an achievement paralleling mathematics is to be found in the
East it must be sought in the discovery and elaboration of the
techniques based on intimate knowledge of the working of mind
and body and the application of this knowledge to specific ends.
In the Far East, in China as well as in Japan, there is a huge field
of applied art which must be appreciated from this same angle.
Nowhere in any known civilization have the tools of daily use, the
whole apparatus which constitutes man's surroundings and
accompanies him from birth to even beyond death, been shaped
with such exquisite taste and cultivated in perfected harmony with
the purpose for which it is meant. Of the utmost significance is it that
in the fabrication of these devices which serve the instincts in both
the narrower and the wider meaning of the term, such as eating,
drinking, housing, dressing and lighting, there has been blended

in the Far East visual finesse with the tactile sense, the sense of surface and the feeling for material. Tools never were permitted to deteriorate into perfunctory and lifeless things. On the contrary they emerged from the status of mere objects and came into intimate relationship with man. They were his companions and friends rather than his servants.

The rich and intricate ceremonial which pervaded life and the instincts, sex and kin relations within the family, the power relations between the patriarch and the family members, between officials and men in daily life and finally between the emperor and the people, must be similarly evaluated. Such rites and ceremonies, in canalizing the instincts, act as a protective measure. Yet at the same time they also confer upon them a higher dignity and refinement. Thus the instincts are neither outlawed nor faced objectively as adversaries. They are surrounded with an artificial framework, the outward expression and psychological and moral accomplishment of which is a true work of art. The ceremonial of medieval and modern Europe cannot compare in subtlety and refinement to that of the Far East. Nor did it ever affect the art of living to the degree that it did in the Far East.

There is good reason to parallel the Far Eastern art of surface and material with this art of ceremonial. Both are seemingly external and superficial. But just as the art of surface led deeply into the life of the material, whether it was jade or silk, or wood, and created out of an instinctive knowledge of the particular material objects which united idea and material in a unique perfection, so the ceremonial, though seemingly an outward form of attitudes, reached to the depths of existence because it was from there that it stemmed.

These characteristics are to be found in Persian art. Persia has a magnificent ability for stylization which achieves an impression of reality that no kind of realistic art can ever hope to reach. This is well illustrated by the reliefs of Persepolis, in miniatures and the like. Without belittling the greatness of Persian architecture it may be said that the significant artistic genius of Persia excels in the art of decoration. As used here, decoration has a particular and profound meaning which separates it from mere adornment and embellishment. The mosaic faïence of the façades and cupolas of the mosques are not mere additions. They melt with the beauty of the architecture into one whole, just as in Persian crafts the decorative colour, ornament or representation of the pottery transform the object. Indeed this decorative element divests the object, be it large or small, of its objective character and brings it nearer to the viewer, to his inner life and his need, by penetrating into its essence. The relation of the exemplary refined ceremonial at the Sassanian court to the art of the period compares to the conditions in China and Japan.

Thus, in the artistry of the East we have a typical example of the unification of world and subject by their relation to the instincts. The life of instinct is both self-sufficient and entire, even though it is divided into a plurality of separate instincts. The proof of this is that a wholly instinct-based life in fact exists, whereas a life relying exclusively on the higher senses is unthinkable and cannot be actually found. Thus, the instinct-based relation of man and world rules the Eastern form of art. All that has been said about the world's relation to instinct and the substantiation of this by art, takes us back to concentration as the life-nerve of the Eastern mind. The result is a specific kind of artistic attitude which is distinct from the aesthetic attitude of the West.

In order to evaluate this attitude it is necessary to consider the Eastern connection with nature. The relation to nature cannot differ from that to the world in general. On the contrary, since the idea of nature comprises all the generative forces and phenomena together with the inanimate world and its changes, the relation of nature to instinct must be particularly profound. To India, nature represents the limitless generative power of the craving for existence. Thus, man's implication is all the more fateful since his craving for existence is pitted against his deeper insight and destination. So likewise the man of the Far East is a part of and one with nature. But nature, there, is not the elementary and senseless power which swallows and vomits up its own creations without beginning or end. In its positive and negative aspect it is a homely atmosphere, an environment less observed and judged than lived in.

Thus, the connection of the Chinese and Japanese peoples with the world of plants and animals as expressed in poetry and painting has been particularly intimate. One of their preoccupations was to grope for the secrets of nature not scientifically but in their purely phenomenal as well as aesthetic appearances. The results are to be seen in two quarters. In the speculation of the Taoist and related schools the unification with and the penetration of nature-objects amounts to their complete domination. Secondly, it is evident in intensified reproductions of nature objects in art. A most illuminating example is the Chinese and Japanese art of garden landscape. To use a mathematical homily this consists in raising to a higher power the skill and achievements of nature which are acquired only after a long process of empathy. Hence arises an incomparable impression of these gardens where nothing seems to have been created by the invention of man but merely as a result of emphasizing the will and achievement of nature. This is in almost absurd contrast to the eighteenth century's French garden where man's superiority teaches nature the perfection it may achieve if it acts according to the rigid laws of well-ordained and mathematically based beauty.

The Eastern work of art must fulfil certain conditions. It invites the co-operation of the spectator. It must permit him to contribute something at once different from and superior to the emotions of comprehension and appreciation. This means that in a very particular sense the work of art must be incomplete. The most exquisite Chinese paintings excel in this delicate art of being seemingly incomplete. There is a boat, yet no trace of the sea. Nonetheless, the boat is seen to repose on and to merge with the sea. The mountains and the weight of their masses can be felt though there is no shadow of a third dimension. And there are those birds where any kind of movement and expression is covered with a few strokes of the brush so that the immediacy of the effect achieved remains a mystery. This great art of omission which is simultaneously purposive and creative, must be appreciated from a two-fold angle. The artist penetrating to the essentials of his object often by a technique of prepared concentration protects himself against the onslaught of the phenomenal world while the imagination of the spectator is invited to complete what is omitted. Unlike in Western art, the function of the subject is more than comprehending and sensitive beholding. It amounts to another perhaps greater contribution than aesthetic contemplation. This attitude points back to the Eastern mind-structure with its denial of an independent object.

The Japanese art of flower-arrangement, seemingly so unassuming and yet so important in the emotional life of the people, follows the same pattern. The singular and yet simple arrangement of one or several flowers or twigs needs to be completed by the eye and mind of the beholder, a need that is all the more enhanced by the asymmetrical arrangement. Just as this delicate art of arrangement is difficult to learn, so only a cultivated mind can consummate what is intimated and thereby complete the real work of art. In striking contrast, our dazzling flower displays with their exuberance and variety demonstrate in their way the self-sufficiency of the object.

However, it is not art alone which is held close to the subject. Every good description of Chinese and Japanese customs of the past, even the near past, shows the close relationship to man of the appurtenances of daily life. Be they household or luxury objects, garments, house and garden, they were regarded more like revered and esteemed friends than as inanimate means to practical purposes. To draw India again into the picture, although in the present context she is not the equal of the Far East, there come to mind the words spoken by the father-carpenter to his son who is about to be solemnly initiated into the craft. In the presence of a priest, the father hands over to his son the tools, the heritage of the family, and he says:

'These are your younger brothers. They want fulfilment and you who have a soul must help them. By using them to create beauty and utility for men you will realize their destiny as well as your own.'[1]

* * *

The structure determines the relation to nature. From early times in Greece the objective character of this relation was demonstrated by philosophy. As a result there has remained

---

[1] Dhan S. Mukerji, *Caste and Outcaste*, New York, E. P. Dutton & Co., 1925, p. 62.

through the whole history of the West a relation between man and nature which is intellectually inextricable and powerful, but emotionally uncertain and ambiguous. This insecurity is admirably expressed in two contradictory poetic enunciations. One is by Homer: There is nothing which is more wretched than man[1]. . . ; the other by Sophocles: There is nothing more powerful than man. . . .[2]

In the Middle Ages, the critical reserve of the Church and at times its hostile attitude toward nature contributed to solidifying psychologically and even over-emphasizing its objective character. In this way, religion unintentionally prepared the ground for the scientific age where the object character of nature reached its fulfilment. Thus, nature as the adequate environment where man feels at home, is soon to be matched by the conception of a world that is cold and indifferent, if not repellent. In the East the subject-other relation is such that the physiological connection between man and nature is primarily contained in the instinct. Such a tie is stronger, more reliable and resilient than sense-perception. Accordingly, nature is man's environment and home, and so it remains acceptable under all its aspects. As is repeatedly said in the Zoroastrian texts:

'Ahura Mazdao made the cattle and Right, made the waters and the good plants, made the Light and the Earth and all that is good.'

Despite the Evil so deeply acknowledged in Zoroastrian religion, the earth remains the good home for man. More than any other people, the Chinese are attached to nature. The depths of their philosophy seem to arise out of the depths of nature and the sayings of their great sages sound as though they had been learned by listening to the nature of things. For it may be said that to the Chinese, nature itself is philosophizing. In India man is one with the insatiable craving for existence and with the endless procession of creation and destruction which carries him away. This is nature as it is experienced and represented. And even if man's fate in the turmoil of existence is illusive and full of suffering, he is still in the womb of nature and, therefore, sheltered and secure.

[1] *Odyssey* XVIII, v. 130.
[2] *Antigone*, v.

Not until he has pierced nature with the eye of deeper insight can he look at it objectively. But then it has ceased to be an effective reality to him.

Accordingly, to the man of the East nature is a living entity which is deeply akin to him. He dwells in the totality and fullness of its life. He is borne by its rising and falling waves. He tries to understand the hidden rhythm of this movement and to translate it into the language of the mind and spirit, endeavouring thereby to work out his own destiny. Indeed, the more one gropes with the manifestations of Eastern life and thought the more apparent does it become that rhythm occupies the place of law in the West. The order that is revealed and lived cannot be clarified by formulas. Not even the law of causality can be said to bear the meaning it has in Western philosophy and science.

To quote a single example—in Buddhism where the conception of *karma* came to be elaborated with the utmost acuteness, only a superficial presentation can interpret the relation between actions and their consequences, or between previous and actual existences and the succeeding ones, as determined by the law of causality. Since no soul-substance or anything else substantial is assumed to exist, there is nothing which might be called cause, and nothing where causality could take its start. The relation between the karmatic tendencies or the cravings which survive death and their concurrent appearances as rebirth cannot be conceived under the image of cause and effect. The only adequate kind of relation is that prevailing in the magic world. This has been formulated as 'if or when there is a, there is b'. Such a relation is foreign to and beyond time and is therefore incompatible with causality though certainly it is no less effective. Everywhere in the East the fundamental conception is that of an order based upon co-ordination and concurrence. For this, the term rhythm seems most appropriate. The predominance of this conception in Chinese thought of all schools need not be stressed. Everywhere the dynamic order of the universe is assumed. To envision and understand it is the unfailing effort. To realize it perfectly constitutes the solution of all human problems individual and social.

Under these conditions the proper position of the human body among the phenomena of nature is no problem in the East.

Participating in every respect in the life of nature, the body is not particularly distinct from nature either by its specific qualities or by evaluation. The immediate reason is that the clear idea of organism which is essential to Greek life and thought, is lacking. The characteristics of life are not the prerogatives of a particular kind of matter. However, this primitive animism is transcended by the metaphysical conception that the driving force is the same in all existence and further that the nature of consciousness is such that it cannot be conceived to be a function of a particular form of matter. Expression, significance, rhythm, the drive to exist are in all things. And this is why man finds himself in affinity with all things. Viewed from this standpoint the human body cannot claim any exceptional position. As to its relation to the subject, it is one of natural union. Even when detachment from the body is required, the soul which wants to disrupt this dependency does not achieve it by violent action directed against the body. On the contrary, the withdrawal is worked out by means of subtle techniques concomitant with deepening knowledge. Instead of a concrete soul fighting against the body, the pure subject, self or consciousness, originates or emerges as the instinct centre is dismantled. All this is evidently in accord with the subject-other relation.

In the Western mind-structure the subject faces objectified nature. Therefore, it must assign to the body its place among all other things. In consequence, once dualism was established in Greek philosophy, it retained its dominant role, and even when it disappeared from sight it was destined to return. Either the subject withdraws from the body and establishes itself as mind opposed to matter or in some way or other it permits itself to be drawn with the body into the physical realm. However, the idea of the body as an organism lends itself to solutions which are more conducive to hide the gulf than to bridge it. Philosophy aside, Western man has at all times insisted within the limits set by his objectifying mind in raising his bodily appearance above the rest of the natural phenomena.

The earliest and exemplary manifestation of this is in Greek sculpture. Here, the human body is exalted beyond anything created. So long as man feels that he is primordially instinct-based and functioning in accord with the whole of nature, he does not look at his physical appearance with the objectivity necessary to exalt the naked body and make it the privileged object of artistic presentation. Obviously more than the art of painting and bas-relief, free standing sculpture personifies the exaltation of the body. Since early times the Greek gods were cleared of fantastic disfigurement and animal shapes, and made to express human beauty in various forms. Thus was the human body set aside as the peak of creation. But while raising the standard of the body among the objects of nature all this endeavour does not alter its relation to the subject.

Medieval Christianity faithfully followed this attitude though with a negative sign. Its sceptical, if not flatly hostile, attitude towards the body conferred upon it an objectivity which it previously had not possessed. Classic antiquity revered in the body the living realization of the organic that was so dear to its heart, and it was this very thing which guaranteed to the body its place at the summit of nature. But to medieval Christianity the body became the antagonist of the soul and it shared with nature as a whole the sceptical evaluation of the Church. Strange as it may seem, this stern objectivation of the body and nature, this setting them off against the spiritual realm, in considerable degree, helped to prepare the modern age with its predominant interest in organic and inorganic nature. For the spirit of the Renaissance had only to substitute a positive sign for the negative one and then it received nature and body from the hands of the Middle Ages as the centre of its preoccupation.

Another very strange phenomenon cries aloud for comment in reviewing the efforts of Western man to assure a distinct place for the body. Beginning with the fifteenth century and reaching well into our own time, there began in Europe a line of styles of masculine and feminine dress which in its absurdity, lack of taste and impracticability defies imagination. A few of these styles may be explained as a reaction to medieval restriction. The ostentatious presentation of the genitals in the tight-fitting dress of Emperor Maximilian, in the well known picture of him meeting his bride, or the emphasizing of the breasts are examples of this. But the overwhelming number resemble an orgy to disfigure the natural form of the body and render its bearing as unnatural as possible.

To enumerate at random some of these monstrosities:[1] In the fifteenth century—extravagant forms of women's headgear, horns, butterfly-draperies, steeple-like structures, high, padded heart-shaped headdress with streaming scarves. The long piked shoes. The short upper garments of gentlemen do not cover the buttocks. In the sixteenth century—the boldly set ruffs for both men and women, this white circle round the neck expanding from the width of an inch to the width of a foot. In the Elizabethan period the farthingale with its fantastic decorations and the padded doublets of the gentlemen. The completely slashed costumes. At the court of Henry III of France—the hip-bolstered skirt and the leg-o'mutton sleeves elaborately decorated. In the seventeenth century—fan collar, a shorter waisted bodice necessitated by cart-wheel topped skirt, and frizzed hair dressed high with jewelled ornament. The perukes of men reach unprecedented heights. In the eighteenth century—the ladies' dress becomes particularly elaborated, 'be-looped, be-ribboned, be-plumed.' The panniers are replaced by hip-pads, then by a crino-lined bustle called *cul de crin* or *cul de Paris* which reappeared towards the end of the nineteenth century. There is no need to enumerate the horrible disfigurements the last century has produced in the habiliments of men and women.

In the Eastern style of dress there is very little to parallel these aberrations. The crippled feet of the Chinese women are not Chinese in origin but were imposed by the Mongols. The highly artificial hairdress of the Japanese women fades away to nothing when compared to that of the French ladies at the time of Louis XVI, those monstrous constructions which bore the model of a ship, or represented vegetable gardens and other phantasies. Generally speaking, the East indulged in free falling garments and comfortable trousers for men and women, and healthy footwear. Decorative and ornamental effects are obtained not by violating but by recognizing the form of the body. The styles in the East conform to the natural environment of the body and they respect

[1] The following mostly from: Millia Davenport, *The Book of Costume*, New York, and James Laver, *Style in Costume*, London, New York, 1949.

the natural dignity and freedom of its attitudes and movements.

But in the Western modes of the last four or five hundred years the body has been treated as a foreign thing which has to be decorated and draped without regard of its needs. What contradicts and derides the body becomes law—unaesthetic, uncomfortable, unhealthy, indecent and perverted. Many of these costumes enforce upon the body an unnatural rigidity of bearing which cannot but reflect upon the inner life. There must be some definite significance hidden in this trend which has persisted with such pertinacity throughout this last period of Western history. Certainly the aggressiveness which is the hallmark of this era asserts itself in demonstrating that it is unwilling to respect any natural data and that it is within its power to deal with them at will. There is an apparent satisfaction in this arbitrary handling of the body and in trying on it whatever whims come to the mind regardless of what its nature requires. All this is but another expression of the experience of freedom in facing the phenomena of nature. However, in the line of our argument this pageant of strange and artificial aberrations comes to be regarded as so many attempts to set off the human body in the most drastic way from the rest of phenomena, while at the same time both preserving and emphasizing its objective character.

CHAPTER XI

The Yoga Technique

The exemplar of the object in the structure of the Western mind is the external world. This does not mean that nature is eternally in the foreground of interest. It simply states the fact that in the relation to nature and specifically in the construction of nature, the working of the Western mind is best exemplified. But what best illustrates the otherness in the structure of the Eastern mind is the human body.

The body is essentially the concretion of instinct. As such it is close to, yet at the same time different from the subject. It constitutes, so to speak, the impersonation of otherness. The body is not considered an object, a thing among other things, pertaining wholly to the external world. For in the East, the external world is intimately related to the body as the incarnation of boundless thirst for existence. And in like manner the body is the foremost representative of otherness in relation to the subject. Again, the predominance of the body as the exponent of otherness does not imply that it claims a constant preoccupation. But it does suggest that we have to look at the special way in which philousia approaches the problem of the body in order to understand fully the technique and process of dismantling.

Upon the distinctive experience of the body the mind builds differing pictures of its organization. These can be traced historically to attempt to establish the seat of life and of the soul within the body. These efforts are as old as mankind and they constitute the first quasi-scientific interest in human anatomy. Blood, heart and breath offered themselves more readily than any other components as being intimately connected with the life principle and the death surviving substance. However, they are neither physiologically nor psychologically of the same order. The first two are tangible, but breath on the contrary is fleeting, perceptible only at low temperature, and easily suggests a transition to the invisible. More important, while blood cannot be called an organ like the heart, yet it is a clearly circumscribed part of the body whereas breathing is a function. And through its regular rhythmic recurrence and its concomitant sensations it seems destined to become identified with life itself.

Under these circumstances it is not surprising that in the East, particularly in India and also in China, a remarkable science and technique of breathing has developed. Almost all Eastern doctrines which are centred in transformation through concentration and meditation include breathing techniques as an indispensable foundation. Their far-reaching physiological, psychological and mental potentialities are fully appreciated. Indeed, it may seem strange that Eastern medicine did not make use of the science of breathing for curative purposes. The reason could be that it was considered a lore, both secret and sacred. But a more pertinent one lies in the simple fact that the art and technique of breathing produce their effect only as the result of scrupulous training. Therefore, they do not lend themselves to medication.

The same reasoning may well answer the same question in the West. In neither its initial Greek period nor in modern times has medicine acknowledged as a curative means the full importance of breathing. Western medicine more than Eastern, even the highly developed Chinese medicine, is of course primarily interested in the respiratory organ, and in respiration itself only in so far as it is an indication of the morbid condition of that organ or of any other indirectly connected with it. So while neither in the East nor West did medicine pay any particular attention to breath, it is all the more noteworthy that the East assigned to it a distinctive role in a realm superior to any purely empirical endeavour. Before this can be appreciated the extolling of breath must be viewed against a broader physiological background.

The difference between West and East as regards the relation to nature and the body is important.[1] The objectifying mind of

---

[1] This argumentation as well as any other to be found in this book, it must be remembered, deals with the ideal type and its outstanding manifestations, the characteristic creations and the atmosphere pervading the civilizations. The degree to which the contingent individual participates in the type is, of course, widely variable.

the West views the body as a thing belonging to the world of physical phenomena. Yet at the same time it endeavours by any and all means to raise it above them. The objectivation of the body rests upon the priority conceded to the higher senses. This priority is linked to the emphasis laid on the cerebro-spinal system. Thus, it is appropriate to say that in the West the cerebro-spinal system is the representative of the physical part of man. This implies that the harmonious interplay of the parts is directed by a superior organ—the brain. In constant touch with all the other parts it receives their messages and communicates to them its orders. Even if the brain is not simply identified with reason or mind, it retains its importance regardless of whether it be considered their mirror, expression, or tool.

All this stands in contrast with the instinct-rooted relation to the body in the East. There the subject-other relation is reflected in this instinct-based relation of the body to the subject. The compound of the instincts represents the body and is considered its essence. On their part the instincts are intrinsically connected with the sympathetic and para-sympathetic systems, which together form the autonomic nervous system. This regulates their functions, and normally escapes partial or total voluntary interference. For in contradistinction to the brain which consciously receives and answers the messages received and is in one way or another inseparable from consciousness, the autonomic system is indifferent to consciousness. Indeed consciousness may even interfere harmfully with its operation. By its very nature the autonomic or vegetative system is not in need of organized leadership.

Between these two systems—the cerebro-spinal and the autonomic—breathing occupies a distinctive place. It is anchored in both and so, in a certain sense, it transcends each. Albeit it is regulated by reflex mechanisms, it can within limits be voluntarily controlled. The interdependence between the holding of the breath, its acceleration and the like and the psychological states which involve the suppression or absence of emotions, would seem to indicate the crucial point at which the lively interplay of body and soul continually transpires. In quite another way, which is abstract and scientifically demonstrated but not experienced, the brain is linked up with the perceptive and intellectual faculties. Therefore, it is reasonable to consider breath the immediate entrance to the immaterial part of man. Such at least is obviously the reflection of the East. Many attempts to widen this opening for deeper penetration are made through elaborating on the voluntary control of breathing, developing the techniques fitting that purpose, and investigating how far the control can be extended.

The effort of harnessing breath for the purpose of exploring consciousness—for this is the East's domain—inevitably must co-operate with concentration, which is the life centre of the East. A deep mutual influence of breathing and concentration exists though not on equal terms. Whereas regular breathing does not alone condition a state of concentration, no state of concentration can be sustained for any length of time without it. On the other hand, concentration may exert a regulating effect on otherwise irregular breathing. Normally it does this indirectly as the result of the subject's facing an object of absorbing interest, rather than by making breath its immediate object.

* * *

This conception with all its far reaching consequences has found classic expression in the Yoga system. Although the essential ideas of Yoga were for the first time systematically expounded in the Yoga sutras of Patanjali, they were stated in the Upanishads and in fact to some extent they form a part of all important Indian doctrines. Thus, in a deeper sense Yoga is less a system of thought and practice than it is a great spiritual movement and attitude. As such, though predominant in India Yoga is equally indigenous in the Far East. There it unfolds in many doctrines, sects and customs, besides those of Indian origin which have been received with congenial comprehension and developed in a distinctively original way as in Zen-Buddhism.

In India, however, we see Yoga crystallized in an elaborate system embracing body, soul and mind. The technique of breathing as the central bodily function is linked with that of concentration in a twofold effort. The end sought is to hoard mental energy for the attainment of pure consciousness. With the utmost transparency the system lays bare the working of the dismantling of cognition and the logic of the Eastern mind. There is an additional reason to give due appreciation to the Yoga technique. For despite the extended literature dealing with it no comprehensive scientific study has yet been made to investigate its physiological and psychological principles and their qualification for the achievement of its purported aim. While in a looser significance the term Yoga is applied to any consistent effort which will bring about the union of the individual self with Brahman there are many forms of Yoga, such as Bhakti Yoga—union through devotion—Karma Yoga—union through action, and others which can be left aside for our argument.[1]

At the threshold to the comprehension of Yoga man's relation to his body appears once again, but in a new light. To the West it is a basic idea that we control our body, and more specifically that the body is that part of the external world over which we exercise an immediate influence. That the body possesses power over us is a secondary insight and therefore a derivative experience. Our emphasis on controlling the body derives from the fact that in our mind-structure the body and the whole external world are relative to the higher senses. The moving at will of the body and its limbs and the changes caused thereby in our surroundings and in relations to the world, immediately impress the eye and result in making an object of the body. Thus arises the unequalled endeavour of the Greeks to shape the naked body according to an ideal harmony of beauty, health and fitness. This dominating positive objectivation is questioned by doctrines which maintain that the body controls us and result in an ascetic attitude of a more or less aggressive character. Announced in various forms by pre-Socratic philosophers this latter was resolutely taken up by the Stoics to triumph in the Middle Ages.

---

[1] All of the Yoga systems derive from the two basic forms of Yoga—Hatha Yoga and Raja Yoga. These two systems depending upon and complementing each other constitute the classic Yoga system, going by the name of Hatha-Yoga-Pradipika of Svatmarama Svamin. The Hatha Yoga of the Pradipika contains only a limited number of postures and exercises, differing in this from the variety of acrobatic performances which Hatha Yoga has developed. The right view is that there cannot be Hatha Yoga without Raja Yoga nor Raja Yoga without preceding or accompanying Hatha Yoga. This the Pradipika indicates from the very beginning by the emphasis placed on breathing exercises which form a natural link between physical and mental Yoga.

The Yoga Technique

The original and deepest experience demonstrates to the East that we do not control the body. This must be so because to the East the body is relative not to the higher senses but to the vital instincts. And over the instincts man does not exercise the direct power he does over his limbs and the whole body as a part of the external world. If there is to be any control at all of the body it cannot be the same as in the West. It must aim at something else— deeper and of wider scope and be attained by other means. Indeed, the East has been granted a more penetrating intuition of the link existing between the body and the subject. Owing to its structure and the resulting orientation, the East bypassed the Western position which stressed the visible and tangible aspect of the body.

The Eastern man feels body and subject to be linked together in a sphere far below that viewed by the West. This sphere is inaccessible to observation and is barred from interference by will or reason. In our body, the man of the East would be prompted to say, we are dragging something along with ourselves which though close to and experienced as intimately connected with us, nonetheless remains unknown. It is independent of consciousness and under its surface. Pretending that we control our body—he would continue to argue—is vain and sticks to superficial impressions. On the contrary, if there is anything over which, in the normal state of things we have no power at all, it is the body. Power is founded on knowledge and those who have no knowledge have no hope of control. The newborn infant moves his limbs automatically. Even the all-important gesture of grasping is automatic. These elementary movements of the legs and arms have only to be regulated in the simplest way to produce what we proudly proclaim to be the control of the body. Thus, our control is limited to a tiny section of the functions of the body. And it remains, in the proper and figurative sense of the term, superficial. This must be so, for our immediate knowledge of the body through distinct sensations extends but little farther. If we in the West are satisfied with calling this capacity of directing the movements of the body and its limbs in space control, we deceive ourselves.

The East is transfixed by the experience of coenesthesia—the sensation of bodily consciousness. This is an inextricably obscure compound of organic sensations which seems to grow more refractory as one tries to penetrate its mystery. And yet it is evident that nowhere else can there be found the key to a deeper insight into the joinder of body and subject. And it is by virtue of this insight that a real mastery of the body is achieved. In order to realize this goal the confused mixture of the bodily experience has to be broken down into its components. Only in this way can the inaccessible be made accessible and the impenetrable penetrated by consciousness. Only in such a procedure can the ultimate sense data which carry the experience of the body's belonging to the subject, be induced to appear in the light of consciousness. As long as they remain below the level of consciousness safely hidden in that chaotic compound of coenesthesia, the body eludes being known and therefore escapes real control beyond the pitiable pseudo-domination which is the only one we may claim to possess.

There is, however, a reverse to this fact. In the proportion that we learn to control our body in full measure, the experience of the body being ours would gradually vanish. It would be replaced by a feeling of increasing estrangement, for then our body would no longer be experienced as ours. But the very condition for its being experienced as ours is that with the exception of an exceedingly small section, the body and its functions operate outside and below consciousness. The superficial direction which we exercise over the body, though not entitled to the pretentious term of control, suffices for all practical means. Nothing short of the complete consciousness of all bodily phenomena could afford the ground for a genuine control. But such a state would inevitably produce a rupture of the natural tie between us and our body— an effect which would make us experience the body as an object. Thus the technique of breaking down the body experience into its elements in order to render them conscious and thereby to exert full control over the body will end in its objectivation. However—and this cannot be overemphasized—this result will come to pass only in a mind which by its very structure is bound to create objects. For the natural intention of the West in adopting this technique would be to aim at controlling the body like any other well known object.

Contrariwise the same technique applied by the East will cul-

minate in a quite different result. For the Eastern mind is oriented
not to objectivation but to the establishment of pure consciousness. Therefore, the result will be just the opposite. As the body
elements come to be controllable at will, the subject, now that he
is assured that the body will no longer exert any disturbing influence, loses all interest in it and dedicates his life and effort to the
freed Self. Under these circumstances the body will resemble a
smoothly run engine whose connection with the subject has been
unhinged. In that condition its relation to the subject is neither
that of subject-object nor that of subject-other. In a metaphoric
sense one might call this state of things the utmost possible
control in domination of the body. Yet one would hardly speak
of domination where what is controlled has definitely dropped
from sight. It would be different if in this process of the dismantling of the body a hostile attitude towards it existed which
would immediately restore to it the object character.

This general background is essential to an understanding of the
operation of the Yoga technique and its potential success.

* * *

The inner logic of the structure of the Yoga technique is no
less scientific than its basic idea. It starts from the principle that
the raising of all body sensations into consciousness is the means,
by unhinging its connection with the subject, of controlling the
body. Then the first task is to diminish the number of potential
body sensations. This means that the bodily sensation in which
all of them merge, some distinguishable, the overwhelming majority
indiscernible, has to be restricted. To achieve this, conditions
must be created which, by excluding disturbing stimuli stemming
either from the body itself or from outside, will guarantee the
smooth running of the bodily functions.

A lonely but pleasant spot for one's house with surroundings—
even flower gardens agreeable to look at, and a palatable and
nourishing diet, both serve the purpose and demonstrate, in flat
opposition to Christian asceticism, that the problem of the body
is best approached with the utmost caution and gentleness. All
this is in accord with that truly Asiatic wisdom that the more we
fight against a thing, the more surely do we become its slave and

the more we try to escape from a thing the more we are liable to become ensnared by it. Mortification of the body and raging against the flesh are of no avail. The last elements of the body consciousness, that hidden borderline between body and mind, must be uncovered. So subtle a task cannot be achieved by violence and direct attack. Even before the technique has started, the general orientation and its effect can be anticipated. As a result of the particular living conditions all immoderate and abnormal sensations are ruled out, their number and variety diminished, and their appearance and disappearance regulated.

Then the technique proper is accompanied by quite a few exercises, some of them rather drastic, to remove eye diseases, clean respiratory passages and the intestine, to increase digestive power and to prevent the emergence of morbid conditions with their unpredictable and disturbing sensations. The principle is thus firmly established. To the physical hygiene corresponds the mental with the usual moral code of doing no harm to anything, speaking the truth, preserving continence, being merciful and the like. But the remarkable fact is, not the contents of this code, but the place assigned to it. Apparently these moral qualifications are considered the strict parallel to the physical hygiene and they are valued more as a natural precondition of the proper technique than as an achievement to be acquired during the procedure.

To complete the picture of the situation in which the Yogin finds himself, another element—this one of a higher, a spiritual character—must be added. The loneliness of the Yogin is not only an isolation in space. It is also a spiritual isolation, an isolation in the metaphysical sphere. True, Shiva, the tutelary god of Yoga, and Ishvara are here and there invoked. But they are no more than mere expedients to concentration and they disappear as the Yogin reaches perfection. But even they do not effectively lessen the Yogin's loneliness. For though the Yogin may turn to them asking for help there is no living communication between man and god, no questioning and answering, nothing resembling the great human drama of the Christian, particularly the Christian mystic, in his search for his god. Thus, as the Yogin advances along his path he may be compared to a closed system protected from any interference from without.

The Yoga Technique

Although the order in which the exercises, almost all of which have to be repeated time and again, are described does not correspond to the order in which they are performed, a thorough analysis divides them into different categories. Avoiding the astounding acrobatic and contortionist performances usually known by the name Hatha Yoga, Swatmarama's system demonstrates only a few exercises resembling our gymnastics. The reason for this is that the basic attitude of the Yoga exercises is the cross-legged sitting posture with the spinal column straightened, whereas the starting point and preparation of all our gymnastics is the standing position. The latter leads directly to all activities important for ordinary life where muscular tension of the whole body or of its parts is naturally directed to useful movements. Such are grasping, striking, all kinds of locomotion as turning, walking, jumping, running; further-on assault, self-defence and the overcoming of obstacles. Nearly all our gymnastics consists in a condensation of these activities, anticipating their execution in an elaborate way. Skill and muscular power, preparedness and elasticity for action lie at the core of our gymnastics, the ideal of which is action in the outside world. Its purpose is to lead us right into the physical world, to give us a good position there, to make us fit to take possession of it and there to defend our place.

The cross-legged posture of the Yoga presents the reverse picture. Not only is it opposed to the standing position but no less to our mode of sitting in which the body is quite unnaturally bent twice. The cross-legged position provides the natural condition for a free and relaxing attitude. At the same time, it brings the parts of the body close together. And thus, all in all, it symbolizes what it is intended for—concentration of the mind and the accumulation of energy. One is tempted to compare this posture to a pyramid or a cone. In any case, it is a pose of steadfast self-sufficiency without any orientation to the outside world. It is indeed the ideal posture since it combines the utmost relaxation with waking consciousness. Under such conditions the expenditure of muscular energy is obviously limited to a minimum. However, the stimulation of most of the proper exercises is not concerned with muscular efforts and the movements of the body and limbs. Rather do they refer to the interior of the body.

Therefore, with only slight exaggeration we may speak of Hatha Yoga as an invisible technique. The basic idea, however, remains the same, namely, first to eliminate all superfluous sensations and their morbid causes—second to raise to the plane of clear consciousness all the rest, the potential as well as the existing sensations. The final aim is to separate them and thereby the body from the subject. What there is of gymnastics in our sense of the term including the variations of the cross-legged posture such as various ways of crossing the legs, holding and moving arms and hands, also serve this purpose.

While this technique is easily attainable when it is applied to the sensations connected with muscular movements, it becomes extremely difficult when it turns to the inner organs and their functions. Yet it is precisely at this point that Yoga must concentrate its art in order to unhinge the link between subject and body. This task is all the more difficult because in normal life the stimuli originating in the inner organs constitute the overwhelming material entering the state of bodily sensation known as coenaesthesia. However, they send but few distinct sensations into consciousness, and these few are comparatively uniform and regular such as those that stem from the digestive tract and the heart. Abnormal and morbid conditions are required to remind us of the existence of our inner organs. To conjure up all their specific sensations, which nature has so wisely kept in the dark, is certainly as difficult a venture as it is paradoxical and contrary to nature. True, there is the fact known as relative analgesia and connected with it the anaesthesia of the inner organs. But if this fact limits the task it does not by any means make it easier.

And so it is all the more remarkable that Yoga has elaborated methods of coping successfully with the problem of awakening, controlling and distancing these inner sensations. To try to break down the coenaesthetic feeling into its components by directly attacking it, would obviously be a hopeless task. No attention, be it ever so meticulous, could achieve more than spurious success. No concentration could succeed in singling out clearly defined sensations of the inner organs, in localizing them correctly, and still less in reproducing them at will. Thus if the way is barred to direct approach, an expedient had to be found to get around these difficulties. It was found in a diagram of the interior and the organs of the body.

The anatomy of Yoga has been generally accepted as a creation of unlimited imagination. Fantastic elements grew like weeds around the original framework, since it did not and could not pretend to correspond to reality. The central part of this imaginary chart are the Cakras. These are often represented as Lotus flowers of which there are six or seven from the middle of the cranium down to the perineum. Then somewhere below the navel there is the Kanda twelve inches above the anus, and there in the Kanda is the source of the thousands of nadis of which the Sushumna is the most important. For at the mouth of Sushumna sleeps the great goddess Kundalini coiled like a serpent. And to awaken Kundalini and to make it move so that the breath may pass freely is one of the main parts of the technique.

A full description of the Yoga anatomy of the body's interior is beyond our argument. Attempts to identify it with the real anatomic conditions have had uncertain and fragmentary results. Some of the Cakras are likely to correspond to nerve centres, as for example the solar plexus and the nadis to nerves and arteries. Be that as it may, there is little doubt that the Indians could have produced a picture of the body's interior closer to the facts had such an achievement been their ambition. But, on the contrary, a kind of vague analogy was all that was needed. In view of the relative analgesia of the inner organs, the sensations which can be identified in a smoothly running organism must be assumed to be relatively few in number. Singling them out and localizing them, however, is a supernormal task which requires unusual preparation. This prerequisite exists in a diagram of the body's interior.

Such a diagram when vividly imagined and mentally incorporated into the body, lends itself admirably to the purpose, particularly in a mind endowed with concrete thinking, creative imagination and an inner bias to realization. In full agreement with this endowment, although the diagram of Yoga constitutes a forceful schematization, yet it presents an animated picture, and of this the previous description of the goddess Kundalini is a good example. For this reason too the diagram is not merely more or less clearly represented, as we may be prone to believe. It is actually incorporated by a vivid and determined imagination. In this way the diagram fulfils all the functions required. It facilitates the awakening of sensations. It singles them out and individualizes them. It permits the localization of the individualized sensations by projecting them on the part of the diagram. And finally it performs the decisive function of externalizing the sensations stemming from the inner organs. Then the result is the externalization of the body as a whole—or, to express the same process from the other angle, it enables consciousness to withdraw from the body. Here again, the psychological insight of the inventors of the Yoga technique is apparent. Only a diagram of the body interior with but a superficial resemblance to real anatomic conditions, is capable of exteriorizing the sensations. A picture reflecting the interior of the body as it really is, might at best facilitate the awakening of sensations. But it would never succeed in separating them and therewith the body itself, from the consciousness of the subject.

*　*　*

Here we arrive at a crucial result which casts into clear relief the cleavage between the Eastern and the Western mind structure. This whole process of singling out sensations, raising them ever more clearly into consciousness, and setting them off from the perceiving object, might seem to bear strong resemblance to the Western process of objectivation. It is, however, the exact opposite. Not only is this obtrusive object the body dissolved into its smallest experienceable elements. But by controlling the sense-data at will and thus making them appear and reappear before the indifferent eye of consciousness, the fundamental intention aims at depriving them of any substantial existence. The result, therefore, is not the constitution of an object. On the contrary, it is the exteriorization of the sensations and thereby of the body as an empty shell void of autonomous existence. Indeed, there is no better and certainly no more consistent example to illustrate what the dismantling form of cognition means and how it works. All the great representative doctrines of Eastern cognition share with the Yoga technique the dismantling of phenomena. But this is not with the intent of reconstructing them anew as the real objective entities. Rather the definite aim is to advance on the way to the pure subject.

For the sake of the clarity of the argument, it has been necessary to lay to one side the dominant role of breathing. Actually, an overwhelming number of the Yoga exercises are directly or indirectly connected with it. From an early moment whenever the nature of the exercises permits, the control of the breath is connected with them. Then, as the technique proceeds the multiple variations of breathing come to the fore as the main preoccupation, and because of the intimate relationship between breathing and concentration, it becomes the content of concentration. With the usual caution the breathing exercises start with the various hygienic devices for the purifying of the respiratory organs, nostril, windpipe, and lungs. Then variations of breathing are probed and trained while the breathing is connected with different parts of the body as contracting the throat or the anus, or assuming different postures. Then follows the regulation of the rhythm of breathing and the technique of restraining and stopping breath and its concentration on the Cakras and other parts of the body. In this way, breathing is not only purified. It is restored to the leadership which belongs to it. Once this has been achieved, this art assumes the role of the foremost ally in the endeavour to exteriorize the inner sensations. Thus, the breath is directed to and let through the organs as they are or as they are imagined. Here is an example:

'Assuming this posture, he should close the mouth and breathe out through the nostrils till the pressure is felt on the heart, the throat and the brain. Then he should draw in the breath with a hissing sound till it strikes against the heart, all this time keeping his body and head erect.'

Moving the breath through the body it may rightly be said is but an illusion. Yet it is no more an illusion than the whole anatomy of Yoga which it is meant to complete and it is real to the degree that it is efficient. So far as efficiency is concerned a superficial training will disclose that when deep breathing is directed to a real or imagined part of the body, whether it be exterior or interior, it facilitates the perceiving and exciting of sensations. In so doing, it helps to project the sensations on the anatomical diagram and thereby it leads to their exteriorization. When, after an unlimited number of years, the exteriorization of all body sensations has been achieved, what will then be the situation? The natural link between body and subject will be severed, and the body functioning perfectly in its own right, will appear to the subject as an indifferent phenomenon.

With this exteriorization of the body the definition of Yoga as 'the restriction of the fluctuations of mind-stuff'[1] has been realized. What is left is breath and consciousness both of which if not identified, are inseparably interlaced and interdependent. Again and again is it repeated that when the breath wanders the mind is unsteady and vice versa. Yet even with this state of perfect steadiness the summit has not yet been reached. There is still consciousness and the content of consciousness, breath being now that content, in fact the only content of consciousness. The aim must be to attain pure consciousness—consciousness without content. To achieve this final state—samadhi—consciousness and breath must be ever more restrained until with the suspension of breathing, empirical consciousness will cease to exist. Consciousness has at last become independent and absolute. But in no way can this state be called the destruction of consciousness, that is to say, nothingness.

*   *   *

In the Yoga technique and its underlying idea we face one of the most daring and ingenious conceptions of the human mind. This great adventure in consciousness is distinguished from all others in that consciousness deals with itself alone and with the sole aim of arriving at its own essence—pure consciousness. All other adventures, particularly those of the West, deal with qualified consciousness, be it religious, artistic, philosophical or scientific, and they achieve something concrete and determinable. Nevertheless, the fundamental assumption which underlies Yoga can certainly claim a higher degree of evidence than can the presuppositions of religion, philosophy, art or science of any denomination.

As with all Eastern philousia, Yoga starts with the self-

---

[1] James Haughton Woods, *The Yoga-System of Patanjali*, The Harvard University Press, 1927, p. 8.

evident truth that consciousness is the primordial and unquestionable datum. At first sight this position might seem in close relationship with Descartes' *cogito ergo sum*,—I think therefore I am,—as the fundamental self-evident truth. His conclusion that thinking implies the existence of the thinker or, to put it in a general form, that Isness derives its validity from thought, is, to say the least, debatable. Descartes' statement is in fact a *petitio principii*—a begging of the question—which could be formulated thus. If I consider real or existent what thinking reveals to be real, then reason is the only safe source of reality. The stand taken by philousia in general and Yoga in particular is infinitely more cautious and consistent. It avoids any involvement in the problem of whether or not thought is the only or the foremost means through which we can be assured of our own or any other reality. Yoga is satisfied with the self-evident statement—there is consciousness. And this without attaching to the word 'is' any particular significance such as reality or unreality or whatever it be. Consciousness is there, and this is the only statement which is beyond any possible doubt. It would be equally erroneous to pass from the being-there of consciousness to the conclusion that some or all of the contents of consciousness are real or unreal. All such moves, however tempting, transcend the simple datum of 'there is consciousness'.

So if we are to avoid quicksand the only matter with which we can deal is consciousness. To express this in a more conspicuous form—consciousness can deal only with itself. This preoccupation of consciousness with itself can have but one ultimate meaning. Consciousness must rise to ever increasing clarity about itself. The clarification of consciousness or the attainment of pure consciousness is, therefore, the only task which can be undertaken without risk of moving in the realm of the uncertain and the deceitful. Placed in this light the task implies that all content must be eliminated from consciousness. And further the connection between consciousness and all that is not consciousness, particularly the body, must be unhinged.

This reasoning is as sound as the basic proposition is self-evident. Likewise the Yoga technique, abstruse and unrealizable as it may seem, is in itself consistent and thoroughly adapted to that purpose. Nowhere is there a fault in theory. Whether or not the goal can be reached is unpredictable and can be demonstrated only by experience. Thus it is impossible to look at Yoga as a fantastic or illusory creation. Yoga theory and practice live up to both philosophical and scientific requirements and its conclusions are drawn with relentless consequence. Whereas at the outset prayers are addressed to the Gods Siva and Ishvara these disappear from the scene as the work progresses. At the end they are thrown overboard as is the anatomical diagram of the body interior. Both diagram and gods are mere expedients, pragmatic means for concentration or exteriorization. To accept them as real would contradict the search for pure consciousness.

Apart from the prayers addressed to the divine helpers, the kind of consciousness that dominates the Yoga exercises is of a particular character. It is prepared by conditions which, by excluding emotion and unforeseen stimuli, induce a state of equanimity. In this calmness of the mind the exercises, though variegated, are monotonous. They produce and reproduce again and again the same sensations. This, however, is not all and it is not even the main point. It should be emphasized particularly with regard to breathing, that these monotonous repetitions must take place unfailingly in the light of consciousness and that any other kind of mental activity must be avoided.

The difficulty in keeping the mind concentrated on a succession of monotonous impressions even when they may present a particular interest is well known. Almost inevitably the mind will either go astray and turn to other objects, or somnolence will set in. In order to stay awake our consciousness requires interest in the object so that it can be active in observation and reflection or at least in emotional reaction. But in the Yoga exercises not only is there no interest in the sensations implied, but it is the very core of the technique that they should be regarded with utter indifference. To ask that the mind should remain evenly awake in this state of monotony amid indifferent impressions is therefore a demand of the utmost difficulty. It is contrary, if not to the working of the mind in general, at least to the Western mind which by its very nature must elaborate on the object. What Yoga requires is a subtle, a disinterested and a steady kind of consciousness which follows the impressions, so to speak, from afar. It is a species of accompanying consciousness which with its discreet light is but the place where the impressions occur. The inner relationship between this kind of consciousness and awareness is obvious. And whatever may be the state of consciousness in samadhi, it cannot differ fundamentally from awareness.

The most demonstrable and the most transparent example of the process of dismantling cognition is provided by Hatha Yoga.[1] The subtlety with which the natural data of our body are resolved into their elements and deprived of reality, and the prudent confidence which prevents any kind of objectivation—all this is but the negative aspect of that positive intent which seeks to maintain everything in relation to consciousness and consciousness in relation to itself. For the aim of dismantling cognition is the pure consciousness or subject. At first sight a definite similarity, if not analogy, occurs between the working of methods of Eastern and Western cognition. This impression is justified only in so far as both, dissatisfied with a merely receptive and contemplative attitude toward the world, deal actively with it. And action means interfering with and transforming the original data. But this is all that they have in common. In flat contradistinction to the East, the West disintegrates the phenomena because they do not satisfy the philosophical or scientific reason which seeks out objective reality, and constructs one world image after another in the tireless hope that eventually it will discover one solid and resistant enough to stand the test.

This is the 'saving through of the phenomena'—that seemingly

---

[1] It is generally assumed that Hatha Yoga has to be followed by and culminates in Raja Yoga—Raja Yoga being the technique for those whose spiritual endowment permits them to dispense with the exercises of Hatha Yoga. Such a sharp distinction between Hatha and Raja Yoga is, however, not unconditionally justified. True, Raja Yoga is the Yoga of contemplation and meditation based upon concentration and breathing. However, in the advanced stage of Hatha Yoga there are quite a few exercises which live up the requirements of Raja Yoga or at least come very near to them. In any case, so far as aim and technique are concerned, Raja Yoga shares with Hatha Yoga the principle and method of dismantling cognition. The difference is that the dismantling process in Raja Yoga operates exclusively on the level of mind and spirit. Indeed this applies not only to Raja Yoga but to all the various branches of philousia in India and the Far East. To quote one characteristic example: The Bhagavadgita is essentially Raja Yoga relying chiefly on meditation. But in order to prepare a sound basis for the spiritual way and to secure it from harm, the Gita appropriates from Hatha Yoga the general physical, moral and mental conditions. (Lesson the sixth, 10–14.)

endless process in which man reduces the world, whose objective reality he is driven to recognize by his instinct and senses, to the rank of phenomena, and in the course of which all the screens of objective world images which he has invented seem doomed to share the same fate. For apparently renunciation is man's destiny. Either he chooses to move and toil in the abundance of phenomena, enlarging their number by endless discoveries at the same time trying to reduce them to fundamentals—free to call this universe the reality instead of resenting it as imperfect. Or he may resolutely turn his back on it, renouncing the variety of outer and inner phenomena, in fact everything which is known as life. Then grasping at the unique datum in the whole spectacle, to wit, consciousness, he makes it his exclusive theatre of action, confident that in this realm if anywhere truth and reality must be found.

* * *

At the height of his fulfilment, the man of the East stands utterly alone. On his way, save for initial guidance, he has been without human or divine help and having arrived at the supreme state he cannot nor does he expect to meet anything that can be thought of as an objective entity. Thus, the result of this dismantling process of decorporealization is another form of consciousness, or to be more exact, it is consciousness itself without limit or qualification. And just as during the toiling years there is no absolute being to appeal to in hope or in despair, so at this moment of consummation there is none to receive him. But what appears to those, who are fashioned by another structure, incomprehensible or super— or inhuman, particularly when we remember the continuous communication between the Christian saints and God—of which 'the dark night of the soul' by John of the Cross may be quoted as an illuminating example—the identical situation of unqualified isolation cannot hold the same emotional and intellectual implications for the man of the East.

The ontological connection of the non-subject with the subject as the other, or the dismantling of the other, or its disappearance or exteriorization—all of these phrases conveying the same general meaning—does not involve the same devastating psychological effect as the destruction of everything objective would necessarily produce in the Western mind. For there, the radical elimination of the object would dry up the very life-stream of the subject. The philosophical idea of an Absolute or the scientific construction of an objective world are congenial to the Western mind. So likewise is any kind of relationship of the subject with these conceptions such as subordination, union, identification, or absorption, because any form of participation in the Absolute means objectivation which is to say reality. In the East on the contrary the subject discovers reality in theoretical and active withdrawal from any object, which in turn is to say, in the dismantling of all other data and in the corresponding discovery of an ever more real existence of itself as consciousness. Accordingly, the great Eastern types present the aspect of a monadic loneliness together with an essential self-sufficiency.

Those towering figures which might seem to contradict this statement are on the contrary the best witnesses to its truth. There is the Buddha who moved by compassion, renounces the nirvana and returns to the world to resume the work of salvation. There is Confucius himself the incarnation of his teaching, who passes his life in expounding the humane attitudes which alone create the perfect man, uphold family and society and support the state. However, when the Buddha makes his decision he is the perfect being. His act of commiseration is by no means the indispensable outcome of his Buddhahood, and his return is entirely contingent, constituting neither an inner necessity nor a higher form of Buddhahood. In the same sense, Confucius and the other Chinese sages conceive themselves to be, and they are entities of perfection. If they decide to work in and for the world they neither cede to an inescapable inner compulsion nor do they grow in stature.

This, we of the West who measure their action by our own standards may regard as the true fulfilment of what they are. The reason for our way of judgment is that in an objective world, action achieving changes claims quite another position and value than in the East. Accordingly, a sage's means of producing effects apart from direct action is his teaching and the setting of an example. However, behind and beyond the example is the belief in an immediate, magic influence, emanating from the mere presence of the superior man. Though not everybody is capable of responding to his radiation, this direct mode of producing effect is one which is peculiar to the Eastern sage. It is, in accord with his monadic being, his self-sufficiency and his perfection.

A deeper understanding of Confucius will reveal him in this respect in no way different from a Taoist sage, and the fact that much against his own will he is wandering, teaching and counselling must not deceive us. What he felt would have been the adequate situation in which he could have exerted his influence and what fate refused to grant him, was to be invested by a prince with full authority to reorganize state and society. The kind of influence he would then have applied can be well illustrated by an anecdote. When Confucius expressed his intention to go to the people of the Western mountains he was warned that they were barbarians. He answered: 'If a sage lived among them what rudeness would there be?' The immediate, quasi magic, civilizing effect is apparently what Confucius had in mind in contradistinction to the influence of an example which would have to be consciously appreciated in order to be followed, or to the teaching of moral behaviour—both of these being forms of education quite unlikely to succeed among the barbarians.

The man of the East having thus arrived at his goal realizes what is contained in the structure, namely the autonomy and self-sufficiency of the subject. Here again does it become manifest that in the domain of the Eastern mind, nature cannot occupy a place similar to that which it holds in the Western where it is the live opposite of the subject. But with the emphasis on the subject, nature does not develop into an entity in its own right on equal terms with the subject—it cannot even have any real impact on him. The only phenomenon which can be detached from the rest of nature in order to become of real concern is the body. The experience of man's corporeal appearance among the other phenomena of nature is the distinct phenomenon through which nature reaches deeply into the realm of consciousness. There the man of the East makes the uncanny discovery that the body is not opposed to the soul, but a psycho-physiological whole connected by an impervious link with the Self. Nature is indifferently the same to all men, but everybody possesses a body of his own. Therefore, the body is the crucial experience, not nature. Seen from this vantage the interest in nature appears as an escape, at least as a detour which after an unpredictably long strife returns to the central phenomenon of the body. With clear determination the Eastern mind-structure expresses that man's true concern is man and that man is essentially consciousness.

CHAPTER XII

The Contrasted Solutions
of Classic Problems

The East is the virtuoso of the ineffable. The great notions of the Eastern mind anticipate conclusive states of being which obstinately resist the conceptual approach. Those of the Western mind, such as Plato's Ideas, Spinoza's Substance or God, or Hegel's Absolute which seem to be of a somewhat congenial nature, are actually of a different structure. They are intellectual intuitions which require a substructure and elaborate explanation and demonstration, and they belong to the same realm of conceptual thought as do all the other creations of the Western Mind.

Man has never been content with his surroundings. The primitive populates his world with beings of his own invention, and even adds another or a plurality of worlds. And the man of higher civilization in his religious, philosophical and scientific dispensations does not contradict this basic attitude. It lies in the structure, and particularly in the fact that cognition is a state of being, that the man of the East seeks this enrichment preferably in new experiences. Even if such experiences are elusive or deceptive, the experiencing itself—this specific form of encountering—remains extant. To the East all cognition is essentially experience. And as they draw nearer to pure consciousness these states of being defy description. They are that from which words turn away. All this is implicit in the statement that the East is the virtuoso of the ineffable.

Moreover, no experience, be it ever so simple, can ever be wholly expressed. First, this is because it is practically impossible to extricate it from the elements stemming from memory, expectation and other psychological sources and those deriving from the necessary participation of the intellect. Second—and this is even

236

more important—it is because our means of thinking are unable to seize and specify what is unique.[1] So far as the experiences of daily life are concerned, their capture by the intellect does not exceed an approximate designation. In fact, it is not much more than a handling by means of counters. In the field of average experience the difference between East and West is perceptible only to the knowing observer, particularly since Western influence has robbed Eastern actions, objectives, reactions and incentives of their traditional atmosphere. Beyond this field the East is still wary of the determinate attempt to translate experience into concepts. The idea that, in so doing, experience can be ascertained, penetrated and made permanent is thus dismissed.

Nothing in the East resembles the creative exuberance, the universal versatility and the penetrating power of the Western concept as it everywhere unfolds and shrinks back from nothing. In the East there is an almost deferential attitude toward experience—a respect felt for its immediacy and integrity which does not permit any assault upon it by hostile means. While experience should not be handed over to, and be processed by the concept, it may be completed or replaced by other experiences. It is the East's inherent conviction that conceptual thought cannot penetrate to the root of experience. How then can cognition be obtained? The first paradoxical answer is—by experience. An experience 'a' is adequately understood by an experience 'b', if 'b' is of a higher order. The general implication here is that the higher understands the lower. And this stands in contradiction to the science-supported Western view that the lower explains and therefore understands the higher.

The East lives in experience and to experience it gives the credit of definitive cognition. This may sound like pragmatism, but the resemblance carries no further than a common distrust in the validity of conceptual thought. Actually, the difference is not mainly that the East refuses to identify experience with sense perception, or to put *a priori* limits to its scope. The distinctive characteristic of the cognizing function of experience resides in the Eastern form of consciousness. Again pragmatism presents an

---

[1] Of this fact certain characteristic efforts and tendencies of contemporary literature and abstract painting give striking examples in their own spheres.

illuminating background. To William James the meaning of experience and consciousness is one and the same. To the East to be experienced does not necessarily imply any happening in the light of consciousness. And still less is consciousness considered to coincide with experience. Consciousness is ontologically before all experience. In like manner, at the end of the transmutation-process of the individual it will be restored to its purity, that is to say, its independence from all content. Hence, there is a clear inference of the cognizing function of consciousness in the East. Ignoring the way of Western cognition which confronts the phenomenon as an object and processes it by its conceptual devices, the Eastern mind, having singled out the phenomenon, faces it and takes pains that its wholeness be preserved. It refrains from altering it for the sake of cognition. The man of the East feels that it is not the phenomenon which must be dealt with. It is he himself—his own consciousness which must undergo a change. Conditions must be created where the phenomenon may exist and act according to its nature.

To achieve these conditions the mind has to be becalmed, to be freed from the incentives of desire in all of its forms—from curiosity, lust for power as well as from any higher motives such as the thirst for cognition, love or any other superior incentive of knowledge. For, not until consciousness has become an untarnished mirror can the phenomenon be reflected as it is. Emptiness of the mind is the condition of cognition. Without it, the phenomenon has no chance of unfolding and presenting itself as it is—the perfect 'being there' without the distortion worked by conceptual tools and the interference of emotion or aggressive interest. Even the question real or unreal looses its meaning. To speak of an identification of the cognizer with the cognized or of an inter-penetration of both can hardly be more than a metaphor. For while communicating something of the atmosphere, yet it is unable to express what really happens.

* * *

Western man created the genuine concept and made it the instrument of cognition. In his hands, it has become an offensive weapon. But, at the same time, it works as a means of defence for it protects the subject from the onslaught of the object. Because it thus operates both ways, the concept has the role of mediator between subject and object. Indeed, this oscillation between subject and object constitutes the very life-stream of the Western Mind. Its function as mediator is necessarily inconsistent with any connection with being or state.

In the concept we possess the object and without a genuine concept the genuine object would not be possible. It posits and maintains the ontological distance between subject and object. A qualified psychological proximity to the subject is, of course, possible, but it does not diminish the ontological distance. This situation may be well illustrated by imagining an abyss. On one side, is the subject and on the other, at some distance the object. The object may draw nearer and nearer to the edge, but the width of the abyss determines the absolute insuperable distance. In other words, whatever be the psychological experience of proximity, the nature of the ontal objectiveness does not change. Of such is the nature of conceptual thought, and by virtue of it objectiveness is determined ever anew. Meanwhile, the foremost task of the preservation of the phenomena is never lost from sight. The meaning of the Western way, therefore, consists in the effort to discover, invent or create objective reality by means of conceptual thought.

Hence, from the beginning has there been an unfailing interest in the world around, the theoretical construction of nature and the urge to explore the globe and all its inhabitants. All these activities spring from the thirst for reality and from a corresponding feeling that nothing that can be known should remain unknown. Hence has arisen the discovery of the microscopic and the macroscopic worlds and the construction of a myriad objects superior in many respects to nature's performances. If it is the immediate purpose of applied science to make nature subservient to man's needs, the inherent significance is something else again. It is the effort to create indisputable reality according to the idea that only what we create can we possess and be sure of. The same is true of the abundant variety of conceptions in the field of the mind, society and state, philosophy and religion, and of the systematic and fanatical attempt to realize them. While a given human individual or a historical period may cherish the conviction that a final result has been reached, the process itself is logically infinite.

Thus the concept's function as the means of seizing objective reality is forever assured. Yet, at the same time, definitive objective reality, with ingenuity and pertinacity alike, seems to withdraw before the advancing concept to regions more remote yet still more alluring. Reality must be possessed in the form of conceptual thought in order to establish closer relations with it. For the nature of objective reality is thought itself. When, therefore, the subject enters into contact with objective reality to the extent that he seizes objective reality, his thought ceases to be his. What is there is objective reality, conceived and thought with any degree of adequacy.

In this case the thought is no longer identical with the concept moving between subject and object—it is not simply the mediator between subject and object. It becomes the higher tertium—the Greek μέσον—which transcends both, uniting the one with the other. To express the fact in Plato's language, the individual mind seizing the idea coupled with the idea realized in the mind, constitute a new entity. This, at least as seen from the human angle, is a higher entity since the individual mind rises to the idea while the idea descends to be realized in the mind. The great achievements of the West can thus be conceived as the work of the concept operating as the higher tertium. In this respect, the Western concept on the supreme level where it reveals its true meaning does not link subject and object on the same plane. Its position and role may be symbolized by an isosceles triangle. The opposite points of the base are the subject and object whereas the point of convergence of the two rising sides represents the concept which is above discursive thinking. Any creative system of thought which is not handled as a counter or an object of discussion but understood in the fullness of its impact, can serve as an example.

The most illuminating confirmation, however, appears in the figure of the Saviour and His identification with the *Logos*. The Saviour mediating between man and the Divine and participating equally in divine and human nature elevates man and brings him nearer to God. Even the fact that in Christian theology the movement is not only one of cognition but also of love extending from God through the Saviour to man and vice versa, finds its parallel in the realm of the concept. Here, the genuine concept far from limiting its action to the intellect, to the extent permitted by its character, summons man in his entirety. And if reason is called upon to support by the reality of its own creations the delusive sense impression and in so doing save the phenomena, in its way it parallels the destination of the Saviour to free man from entanglement in the world by substituting for it another realm which, by thus assigning the world of appearances to its proper place, saves it.

From this perspective a new light falls on the reception of the Christian Faith by the man of the West. The successful penetration of Christianity occurred after the concept had processed the assignments, theoretical and practical, that the spirit of classic antiquity had entrusted to its organizing power. In the specific shape, both universal and secular, that it had assumed in the thousand years of Greek and Roman civilization, it had come to an end. Yet as the perfect expression of the Western mind-structure it was not dead. The figure of the Saviour-Mediator formed by the Judaeo-Greek mind of Saint Paul called forth a rebirth in new splendour. There is no need to point out what separates the dying and resuscitating gods of the Near and Middle Eastern mystery religions from the Christ. It is enough to stress that with the mystery god who, through the ceremonial participation in his death and revival, confers upon the initiates the same privilege of immortality, the role of a mediator is not necessarily connected. Though the result be the same, the way and apparatus differ entirely.

In the course of our argument this difference is what counts. One the one hand, there is the immediate union with the mystery god, himself inaccessible to and inexpressible in theory—on the other, there is the central figure of the Saviour-Mediator where the two natures, divine and human, invite theoretical investigation. The Saviour-Mediator is the impersonated concept, the *Logos*. Indeed, the philosophical effort of scholastic thought revolves around the enigma of the Saviour-Mediator, the possibility of His two-fold nature, the clarification of their interplay,

His redeeming function, and His relation to God the Father. In the abundance of these appalling problems the power and subtlety of the classic concept is put to test and reaches new heights. And thus does it train and prepare the mind for the philosophical and scientific activation of the concept in modern times.

From the psychological angle the function of the concept appears Janus-faced. The concept is an aggressive instrument of cognition separating for cognition's sake subject and object. But in interpolating itself between the two, it bridges through its constructive work the gulf it has itself opened. And thus does it become the creative mediator. Mediation means moderation. If the concept intercepts the onslaught of the object, it achieves the ontal distance and the space needed for its constructions.

In the physical world the tool is the parallel of the concept in the sphere of the mind. In his most primitive state man glories in tools of astounding precision based upon an intuitive knowledge of physical laws and keen observation. Of such are the blow-tube and the boomerang, while prehistoric rock-and-cave designs, paintings and pottery demonstrate what can be achieved with primitive tools. These basic facts alone constitute a convincing proof that technology with its variety of tools, is by itself an insufficient measure of civilization. However, the explosive efflorescence since the end of the eighteenth century of a new kind of tool with a dynamic character is the confirmation in the material world of the genuine concept which from its start in Greece fell to the West as both its endowment and its task.

THE DECEPTIVENESS OF PERCEPTION

For Western man, who was always oriented towards objective reality, the discovery of the fallaciousness of sense-perception was a disconcerting and frightening experience. This was exacerbated by the circumstances that his form of cognition and thereby the world around him and his own body were closely related to the higher senses. The shocking effect of this experience dominated Greek thought from its start, and it has never lost its impact on Western philosophy. To isolate the deceptive and subjective elements in our world perception from the objective, to determine the cause of fallaciousness, and to construct a more valid philosophical and scientific world-picture for the sake of these delusive phenomena became the foremost task. Inevitably, the devaluation of sense-perception was reflected in man's conception of himself, and particularly in the evaluation of his apperceptive, emotional and appetitive capacities. Thus, more than the impermanence of things, the deceptiveness of sense perception became the great incentive which set and still keeps in motion the cognitive process of the Western mind.

It is on the Eastern Mind that the ghastly impermanence of all that exists leaves an indelible impression. The corrosive effect of this experience differs from the turmoil caused by the fallaciousness of sense perception because it throws open the frailty of our own being. Threatening the will to live it deprives life's values of their significance. The deceptiveness of sense perception, confusing and disorientating, causes a deep feeling of insecurity, but the mind instantly appeals for help to reason. But against impermanence reason has little to offer. Its arguments and consolations seem flat and stale. The fallaciousness of our sense organs touches first of all the external world and only indirectly reflects on what we are ourselves.

Impermanence, on the contrary, even if it be observed in the phenomena of the world outside, is instinctively felt to be of immediate concern to us. Then the experience of our own impermanence is inexorably confirmed and a thousandfold increased by the knowledge that it is the fate of all that exists. One must bear in mind that with the Eastern man the experience of the self as well as that of the world is physiologically related to instinct. The instincts with their delusive promise of fulfilment and definite satisfaction rise and fall endlessly only to repeat after a moment's illusion their meaningless performance. This we know. Yet with open eyes we fall victims to ever the same error. One may expect to rectify the delusion of sense perception with the help of reason and so build an objective world, but there is little hope that reason alone will ever save us from the fetters of impermanence.

The connection of this difference with the two forms of cognition is obvious. A mind which moves in states of being cannot but make permanence its ideal. For the impermanence of the outer and inner world is its perennial antagonist. This is the source of the inherent disinclination, toward radical changes of social and political conditions, even more of systematic and progressive evolution. So likewise the potentialities of discoveries and ideas are left undeveloped. And in the fields of philousia and religion there is a strong bend towards conciliation, amalgamation, syncretism, peaceful symbiosis or interpenetration.

All this has been and is impressively demonstrated by the basic attitude of India towards foreign creeds, by the receptivity and creative assimilation of Buddhism by China and Japan, and by the benevolent and unprejudiced admission and examination of the Christian faith by India, China and Japan. In this way, the Eastern mind tries instinctively to stabilize conditions here below while moulding them in harmony with its idea of the immutable absolute. The Western conception of the Absolute is by no means irreconcilable with movement and evolution— neither in philosophy nor in Christian religion, where since the creation of the world God is constantly active. But the supreme ideas of the Eastern absolute are beyond such anthropomorphism.

Such are the roots and the implications of the Eastern experience of impermanence. Those that pertain to the experience of fallaciousness are quite different. When the mind starts to construct by means of conceptual thought, objective reality in philosophy or science, it is not immediately directed at permanence. It is seeking for the undeceiving, objective truth—its function being to save the phenomena. To fulfil this function the relation which is either assumed or found to exist between the phenomena and the objective reality, must be constructive—that is to say, it must be logically connected with the phenomena, it must be right, demonstrable and refractory to doubt. Though there may be a relationship between the permanent and the right that relationship is by no means essential and the permanent no more implies the notion of the right and its function than what is right necessarily implies the permanent. The relation of the deceptiveness of sense perception as well as that of inner perception to the objective reality which has been constructed to save their respective phenomena, may be compared to one's experience of the stick which appears bent when it is dipped down into water. The right knowledge explains the phenomenon of the bent stick.

But it does not make it disappear and the phenomenon continues to belong to our world.

Impermanence is of another order than fallacy. It is a fact and to eliminate it another fact must take its place, not only a new insight. This is clearly in accord with the nature of Eastern cognition which is becoming and being and which proceeds in states of consciousness. The mere knowledge of the impermanence of all that exists, even the theoretical knowledge of its causes is sterile. Only when this knowledge begins to transform the knowing subject, does it become cognition and creative. And this is in contradistinction to the deceptiveness of perception where the discovery and cognition of causes are themselves parts of the constructive theoretical process.

FREEDOM OF WILL

Primitive man lives his life in the presence of threatening powers. Though his ideas about them are none too clear, he is certain of their existence. At the beginning of their structure-based civilization, the insecurity of the Western and the Eastern man was of another kind. Having left the shelter of tradition behind, their minds were transfixed in an attitude of boundless wonder and a state of awe in the face of the world. Both were conditions of tormented confusion from which they aspired to the heaven of certainty and finality. And so each started on the road towards its destiny.

Objectivation, the West's allotted task, seized upon nature as its first and favourite field of action if only because the world of matter offered the easiest opportunities to evolve and to test conceptual thought. Disillusioned by its precarious results the mind was thrown back on itself. It had to examine its instruments of knowing, and thus originated a general objectified picture of mind and soul in their own right. The East admitting the non-subject only as the other and so rendering impossible the true opposition of subject and object, strove for fulfilment in the sphere of the subject which it recognized as consciousness.

This assertion, however, must not deceive us. For both the Eastern and the Western mind transcend subjective consciousness in the common sense of the term. The attainment of its respective consummation is both motive and motor in each civilization. It can never be overemphasized that the absolute object of the West does not coincide with the objectivation of the physical world. While this latter presents the most successful realization of objectivation the intrinsic aim is the cognition of thought through its own means. In strict parallel the consciousness, which inspires the Eastern mind and stands at the end of the process, is not identical with the psycho-physiological subject although this latter is the starting point and the field of action as well.

Whatever the success of the Western mind in objectifying the outer and inner world, the basic opposition of subject and object remains unchanged. But the historical position of the subject is ambiguous from the start. For in constructing the objective world, the subject cannot halt before its own psycho-physiological appearance. Were it not for the fact that through the objectifying process the subject hopes to arrive at the final knowledge of itself, one might say that in trying to objectify itself, the subject is trapped in its own net. This process, however, reflects decisively upon Western man's position in his world. He does what he can to make it an independent world in its own right, be the price ever so high.

So the idea of nature ruled by the law of causation, which was introduced as the strongest guarantee of an inviolable order of the universe, could not stop in front of man himself. The belief in *moira*—that inexorable fate which rules over gods and men— which accompanied the Greeks into the times of the tragedy, had somehow coexisted with human responsibility though it was hardly compatible with it. Yet the law of causation stemming from reason claimed an unconditional validity. Moreover, the same subject which had built the objective world could not acquiesce in the consequences of its doings and, in keeping with the subject-object opposition of the structures, oppose to nature-causality the idea of freedom of will. However, the fact is that freedom of will appeared in philosophy as a reaction, an answer and a protest to the well-established causality. And so it remained problematic, being summoned to plead its cause before a hostile tribunal. This is the reason why in the West until the end of the last century the freedom of the will figured as one of the burning philosophical problems. Even today it is reappearing in the considerations of philosophically minded physicists in connection with the statistical law of probability.

In the East one looks in vain for a comparable impact of the problem of the freedom of the will. The subject-other relation excludes the pairs of opposites that are rooted in the subject-object relation. Therefore, neither the conception of freedom of will nor the lack of it carry the same significance in the East as in the West. Since the non-subject is not relative to the higher sense-perception but to the vital sphere of the instincts, nature ruled by its own laws and independent of man, is unknown to the East. Nature, therefore, is essentially life—not conceived as the opposite of the inorganic, but felt as the power which permeates all that exists. Though man is one with nature, the preponderance held by the subject in the Eastern structure reserves to him the central place and potentially the immediate power over both nature and himself.

The decisive datum then is the intrinsic relation between man and nature without the primary interference of the Western concept, which itself is connected with the higher senses. In India this immediacy is metaphysically and psychologically founded in the insatiable thirst for existence. But it is man alone who may quell this craving and in so doing redeem creation. The particularly human character of Chinese civilization expresses this same immediacy in a less dramatic but no less determinate form. The great words of Protagoras—'Man is the measure of all things, of the existing that they are, of the non-existing that they are not'—could be said of the Chinese. And this without the negative connotation it carries in the mouth of the sophist who thus formulates his thesis of the relativity of knowledge and the impossibility of truth, for such is not the Chinese position.

The spirit of man and nature being one, man becomes the trustworthy measure of truth. What is below and what is beyond proves its reality and its truth by its immediate bearing on human conditions. To compare this view with pragmatism would be erroneous since it is based upon the idea of the harmony between man and cosmos. The Eastern images and experiences of nature are not a fertile ground wherein causality may take root and grow. Causality of course is recognized in daily life and in philosophical context and science so far as it has developed. But even in these regions it could never play an all important role and become the backbone of philousia without the injection of the magic connections between things. Nature to the East is not the mere environment and at times the hostile power. It is nature that is lived even in its evil aspects. And it is lived as the inner life is lived where the psychological phenomena while penetrating each other emerge one from the other. There the case is comparatively rare when a sharp cut occurs as the result of wilful interference, an outside interruption or the implosion of an idea.

Neither nature nor inner life lack either order or organization. But it is not causation which is called upon to perform this function. What the East feels is the regular, periodical occurrence of the phenomena which succeed each other independently of their being connected as cause and effect. There is the regularity of the movements of the astral bodies, of such processes as ageing, the periodicity of the moon phases, the seasons, life and death, the periodical recurrence of the need for sleep, the instincts of hunger and thirst, and of the sex drive. Indeed, this idea of periodicity as the great regulator of terrestrial and heavenly events has impressed itself on the human mind from immemorial times. It has, for example in Greek thought, maintained a part of its influence in the face of the steadily expanding realm of causation. While in all agricultural civilizations the periodicity of plant life, of sowing and of harvesting reflects upon mental and emotional life and the social institutions, it is the East and particularly the great Far Eastern societies which reverently bow to this periodicity, as manifested in nature. And from this recognition they derive the harvest of their wisdom, achievements and forms of life.

The East, in living in and with nature as the other, lives with itself. In yielding to the great order of nature—harmonious and friendly or terrifying and hostile—the East recognizes its own being. Thus, when it turns to nature it does so to be reminded of its own essence. In India this is to face knowingly what man or nature are, but should not be. In the Far East it is to experience the instinct-related essence of nature and to learn from it the perfection neglected by man. Nowhere is there the fundamental opposition of man and nature which gives rise to the law of causation claiming to embrace man as well as everything else. Whereas Western man has to defend himself and his freedom against an objective power, the man of the East finds himself in a different position. From the beginning, the subject-other relation permits him to live nature instead of facing it as the antagonist and to live it without the scrutinizing suspicion resulting from the subject-object relation. Thus, as he awakens to full consciousness, the man of the East discovers that he is bound, not by the law of an objectified nature, but by a power within himself. And this is the vital urge of instinct to which nature is related, and in which he recognizes and feels the life of nature as his own.

*   *   *

Under these circumstances the problem of freedom of will assumes a different aspect. In Western philosophy and psychology the net result of all the effort to solve this problem is uncertain if not negative. No system has been vast enough, and no argument sufficiently subtle or sagacious to ward off the onslaught of the determination of will by the law of causation. The necessity of free will as an indispensable postulate of ethics and religion has been well defended. But the compatibility of free will with causation has never been demonstrated nor has there ever been a mind bold enough to dethrone causation and make freedom the sovereign ruler. The psychophysiological determination of man's actions is held to correspond to causation in nature. There is, of course, no sufficient direct or scientific proof for this assumption. But since causality is of a theoretical nature—a product of thought—its universal validity in the world of experience cannot be contested without an adequate reason such as is provided by the law of probability in modern physics.

In the Eastern mind the necessitation of the will is not derived from any universal law of causation. It is not a product of conceptual thinking. It is primarily localized and is lived in the system of drives and the whole fabric of contents dependent thereupon. This compound is not and it cannot be considered the cause of the necessitated will. For it is itself the impersonation so to speak of the necessitated will—of an unconditionally fettered existence. In such a world-conception causality will claim its place in daily life for practical purposes. But it will not determine the innermost belief and experience. Such belief and experience are determined by the irresistible recurrence of instinctual life, its impermanence and its inanity. When the world and nature are relative to this vital system of drives, the forms of order will differ from those posited by a mind which establishes its relation on the basis of the higher sense perceptions. With respect to the latter, the law of causation may reign unshaken though not uncontested in an independent objective world.

Although this all-pervading creative power appears aimless if it be taken in its dynamic aspect, it does not lack order when one starts with the endless recurrence of the great cosmic periods down to the tide of human instincts and animal and vegetative life. Periodicity, recurrence and regularity are first lived physiologically and psychologically, and are then confirmed in surrounding nature before they are applied to human history. The fact that this idea of recurrent world periods exists in Greek pre-philosophical mythology reaching well into classic times and that it reappears in the Middle Ages and in modern philosophy of history, at least in two important instances—Gian Batista Vico and Nietzsche—is a sufficient proof that it is rooted in deeper strata than is discursive reason. Assuredly, a world based upon the experience of these vital forces does not cede to the world of causation in the firmness of its order, or in its power and impressiveness. Such a world consisting of regularly recurrent phenomena permits perfect orientation and, within limits, prediction. With the experience and knowledge of these cycles man may be satisfied. He may not feel the pressing necessity of causal explanation. It is a conservative world. In the end it yields a security and definitiveness which a causation-based world conception proceeding endlessly between no beginning and no end, is unable to convey.

Determination by instinct is just as binding as that by causation, and so long as it reigns it does so unconditionally. But its relation to freedom of will is not the same as that of causation. While a discussion of the entire problem of the freedom of will lies outside the scope of this argument, it can yet be shown that in Eastern thought it assumes an entirely other aspect than in

Western. This results in the last analysis from its mind-structure where the subject faces the non-subject not as the independent object, but as the other. Since nature is relative to the instincts, it constitutes in all of its aspects the genuine environment of man in an infinitely deeper sense than when it opposes the subject in its own right. The dismantling of the other—that great concern of the East—therefore necessarily results in a dismantling of the instinct-determined parts of the subject. If, then, freedom be equilibrated with freedom from the power of the instincts, at first view we find ourselves on well-known ground. Indeed, nothing has been gained for it will rightly be objected that in this cardinal point no discrepancy exists between the Eastern and the Western view.

And yet, though this objection be obvious, it is by no means valid. In the Western view, instinct-determined life is the precise place where the causal bondage of will can be observed. However, even if the instincts were neutralized, a causation-oriented philosophy would for two reasons find its position unaltered. Not only would it discover that one bondage has simply been exchanged for another, but above all it is wholly unintelligible that the overpowering of the instincts should coincide with the liberation from the law of universal causation. To arrive at this conclusion we have to turn to ethics and religion. Here, for the sake of their premises and the possibility of their realizations, the freedom of will is assumed but not proved.

So soon as causation ceases to be the dominating category the outlook changes. While it is limited to a comparatively small area, and even there is intermixed with magic beliefs, it gives way to the eternal rhythm of cosmic and vital drives, the compulsory force of which is quite the equal of causation. And now that the power of instinct is recognized as the most important determinant, the situation as to the problem of freedom of will becomes entirely different. Under these circumstances it is not unreasonable to hold that having subdued his instincts man has attained freedom. How man within the reign of Western structure should overcome the rule of a law which is as objective as nature itself is beyond comprehension. Still it seems possible that in the subject-other relation, where nature deprived of its objective character is of essentially the same stuff as himself, man may become free in freeing himself from the domination of the drives. For, contrary to the Western structure where man in striving for the liberation from instinctive life fights causation-based nature as his opponent, in the Eastern structure he gives up a non-essential part of himself and in so doing follows his usual course of dismantling the Other. Such is the intuitive assumption of the East. It implies sometimes the significant and not illogical belief that this acquired individual freedom may radiate effects upon others, perhaps, since there is one force pervading all, even at a cosmic level.

Another approach leads to the same result. In Western thinking it is an uncontested affirmation that freedom is the genuine opposite of necessity that is to say, causation. True, a rather striking difference exists between the two terms. For necessity permits a clear definition which precludes any doubt about its significance, but freedom does not enjoy this privilege. Idea and definition reveal freedom to be nothing more than the negation of necessity. Nor does the appeal to experience come to our rescue since the consciousness of freedom easily accompanies acts which under examination cannot be considered free. A universal rule of necessity represents a perfectly clear idea whereas the idea of a free universe is unthinkable. Since freedom can only be the prerogative of man, its assumption opposes him to the rest of the universe.

Considerations such as these suggest that the traditionally accepted opposition of necessity and freedom cannot stand the test. It must be revised in favour of another which better satisfies logic and reality. Indeed, the true opposite of necessity is not freedom but contingency. The introduction into our causation-determined world picture of the idea of contingency did not have to wait for the probability-calculus of modern physics. Deeply significant is it that in the philosophical system of Democritus, the first in a long line of materialistic and thus necessity-based theories, the primordial fact is one of pure contingency. This is the free fall of atoms and their haphazard unions in composite forms. Whether or not contingency as the characteristic of the movements of the smallest particles of matter can be used to explain freedom of will, lies beyond the scope of this argument.

252

It seems unlikely, however, that contingency is less incompatible with freedom of will than necessity or causation. However that may be, the only point of relevance is this. In a theoretical world conception with causal necessity as the main principle of order there is not even a side-door for freedom to enter. Necessity and contingency dominate the field and they preclude the theoretical possibility of freedom.

This view differs entirely from the Kantian which after demonstrating the theoretical impossibility of freedom as that of God and immortality, then reintroduces them both as postulates of practical reason. In Western world conception, then, freedom appears as the strict opposite of causal necessity. From this opposition it derives all its weight and the accompanying uncertainty and abysmal hopelessness as well. However, freedom and necessity are one of those pairs of opposites in the Western mind which, despite its stimulating and creative effect, is artificial and misleading. How it came to pass that freedom so presumptuously asserted its place as the true opposite of necessity is explained by the desire for the freedom which protests against necessity. But this protest is only the negation of necessity. Far from constituting the real opposite, freedom does not possess a demonstrable meaning in its own right. This prerogative falls to contingency.

Necessity and contingency belong to one and the same world—they are real opposites. This is a thesis which can claim the approval of modern physics. In this world picture freedom cannot aspire to either a logical place or a definable meaning. It soars as the object of an irresistible longing—all the more so as it cannot help feeling a stranger in a world which is not made for it. Were this not so, freedom of will could not have been the burning problem it has been in the West in contrast with the modest importance assigned to it in the East. The problem of finding his way out of the labyrinthine and senseless world of contingency and of overcoming the fetters of causation has long haunted Western man. And this regardless of whether the insight into the true opposition of necessity and contingency came into the focus of some discerning minds or whether it was subconsciously active in metaphysical anxiety. Yet, in spite of all efforts, a convincing positive philosophy of freedom has not yet been written. Nor can it be conceived until the structure will have lost its ascendency which is to say before the end or transformation of Western civilization.

*　*　*

It fell to the East to reveal a philosophy of freedom consistent with its structure. Indeed, it is not an exaggeration to regard philousia in all of its manifold aspects as one great philosophy of freedom. In line with this is the lack, compared to Western philosophy, of elaborated theoretical thinking and of perfectly constructed systems covering the whole of human experience. Within the realm of the Eastern mind-structure freedom finds a natural and intelligible place. There it is the *true* opposite of the determination by instinct, which though equally as compulsory as determination by causation, is of an entirely different nature. It is not to be viewed as a subdivision of causation. It is original and immediate—concrete and lived and is not, as causation is, a form or category and a creation of reason. The mere fact that the Eastern mind-structure maintains an unmistakable relationship with the magic world makes it *a priori* impossible for causation to occupy a dominating position in the world picture. For the main creations of philousia do not avail themselves of causation as the main instrument. Even where a superficial view seems to contradict this statement, a closer analysis will reveal it to be valid.

To quote two outstanding examples. First there is the Buddhist 'chain of causation'—'from ignorance stems action, from action consciousness, from consciousness name and form, from name and form the senses, from senses feeling, from feeling craving, from craving attachment, from attachment becoming, from becoming birth, from birth age and death.' This so-called chain of causation is by no means held together by causation. In reality, the links of the chain proceed out of each other just as do the consecutive states of an organism—say childhood, adolescence, mature age and old age. The same is true of the consecutive states of psychological and mental life. To some extent these proceed in a subtle and inextricable way from each other but they are not the cause of each other.

To speak of ignorance as the cause is to use the term cause so loosely as to deprive it of its real significance. The only respect in

254

which the relation of cause and effect carries proper significance—for there something new springs from the cause—is the assertion that all the links of the chain from ignorance to death are the cause of suffering and pain, this with the pertinent reservation that ignorance is the progenitor of the whole chain. However, the nature of the non-causal determination of the Buddhist chain is best illustrated by the fact that the end joins the beginning. For with death ignorance subsists and karma starts another existence in an endless repetition of rebirths. Thus do we find ourselves again, not unexpectedly, in the sphere of periodicity and recurrence which transcends causation. The only place in the chain where the question of causation may legitimately be asked is with respect to the cause of ignorance. But such a question is as to the cause of the chain itself. Whether the craving for existence or karma be offered as an answer, is of no interest to our problem since both push the cause indefinitely back from one existence to the other.

The second example refers to the Bhagahadvita—'He who thinks This to be a slayer, and he who thinks This to be slain, are alike without discernment; This slays not, neither is it slain.'[1] Here causality is led into absurdity. In China the Great Order ruling the universe is equally adverse to the acceptance of causality as a constituent principle. Whether the Great Order assumes a dialectical character based upon the magic correspondence between the parts of the universe and particularly between man and the universe, or whether it represents a type of metaphysical ethics which implies that the virtue of the perfect man radiates because it is in harmony with the cosmic order—nowhere is a significant effort made to understand the structure and the ways of the universe by means of causal thinking in the Western sense. Here, more than anywhere else, is to be sensed the continuing effect of the magic world on the creations of philousia. And this means either the elimination of causation or its relegation to an insignificant place.

In these circumstances the problem of freedom acquires a new shape. Compulsion by instinct requires as its opposite another state of an equally positive character. In like manner, the opposite of causal necessity is not simply the absence of necessity which

---

[1] Lesson the second, v. 19.

has been erroneously identified with an ill-defined idea of freedom, but contingency. And contingency is both a positive and tangible datum in thought no less than in experience. Freedom is the true opposite of compulsion by instinct. If there be anything which survives the elimination of instinct it must be freedom. But it is not the empty idea of freedom which Western philosophy opposes to necessity, a pseudo-freedom which must be saved by such formal terms as self-determination and the like. To stand the test, freedom in Eastern philousia will have to prove its independent significance. Once again, we return to the Western mind as a background. The attitude there is the same with regard to the inner and the outer world. In both of them the alluring phenomena pretend to be real only to prove deceptive to the eye of scrutinizing reason which must then function in order to save them.

And so it is with freedom. In a primitive sense we feel free. But the first introspective thought reveals that our decisions and actions, even our thoughts and emotions, are widely dependent upon forces which in reality are not our own. Outside authority and the persuasion of others, for example, operate from within ourselves. This deceptive consciousness of freedom of will itself then requires to be saved. Thus does the tireless endeavour of Western man to prove to himself the possibility of freedom arise and thus appears his readiness to accept even opposing arguments rather than fall a victim to deception. However that may be, the point of differentiation is the reflective consciousness of freedom as contrasted with the simple experience of freedom. This consciousness asks for certainty which can only be offered by theoretical demonstration. The question is: can consciousness of freedom be justified? And if it can, then comes the second question. How can this now authentic consciousness coexist with causation?

This Western attitude presupposes the basic opposition of subject and object and the corresponding relation of the world to the higher sense organs. The East does not start from any trust in the perceived world and the consequent discovery of its fallaciousness. The Eastern mind, where the closeness to the subject of the Other expresses itself in the relation of the world to the instinct, both lives with nature and lives nature. Against this fundamental relation deceptive experiences cannot prevail. Man

256

is embedded in nature—his own and the great nature are in essence one and the same. There is no need for the problem of freedom and necessity. Experience is indifferent to the alternative, and out of this experience, at once naïve and profound, there stems the standing power of the East. Not even when consciousness awakens to greater clarity does the feeling of compulsion as opposed to potential freedom stir and occupy the mind. The determination by the forces of instinct remains natural and unquestionable.

When the great turn occurs it moves in another direction than that taken by reason. Struck by the impermanence of things, the East recognizes the lack of limitation, meaning and aim in the drive. To command a halt to this endless tide, to unhinge the process of creation and destruction becomes the central problem. If nothing more could be said about the Eastern idea of freedom there would be this remarkable difference between the Western and Eastern dispensations. The West moves in reflective consciousness and decides by conceptual thought on the theoretical freedom. The East conceives existence as the irrational power of the instinct, but at once an inner voice, without the interference of discriminating reason, revolts. And the revulsion is against the fact discovered, not against the validity of the discovery. Thus, what stands up and raises its protest against the primordial data is not reason, but another stratum. And this for the time being defies definition.

Against this background it is apparent that in the East freedom does not coincide with the freedom of the will nor must it necessarily refer to a consciousness of freedom. Freedom in the East means freedom of consciousness both before and beyond all potential contents. The positive significance of this statement dovetails perfectly with the Eastern essence of consciousness. The primacy of consciousness in the structure implies that it is the very life of the subject. It is not a mere possession or attribute. The stages in the path of the dismantling of cognition which lead to pure consciousness are not marked by mere theoretical insight. For to cognize is to become and to be. Therefore, the states of consciousness in general, and the state of pure consciousness in particular, possess all the fullness of which the Western meaning of the term has been increasingly deprived. Since pure consciousness is awareness, independent of and indifferent to objects and contents, it overshadows the opposites of thought and will in the same way that it transcends any other pair of opposites. If there be any freedom at all it is in the freedom of consciousness. Hence, the subject and agent of freedom is not will. It is consciousness. Whereas in the West freedom means freedom of will, of decision and of action, in the East it is a state—the state of pure consciousness.

The whole problem of freedom that haunts the philosophy and religion of the West contains a limitation of consciousness as well as of that which shall be free. This must be clearly understood. Whether or not the will be free remains unanswerable as long as it is viewed as the equality of freedom and freedom of will. Freedom in the East is a prerogative neither of will nor of reason, and if it can be attributed to either it is only because there is freedom of consciousness. Freedom is inherent in pure consciousness. And only when and to the extent the state of pure consciousness is achieved may we speak of freedom. Thus, it acquires a positive meaning. This does not mean—to emphasize it again—that freedom has no place in the West, but it stresses and explains why in the West there is no way of demonstrating it nor of imbuing the term with a clear and positive meaning. The reason for this is that it is sought and can only be sought in the wrong direction.

Freedom of choice and decision comprises the Western definition. Empty and formal because it contains nothing but the negation of causation, this definition calls for some intelligible principle that will guide the will and make it free. None of the many principles offered by philosophy has been able to measure up to this task and set the mind at rest. The East looks at these tentatives as vain efforts if only because all such principles are inevitably marked by the flaw of limitation. Pure consciousness, which can alone be reached by dismantling cognition, guarantees and implies freedom. This freedom of consciousness is not to be found in reason nor is it relative to will. It is an unconditioned state of being. A great conception, inexorable and almost unattainable, it is an autarchic state. It does not point beyond itself, and it achieves its purpose in the transmutation of the ego and the freeing of the Self. This state of pure consciousness which is tantamount to that of freedom is known in India under varying names. It is recognized in the Far East in the conceptions of Lao Tse's Tao, and in Confucious' Golden Mean which is not the middle way, not simply that of compromise and the avoiding of extremes, but rather the undefinable position above and beyond the opposites. Also, there is the void of the Buddhist-influenced doctrines, above all of Zen Buddhism.

A comparison with Western ethics will throw into clear relief the impact of the state of pure consciousness which is freedom of consciousness. Western ethics relies on either a system of commandments such as the Decalogue emanating from God, the natural law and the like, or it is founded on some rationally demonstrable, be it love, altruism, the common good, the well-pondered right of the individual and the like, up to such formal definitions as Kant's categorical imperative. The application of these moral principles to the variety of emerging situations forms an essential part of ethics. There is no need to dwell on the substance of the Eastern ethical values which do not differ essentially from those of the West. Though their hierarchy may not always coincide, their general appreciation and the place assigned to them must be stressed. In the West the values of ethics even if they are derived from metaphysical or rational premises enjoy autonomy, and a life and evaluation of their own. This is also true when ethics becomes a part of religion because the values of religion, such as absolute love, self sacrifice and obedience are the consummation of ethics.

In the East the relations between ethics and the state of freedom of consciousness are the inverse. The ethical values and the ensuing precepts are not theoretically deduced from the state nor in turn, is it possible to infer from them the existence of that state. In fact, they constitute no more than stepping stones leading to the entrance to the state of pure consciousness which, unqualified and undemonstrable, towers above them. Contrary to Western ethics, which, conditioned by the subject-object structure, aims essentially at action, the realization and the verification of the state of freedom does not point beyond itself. Its effectiveness does not imply activation. It consists in the setting of a paragon and the supposed emanation of an immediate quasi-magic effluence. Indeed, apart from this impassive exertion of power, any activity would seem incompatible with the state of freedom which has been attained at the price of dismantling the non-subject and is therefore characterized by the absence of any content of consciousness.

The question—'can freedom of consciousness act without denying and destroying itself?' admits of only one and that—a negative answer. An ingenious way has been found to circumvent this negative issue. No doubt is permissible that freedom is freedom of consciousness and that this latter implies the dismantling and hence the disappearance of contents. However, apart from the radical absence of all content, the essence of the state is fully satisfied if mere images of the phenomena continue, but deprived of substance and bereft of relation and importance to consciousness. This, then, is the non-attachment or the emptiness which is so inseparable from the picture of the sage.[1] It describes a more accessible aspect of the state of freedom because the continuing phenomena are present only as empty frames and do not affect pure consciousness. So there may even be action without the real participation of the subject, such action consisting merely of its outward sign and result. This ingenious and felicitous effort brings the fulfilment of wordly duties into accord with the spiritual state without contaminating it.

But two Western doctrines bear any outward resemblance to this Eastern conception. The one is the idea of Christian mystic theology that the soul must be made empty in order to permit God to enter. This emptiness however refers only to the removing of all content which is alien to pious thoughts and feelings. Moreover, when later God himself enters the soul he will fill it with all his glory. Then again the Stoic idea of the imperturbability of the wise must not deceive us about its totally different character. Reason being in Stoic philosophy the essence of man, the Stoic

[1] Cf. Brihadaranyaka Upanishad II, 4.5. . . . Verily creatures are not dear that you may love the creatures; but that you love the Self, therefore are creatures dear. Verily everything is not dear, that you may love everything; but that you may love the Self, therefore everything is dear.

Bhagavadgita, lesson the fourth, 20: Free from attachment to fruit of works, everlastingly contented, unconfined, even though he be engaged in work he does not work at all.

refuses to assent to the perturbations of the mind which result from world-affected drives. The rational personality never loses the world out of sight, and in some way the Stoic needs the world in order to stand the test.

To know that the world cannot harm him is the Stoic's pride. Yet his victory conveys easily the hue of renunciation. This cannot be otherwise because of the Western orientation to the object. Even the Stoic's withdrawal from the world to within himself is achieved in the face of the world. What is more, he wants to build state and society out of the treasure of his innate ideas. There is none of the metaphysical desire of the man of the East for the transformation of the ego which is accompanied by the dismantling of the non-subject. The Stoic's triumph over the passions occurs on the psychological and rational plane despite his background of a rationalistic metaphysics. The objective world stands fast. It is man's home and field of action, but in order to fulfil his duties he must be sure of himself by extricating his mind from the threads of instinctive and passionate reactions.

The East's freedom of consciousness is that original and spontaneous state which, while remaining aloof from the concerns of the world, may deal with them. Imposing as it is as an achievement, the Stoic attitude bears the character of a reaction to the disturbing influences of the world and the passions it arouses. Or, to regard the same fact from the opposite angle. In appreciating the whole complex of the dismantling form of cognition, the feeling is irresistible that one moves in more than a psychological atmosphere and one seems to touch the metaphysical realm. Not so in the Stoic example. There with good reason the impression of an intellectual and psychological attitude prevails. And the metaphysical background, so far as it is relevant at all is more of an *additum* than an inner necessity.

IMMORTALITY

The divergent Eastern and Western approaches to great issues also come into clear focus with the problem of immortality. So far as the possibility of immortality is admitted by Western philosophy it has been restricted since Plato to the rational part of the soul. This cedes to religion, mystery religions and Christianity, the conferring upon immortality of a richer significance. The uncertainty as to who or what is immortal is linked with the idea of immortality as duration, that is continuance in time. Hence, immortality or duration appears as the opposite of mortality or finitude. Immediately we are reminded of the identical situation found in dealing with the problem of freedom. There, freedom presented itself as the negation of necessity and was erroneously considered the true opposite of necessity. So here again the question turns up in this form—Is immortality conceived as duration the true opposite of mortality or is it its mere negation? And further—if the prevalent Western idea of immortality as duration, that is as the mere negation of mortality, is untenable, then all attempts to determine its substance must remain unsatisfactory. In like manner, it will be impossible to solve the inconsistencies implicit in the concept of infinite duration itself.

Immortality then, means that what is immortal endures in time. Also in this sense it is timeless because time has no power over it. The logical contradictions and psychological absurdities implied in this are obvious. There is, for example, the incompatibility of an entity having a beginning in time with its living on without end. Then, there is the other fact that before our scrutinizing eye the supposed entity itself, the ego, becomes ever more fluctuating and escapes identity. On the other hand, only a simpleton would not be horrified at the idea of continuing indefinitely. Indeed the very conception of this idea is comprehensible only because of the fear of destruction. We cannot think of any condition which could be sustained without an end in sight. Even if we substitute for the duration of ever the same qualitative entity, that of a continuous after-life evolution,[1] the perplexity still remains. For there must be an end of evolution, and so the questionable eternal continuance of a final state would only be deferred. It would not be eliminated. It appears that when one opposes immortality as endless duration to mortality, this fails to establish the possibility of duration because it is unable to animate the idea of immortality itself with

---

[1] The idea of an evolution to ever greater perfection after death which would seem to accord so well with the Western mind was admitted by Plato as a doctrine of reincarnation. But strangely enough it never found a place in philosophy and was reintroduced only recently by theosophy and anthroposophy, both popularizing Indian beliefs.

a definite meaning. Thus, the genuine opposite which would confer a creative meaning on the idea of immortality, must be found elsewhere.

The pure or absolute present is the real opposite of time and triumphs over time. And this is the only significance which Eastern wisdom at its peak considers adequate to be connected with immortality. What is the significance of the pure or absolute present? As it is known to us the present is the real, the immediate and the live experience. Even past and future can be reached only in present acts of the mind—the past in acts of recollection and the future in acts of prevision. To these acts for the majority of men the present owes most of its content. At the same time, the moment we want to grasp and give an account of the present, it turns out to be the most unreal and evasive of data. While such an attempt is a present act of thought it would almost certainly seize upon data either belonging already to the past or about to merge with it. This must be, since we possess the present in the presence of objects of inner or outer perception which are continously dis-appearing into the past and entering from the future. Seen from the angle of consciousness there is nothing but the present. However, this consciousness of the present varies in clarity because it is determined by the contents of consciousness—by the distinctness, the order, and the rhythm of the conscious objects. Thus, in the face of rapidly changing objects and of interfering acts which aim at past or future, a clear consciousness of the present must be exceptional.

In any event it is an accidental and transitory experience. Indeed, to live the present in the clearly perceived intuition of an outer or inner object and free from any emotional and intellectual perturbation and the interference of associating memories or expectations, is a rare gift. It is rarely even desired, still less evaluated, and is entirely ignored as a means of cognition and as an inexhaustible source of energy. While in the course of normal experience the integral consciousness of the present is bound to the presence of something, it would not be paradoxical to assume that a consciousness of the present may be experienced without any demonstrable content being present. On the contrary, the consciousness of the present as such, belongs essentially to pure consciousness. And the dependence upon the accidental content of the consciousness of the present, describes only the prevailing conditions which usually obliterate the essential condition. There, the consciousness of the present, if it does not choose to bring an object into its focus and raise it to full clarity, reigns unimpaired by the passing content. Indeed, pure consciousness can only be the consciousness of the pure present.

At this point pure consciousness assumes its full and final significance. The pure consciousness of the present must coincide with the presence of pure consciousness. And with respect to immortality this is the only meaning that can be attributed to it without involving it in contradictions and finality. It elevates immortality beyond temporality and duration and rescues it from being a mere negation. Thus, immortality refers to the state of pure consciousness just as does freedom. Herein there is no reason for wonder or disappointment. If the state of pure consciousness corresponds in truth to the Eastern structure and if this state is the core of the Eastern mind, then it is bound to appear whenever one of the great human issues is at stake. It will offer itself as the solution and in so doing will testify to the wealth of its potentialities.

The state of pure consciousness having first revealed its metaphysical essence confers upon freedom a *raison d'être*. It proves equally effective in elucidating immortality by defining it as the pure consciousness of the present or the presence of pure consciousness. And this is precisely what has been termed awareness. Thus do the opposed ideas of immortality depend upon the respective structures. On the Western side, immortality as duration stands in necessary connection with the objectifying structure, and involves the idea that if there be immortality at all, there must be something, at least theoretically determinable, which endures. On the Eastern hand, immortality as the consciousness of the pure present or the presence of pure consciousness does not require anything beside or beyond.

*   *   *

Strange as it may seem a deep relationship exists between this conception of immortality as the pure present and the other totally different and even antagonistic conception, that of the eternal recurrence of the world process. The ghastly idea that all that is, has been and ever will be, has already occurred exactly the same an infinite number of times and will be repeated over and over again, has found a grandiose shape in India where the world of gods and men are re-absorbed into the divine essence only to start in again in endless repetition.[1] This conception is the negation of one-dimensional time where nothing can ever be entirely identical with anything that happened before or will happen thereafter. Another aspect, however, is of greater import. The endlessness of its recurrence derives the cosmic process of significance. The intuition that the same situations have occurred an infinite number of times and will similarly reoccur in the future testifies to their vanity and emptiness. The notion of time thus loses its impact, and the happenings dissolve into unsubstantial, delusive phantasy.

This insight will either leave the spectator a victim of despair in the face of nothingness or it will open his eye to the vision of reality as the eternal Now. Just as Plato in a poetical metaphor calls time the moving picture of eternity,[2] so may we speak with greater precision of this eternal recurrence as the self-refuting travesty of the pure present. The inexhaustible import of pure present or awareness can only be negatively expressed in the self-contradictory image of eternal recurrence which transcends human comprehension and crushes itself under the weight of its own impossibility.

Pure thought—the thinking of thought—is the Western counterpart of pure consciousness as the core of the Eastern mind. In the West the subject as the agent and effector of thought has to undergo the objectifying process itself. Here again we touch, not unexpectedly, a decisive and conclusive difference between West and East. Whereas the idea that a state of pure consciousness can be reached by man is not beyond understanding, it is wholly inconceivable and even absurd, to assume that the thinking of

[1] As to the conception of the rebirth of the world after the dramatic twilight of the gods and creation in the North-Germanic Myth, it seems uncertain whether it was believed to happen more than once. In Greece the recurrence was limited to the periods of human history.

[2] *Timaios*, XII

thought could ever be realized. The reason is that this formulation—the thinking of thought—is only a very concise definition of the great vision of the Western mind which wants to preserve the phenomena by means of its objectifying constructions. Thinking of thought is thus a theoretical creation and it carries a purely theoretical meaning. Although it defines the logical aim of the Western mind, it is clearly apparent that it is beyond man's capacity even to approach the situation which the formula implies viz. the situation arising when the conceptual mind, after having objectified all phenomena, faces itself with the same attitude and intention.

The described difference between East and West results from this distinction. Becoming and being—the Eastern form of cognition—aims at an immediate realization. The concept, there, is only admitted as a means and to the extent that it is useful for the preparation of realization, and it culminates itself in a state of consciousness. Conceptual thought on the contrary leads an autonomous life within the subject. For this reason alone its exteriorizations have an apparent objective existence such as philosophy and science, state and society, and other creations, regardless of whether or not theory confers upon them the character of genuine entities. Conceptual thought constitutes the life-stream of the Western mind whatever be its object-matter. Thus, the consummation of this mind is in the infinite and it can only be anticipated in the formula—the thinking of thought. And not until conceptual thought has objectified itself will absolute reality be reached.

The divergent significance of Western and Eastern individualism is one of the relevant conclusions from all this. In Western history associations created by the intellect began from early times to supersede instinct-based forms of togetherness such as that of society founded on family or race and political autocracy created by magic or secular personal power. The varieties of Greek statehood, of Roman civil and political associations and the increasing complexity of overlapping unions of all kinds in modern times, are deliberate organizations inspired by definite rational ideas. They result in undermining the confidence in the instinct base of life and they are designed to curb those instinctive forces and mould their expression into social and political forms. They are the manifestations of the objectifying mind which proceeds by breaking up the data to rebuild the fragments into new units. Togetherness and co-operation thus move on the plane of intentional consciousness and in the name of ideas. Under these circumstances individualism consists either in the assertion of personality by processing into a superior form the influences stemming from the organized spheres of existence, or in defensive aggression and creative opposition. Yet the fulfilment of the Western aim demands purposeful co-operation. And indeed this co-operation has asserted itself again and again despite enmity, misunderstanding and suspicion.

The Easterner's relation with his fellow creature has at all times been founded on the immediacy of elementary instinctive forces. The explanation is that within the Eastern mind-structure the subject lives in being whatever its content. Hence, there is deep resistance to embarking on a life based predominantly on conceptual thought which is unable to guarantee the achievement of another form of being, safer than the traditional and the actual. Hence, the greatness of the instinct based world is recognized and admired. Even when it has become apparent that it must cede its place to a higher form of existence, the cautious and subtle way it is dealt with, testifies to the esteem in which it is held as the great protecting mother who provides for all needs, but asks in return the acceptance of destruction as well as creation. Moreover, there is within the reach of man that other plane of being—the realm of pure consciousness—where the finality of his state releases him from bondage. Though these planes are incompatible, they do not constitute a pair of opposites as the West would like to believe. To assume an attitude of aggressive hostility in the relation between these two forms of being would mean indulging in an all too human attitude bent upon nullifying from the start any effort to overcome the one and attain the other.

A strange and unexpected phenomenon occurs in the Western mind when two of its most original creations illumine its consummation. A dazzling light is shed upon the difference between West and East. In its matured mathematics and music the Western mind shows a marked inclination towards the state of pure consciousness. True, the origin of both mathematics and music connect them with the essential needs of life—mathematics with the necessity of counting and measuring, and music with the urge to express the emotions and to stimulate them in others. Yet, as they move away from the field of their origin—a momentous evolution peculiar to the West—they exhibit an unmistakable trend toward severing the bonds with experience and unfolding in their own right. Mathematics becomes a self-sufficient science, exploring the laws of numbers unconcerned not only with practical application but with any kind of reality.

Music in its purest and exclusively Western manifestation as absolute music, dematerializes its materia, the fleeting sound, and denies any relation to an extraneous object and purpose. Thus, in turning away from anything objective, mathematics and music seem to forsake the cause of the West and to draw nearer to pure consciousness.

This impression, however, does not stand closer investigation. No doubt, number is the most general denotation of things, and absolute music the least material phenomenon in the perceivable world of matter. And yet while both move far, neither mathematics nor music abandon the world of matter. On the contrary, just because they free themselves of this world to the utmost degree, their relation to the world as a whole can be all the more effective. Indeed, it is their autonomy, their not being specifically involved in the phenomena and their concerns, which confers upon them the most creative and extensive power over both the outer and the inner world. Thus, while with mathematics and music, compared to other realms of science and art, we may feel as though we were breathing the air of the world of pure forms, yet in neither of them is there any resemblance to pure consciousness. Both remain strictly within the frame of Western structure.

What can justly be said is this. At the present stage of evolution of the Western mind, pure mathematics and absolute music represent the closest approximation to the ideal goal of Western mind—pure thought, thought thinking itself. They too, like pure thought, have their objects—numbers and musical sounds—which they crystallize into ideas and architecture of ever increasing abundance and clarity. Yet the distance which separates them

The Contrasted Solutions of Classic Problems

from pure thought remains infinite. Therefore, pure thought is not only the unattainable goal. It is also the paragon and the innermost moving force of the Western mind. It follows that between mathematics and music and pure consciousness no relation whatsoever exists. Nor can it be otherwise since the rule of the structure is the more inexorable, the higher the level. Both remain strictly within the objectifying structure.

There is a logical parallelism between the two goals of pure thought and pure consciousness and between the two roads leading up to the respective goals. But there is no approximation either between the goals or between the roads. In point of function and value the two goals equal each other. Even the fact that pure consciousness must be considered realizable whereas the realization of pure thought is possible only at infinity, does not interfere with this balance and equality. For any theoretical preference of the one or the other is the evident outcome of subjective evaluation. Both are forms of consciousness. They are the only ones known to us and they constitute the range and experience of our consciousness. Their exploration shows them to coincide with the mind-structures of West and East. And it is for this reason that the interpretation of the Western and the Eastern mind becomes inevitably a philosophy of consciousness.

CHAPTER XIII

The March of the Mind

All this have we learned and stand ready to believe. The nature of the universe is far different from what we perceive and think it to be. The earth, and the solar system even, are but a speck of matter, and matter itself dissolves into many determinants which can only be understood by the constant invention of new intellectual configurations. Life can and it will one day, be explained and scientifically produced, although at present neither its origin nor its chemical composition are fully known. On our planet, life and consciousness evolve within a measureable time through demonstrable forms of which one conditions the other. And man, in brief, is the end product of this evolution, and in his physical and mental endowments he is the product of this chain, his origin determining his capacities.

A one-dimensional way of thinking might endeavour to follow and connect these phenomena by trying to transform them into objective realities and thereby establish an unbroken evolution. But this obliterates the astounding fact that the mind emerging at the end of the process, possesses the power to retrace its own history beyond its beginnings and to reconstruct the history of the universe. Indeed, were our knowledge limited to the evolution of life, an imaginative biological and physiological theory might assume that from the emergence of the first protoplasm, the living cell preserved and transmitted the road travelled so that a highly differentiated organ such as the human brain could be led to the discovery of the unity and the unfolding of life. Yet it baffles comprehension how the brain, with nothing but the sense perceptions as working material, can embrace the universe, dissolve it into its subtle constituents, and return enriched by this knowledge of the physical world to attempt a new interpretation of its own functions and of life in general.

The March of the Mind

This scheme alone suggests that the basic idea of the natural world-conception stands in need of correction. It would seem more logical to start from the mind in which this whole world-drama is reflected, and whose creation, in a way which is still to be determined, it must be. Such an attempt to reverse the standpoint and directions, however, is immediately met by a grotesque and almost destructive paradox. The nearer the mind draws to itself to know its nature, the more insecure does knowledge become. So likewise do the modes of approach. Contrary to what must logically be expected, the degree of certainty of knowledge increases with the distance separating the subject from the object. And inversely it decreases the more the nature of the object participates in that of the subject. Therefore, it reaches the high point of unreliability when the subject seizes upon itself as the object of investigation. Thus, since physics began with the study of astral bodies and simple mechanical phenomena, it has been considered the paragon of unqualified knowledge, and compared to it all other branches of knowledge appear indistinct. The strangeness of this fact is obvious. For science, built as it is upon sense perceptions which are the most deceitful source of knowledge, at once humbly and proudly glorifies in this parentage and in the pretention of being but the logical extension of the natural world picture.

However, the same brain which is responsible for this construction and performs the miracles of science, proves less efficient when it is applied to what seems to be its proper domain—the mind. Although it evolves the immeasurable abundance of creations which stud the history of mankind, the fact cannot be gainsaid that when thrown upon its own resources and assigned to its own realm—the mind—the brain has been unable to find satisfactory answers to those innate questions which have haunted man from the beginning—the What, the Whence, the Why and the Whither? Nor, silencing for a moment the inner voices which claim to be heard, does the pursuit of perceptions do anything but obscure and taint the real issue.

Whenever the immediate occupation of the mind with itself fails to produce satisfying answers, discouraged and chastened it turns to the objective world, to nature and to history. There it

271

receives from science new suggestions which often strongly resemble the old errors for which it has to pay heavily. Then history grants conclusions which cannot but be influenced if not determined by the questions asked. This cannot be otherwise. Science, ever more depreciating and deprecating pictorial representations, within possible limits sacrifices description to mathematical formula. Philosophy and psychology, which move in concepts, cannot do without the images of experience or intuition that alone fill the concept with meaning. History, in order to mitigate the mind's uncertainty about itself, must be raised from mere historiography to the level of philosophy of history. Thereby inevitably does it become a victim of the intricacies resembling those to which philosophy is exposed. Thus, it depends upon the conception of philosophy itself whether or no the circle so enacted is a vicious one. Science is the great solvent and constructor of nature, history the great treasurer and custodian of the human legacy, each presenting the mind in decisive but qualified action. Yet the mind yearns to seize and know itself in its wholeness without any intervening medium. And so, thrown back upon itself, it repeats the process over and over again.

Unless man resigns himself to his fate or shuts his eyes to his predicament, this dilemma seems inevitable. Yet it is not. This situation is confined to the West. It has no bearing on the East.

The East—in the definition which has been adopted here, comprising the Asiatic countries from Iran to Japan—lacks a science such as that known to the Greeks and to the Renaissance which, rooted in philosophical concepts, derives from this origin its irresistible progress. Nor has the East developed a science of history or a philosophy of history in any sense comparable to Western achievement. It follows that the East, no less tossed and torn by the storms of the mind, lacks these diverting refuges and resources which constitute so much of the intellectual life of the West. To make out of inanimate nature, remote from immediate interest, an increasingly important object of investigation—to objectify history which by its very essence is something lived and to be lived, to shape and reshape it in order to arrive at the reality and meaning of history and of man—all this toil may seem strange and even uncanny to natural man and perhaps to a mind of another structure than the West's. However, no judgment, positive or negative, can carry any significance in the face of such a fundamental realization of the spirit as that constituted by the Western mind and civilization. That of the East, of no less authentic dignity, is by its structure confined to itself. And owing to the different relation of the Eastern mind to itself and to the world, heterogeneous and original results have transpired.

What has been unfolding with ever increasing certainty is now apparent. The difference between West and East does not consist in their qualified manifestations. It reaches deeper. It is rooted in diverging forms of consciousness. This term indicates that beyond the concrete minds expressing themselves in their respective civilizations there exist specific forms of consciousness of which the Western and Eastern mind are the representatives. Indeed, what the preceding pages contain is a philosophy of consciousness —more particularly the interpretation of the two great forms of consciousness, Western and Eastern. So far, they are the only ones to be clearly distinguished in the past and present of mankind. Beside them no others can be imagined.

There are the ancient civilizations of the Near East the achievements of which may be said to equal, even to surpass, in splendour those of the West and East, and certainly so in the decisive role they have played in the progress of humanity. While the debt that rising Europe owes to the Near East as a source of inspiration and instruction is fully recognized, the veil covering the Near East's influence on the countries of Eastern civilization is only now beginning to be lifted. If we compare the Near East to a human person and acknowledge the lavishness with which it has expended its gifts on the world, its role must be called one of unselfish generosity. In the Near East the mystery religions of the dying and resurrecting gods permitted the initiates to participate in the drama of rebirth and regeneration and thus culminated in the figure of the Christ. Hence, the name of a saviour might be appropriately conferred on the Near East since at least it raised Western man from primitive and half-primitive conditions. True, the West has paid back its debt in part through its essential participation in the building of Hellenistic and Islamic civilization.

But, all in all, the Near East did not succeed in maintaining its ascendancy over West and East.

Were it possible, in the absence of a recognized standard, to speak of Western and Eastern civilizations as superior to that of the Near East, such superiority could not be found in the quality of their achievements. What distinguishes Western and Eastern from Near Eastern civilization or from any other is not the excellence of concrete creations. It is the fact that beyond any substantial qualities, West and East alone represent clearly demonstrable forms of consciousness. That of the West has been expressed as unity in variety—that of the East as juxtaposition and identity. These forms preside over the structures of Western and Eastern mind and civilization, their historical aspects as well as their main creations. At the same time, they contain conclusive ideas and ways to man's consummation.

History and the philosophy of history have thus far determined the unities and agents of the historical process by their concrete aspects. Starting from the simple recognition of states as politically united peoples, to Spengler's profound and refined distinction of a few incommunicable and not transferable civilizations, or from a naïve chronological enumeration of events to the digging up of hidden forces and trends spreading over space and time, it is clear that criteria other than concrete empirical data must be applied to penetrate the structure of civilization at its highest level. However, the attempt has here been made to understand Western and Eastern mind and civilization as the manifestation of two different forms of consciousness. In consequence, not only has the definition and characterization of these civilizations been raised beyond possible doubt, but the whole panorama of human civilization receives a new framework.

This view is not and it cannot be primarily the product of induction and analysis. Hence, the accumulation of examples would not have been the right method of presentation. In fact it would only have diverted the attention from the progress of the argument. Inner consistency and systematic philosophy must constitute the adequate proof of our theory. Therefore, illustrations have been confined to the most expressive phenomena. But from their platform the perceptive reader has no doubt discerned others. However, cases are not lacking which do not agree with the norm established by the recognized forms of consciousness. Such deviations do not interfere with the validity of the forms. For in the realm of the mind and the spirit there is no crushing autocracy. No more than a majority rule. Inner weight, conclusiveness and dignity as impersonated by the essential, stand beyond the one and the other. And the light which shines from the forms of consciousness, illuminates not only what they themselves have brought forth but also any diverging and foreign elements.

* * *

Looking back over the road we have travelled, we cannot but be aware that it has led from the simple ultimately to the simple— from the structure expressible in categorical form to its transcendent consummation which is no less clearly definable. Unity in variety, the structural form of the Western objectifying mind, in the effort of saving—which is to say objectifying—the phenomena, reduces them to all-embracing thought so that at the ideal end of the process, thought faces itself. In the course of the realization of the structural principle of the East—juxtaposition and identity —the phenomena representing the Other are successively dismantled until at the end the identity of pure consciousness is achieved. Between the clearness of these structures and their attainable or ideal consummation there unfolds the millennary pageant of the civilizations.

While the appearance of the structures and with them the proper beginnings of Western and Eastern civilization can be clearly determined, the coincidence of the empirical conditions rendering their appearance possible defies explanation. To make the rise of Western civilization seem less of a miracle it is well to point at the privileged geographical position of Attica, the natural endowment of the Greeks, and the stimulating power of the Near Eastern influence. So likewise is it legitimate to combine the climatic conditions in the Punjab, the mentality of its pre-Aryan inhabitants as it can be reconstructed, and the racial qualities of the invading Aryans, in order to understand the origin of Vedic civilization. But at best, these *ex post facto* derivations can make the general possibility of the great phenomena look plausible.

They cannot explain what happened or that it had to happen. To Iran, even, these inadequate attempts at explanation seem hardly applicable, and not at all to China where the structure-inspired manifestation emerged within a practically secluded country and people. The problem of origin persists as it inevitably does when the great and the new appear.

However, if the manifestation of the structures in their first realizations depends upon a singular configuration of circumstances, the sphere of their action cannot remain confined to the lands and peoples within which they sprang into existence.

The expansion of Western and Eastern civilizations, and their hold and growth wherever they went, cannot be explained by conquest whose part in fact is but a modest one. The unequalled radiation of Greek civilization particularly after the incorporation of Greece into the Roman Empire, is followed by the Roman influence after the Fall of Rome. And in modern times the attraction exerted by Western civilization cannot any more be reduced to enforcement and practical needs. So far as radiation is concerned the civilizations of the East, united by their structure, though they did not co-operate in common achievements as did the national cultures of the West, present a picture similar to that of the West. The expansion of the Chinese civilization to Korea, Japan, South-East Asia, Mongolia and Tibet is attributable only in part to conquest and the same is true of the Indian spreading across the whole subcontinent and its ramifications in South-East Asia and Indonesia. The Iranians, while abstaining under the Achaemenian kings from imposing their civilization on the subject peoples, began during the Hellenistic period to spread their influence and together with the Arabs built what is known as Islamic civilization. If it penetrated far into Central Asia and particularly to India, it did so because the conquerors had previously come under its spell.

While many reasons may be adduced to explain the expansive power of Western and Eastern civilization there is one which reaches deeper and transcends them all. This is their structural foundation. The fact that each is based on a clearly demonstrable principle implying a distinct form of consciousness, confers upon them the potentiality—perhaps even the inner right to a universality that no other civilization can claim, whatever its excellence. It must be understood however that this dimension of Western and Eastern civilization does not in itself represent a positive value nor does it necessarily involve a specific superiority. For whether the achievement of universality which is to say the unification of the world in the name of one civilization, is to the advantage of humanity or, for that matter to that of the privileged civilization itself, remains an open question. However that may be, Western and Eastern civilization owe their universality not to concrete qualifications but to their being founded in a form which rules both aspect and process as well as achievements and behaviour. More than any specific quality form tends to guarantee universality.

This is not all. Whatever dignity be assigned to the structural form—a category of reason, an ontological or a metaphysical existence—when it alights on a civilization, it constitutes a form of consciousness. Whatever being partakes at all in consciousness, moves in the last resort for the sake of consciousness. Even in the objectifying mind of the West the cognition of the object for the object's sake does not stand out as the final goal. Rather is it the pure self-realization of the objectifying form of consciousness itself. True, what presents itself to the eye of both actor and observer, and what almost everywhere seems to matter, are the immediately intended objects which satisfy the instincts, the needs and the ambitions. However, the higher we ascend the scale of values, the clearer does it become that what really counts is the particular kind of consciousness connected, not with the object itself, but with its own attainment.

So it is with the two great forms of consciousness represented by West and East. Western and Eastern civilization alone—beyond all others and in contradistinction to all others—promise to offer with universality. a determined and final form of consciousness. It is not too much to assume that it was and that it is the more or less distinct feeling of this distinction which impels other civilizations to surrender the contingency of their own existence and to share the security and finality of way and aim which are inherent in the two forms of consciousness.

This, then, is the picture of human civilization as viewed from the standpoint here assumed. Rising above primitive and half-primitive societies, the next stratum is chiefly formed by national civilizations such as the ancient cultures of the Near East and of Central America. They are national not only because each of them bears the characteristic mark of the people who created it, but also because with the exception of specific arts and inventions, they did not radiate beyond the lands subjugated by their armies. Among these Egyptian civilization would seem to occupy a distinctive place. The secretive fanaticism of the Egyptians which marked their toil to widen the spheres of secular knowledge and sacred wisdom and to secure for themselves a happy life here and hereafter, and their jealousy guarded isolation and self-sufficiency over almost three thousand years, bewray the potency of an outstanding national civilization.

The layer above the national civilizations—this metaphor, let it be said, implying no higher evaluation—is occupied by those civilizations which are the result of the creative coalescence of different civilizations and which are generally described by the word syncretistic. Here, the Hellenistic and the Islamic are the most influential examples. The concrete character of syncretistic civilizations, the fact of their being exclusively determined by a specific outlook upon and conception of world and man, is no less patent than that of the national civilizations. The process of coalescence and of creative interpenetration of the various national contributions constituting Hellenistic civilization occurs in the atmosphere and under the influence of iridescent saviour-metaphysics and religions. So likewise the world of Islam, despite the variety of its components and achievements, derives its strength from religion. Because of their concrete character, descriptive analysis of these national and syncretistic civilizations is the perfect means of their comprehension and interpretation. Beyond the syncretistic lie the structure-based civilizations of West and East.

Here we breathe another air. Description and analysis are no longer the adequate means of comprehension unless they are preceded and illumined by recognition of their structural bases. Then it becomes apparent that the structures relate to and condition two divergent forms of consciousness. In point of fact, they are the only fundamental forms actually to be distinguished. It falls to each to realize both in the entirety of its process and in its

278

individuals, the pertaining form regardless of whether the aim can ever be attained. This is the reason why within Eastern and Western civilization man moves in a sphere of universality and spiritual breath nowhere else to be found.

In these circumstances the question arises as to why Eastern civilization has not been called to spread and dominate in serious contention with the West. The answer is contained in the foregoing pages. Transcending all the well-known psychological reasons for the West's superior aptitude for this role, is the objectifying form of its mind. The political and intellectual conquest and reconstruction of the world according to its law is but a minor manifestation of a mind which, in both the inner and the physical realm, is constantly occupied in positing objects and replacing them by others, joining them into units, only to release these combinations for the sake of more satisfactory ones—and all this primarily a theoretical process. The individual may find his fulfilment in objectivation through creation, work, knowledge of himself and the world and the relation to an Absolute of some kind. But the main line of Western civilization points to a common, organized and objective effort which is amply documented by the history of its tools and institutions. Against this background, world-domination cannot mean more to the Western mind than a poor mundane symbol of the All it mentally wants to possess, just as knowledge of the cosmic universe is but a mirage which hides the eternal aim of the objectifying mind—its self-objectivation through conceptual thought.

In the East the situation is not quite as simple and obvious. It is not that its claim to universality and to world domination is any less legitimate than that of the West. But the whole essence of Eastern mind and civilization is, above all, aimed at the individual personality. And there it achieves its main realization. To this, must be added the fact that Eastern consciousness moves not in concepts but in states. Then it will be understood why the incentive to military, political or intellectual world-domination did not thrive in the East as it did in the West. Indeed, the only exception to be found is, significantly enough, in Iran which in so many respects points to the West, where the Achaemenians conquered the largest part of the then-known world and united it in an empire guided by a central idea. For the rest, it needed the modernization of Japan and her alliance with Nazism to inspire dreams of world-domination. China, despite campaigning and conquest on a moderate scale, kept to her secluded and self-sufficient existence. India had never been united until under British rule—the Mogul emperors did not extend their empire to include the whole subcontinent.

Particularly significant is it that the great figures of the West who aspired to world empire—Alexander, Caesar, Augustus, some of the emperors of the Holy Roman Empire like Frederic II, Napoleon, the founders of the British Empire—impersonated almost without exception the characteristics and the best endowments and traditions of Western civilization. In striking contradistinction, again barring the Achaemenian kings, the only real world conquerors, the East produced—the Hun, the Mongol and the Turkish—emerged from areas outside the realm of Eastern civilization.

Even in the realm of mind and spirit little imperialism is to be found in the East. The great exceptions are the zealotry with which the Manichaean teachings spread from their Iranian homeland to the countries further East and to the West, reaching in various ramifications and disguises as far as Western Europe, and —the expansion of Buddhism. But Buddhism, in contradistinction to Manichaeism and Christianity, owed its all important penetration of the Far East less to large scale missionary organization than to individual initiative. All this illustrates this patent point. Although the Eastern structure and thereby its creations as well as its forms of life, are in principle equally capable of world-wide diffusion, the East cannot hope to compete in point of expansion with the objectifying mind of the West. For the Eastern mind and civilization necessarily lack the dynamic which is the monopoly of the objectifying mind. Were the West not what it is, Eastern civilization in a slow and static process would no doubt be on the way to world civilization.

*   *   *

The divergence of Western and Eastern mind and civilization must have evoked serious doubt as to whether, beyond the sphere

of mere pragmatic exchange and understanding, any real communication between them can be possible. The standpoint from
which the problem may be evaluated can be found only in the
answer to this seemingly paradoxical question—Can two antagonistic forms of consciousness coexist in one and the same mind, and
if so, how? It would appear that conciliation of this antagonism
can take place only in a third and higher form of consciousness.
This, however, is nowhere to be found, nor can it be imagined in
theory. Not even mysticism, which is summoned to so many uses
for which it is not made, can produce this conciliatory effect since
the rift between the two forms of consciousness runs equally
through both Western and Eastern mysticism. The West cannot
give up its evolutionary nature and its conceptual thought nor
can the East abandon the state-character of its existence and
cognition. For either to do so, would be to deny and to end its
true life.

Despite these difficulties, there still is a way out of the intricacies and it points beyond mere theory. True, the burden of the
proof of possibility falls exclusively on the East. Representative
Easterners often express the view that Western civilization can
be successfully assimilated without affecting the core of the
Eastern essence. Whether this conviction arises out of hope or
national pride, it is significantly confirmed by the structure of the
Eastern mind—juxtaposition and identity. Thus it would be
possible for the adopted civilization to coexist with or in the
unimpaired Eastern mind without the one interfering with the
other. This would constitute an inner situation comparable to and
directly reflecting the attitude of non-attachment.

There is little doubt that given the opportunity of peaceful
development, the East in a few generations will be ready to compete with the West in any field albeit it is impossible to predict
whether it will ever be able to produce a pioneer mind in the
adopted civilization. But to perform these tasks against the background of that inner conflict must seem, at least to us in the West,
an almost superhuman aspiration. And certainly it would remain
the privilege of a small number of select minds. This restriction,
however, far from being an objection would actually testify to the
importance of the phenomenon. For not only has the creation of

civilization at all times been the work of the few, but the men of the East who will succeed in moving creatively in Western civilization while standing firm on their own ground, are those who alone possess the sovereign freedom to conceive what may unite the two civilizations if such a portentous happening be within the design of providence.

Western man does not face this dilemma. If he did, and if it fell to him to adopt Eastern civilization, he would not even if he wanted, keep it at a distance while plunging into it. His structure —unity in diversity—would bid him assimilate it with his conceptual apparatus because only through that process of penetration could he feel that he had accomplished its comprehension and possession. From then on, he would live the new life according to his own understanding of it with full affirmation just as the westernized Easterner would move on a new road. It might be rightly objected that the East, as thus conceived and lived, would not be the true East, but an obscure and veiled East. In any case, it must be admitted that if the West were in this position, the nuisance coefficient introduced into the reception of the other civilization by the structure of the receiver would be considerably greater. This results from the nature of the concept. It is necessarily imperative and aggressive even when it adjusts to its object with subtlety and caution. The reserve of the East, however, in respecting and so in its way preserving, what comes to it, would preserve itself. The West, perhaps less reverential, but filled with the thirst for objective knowledge would break up the data in order to construct them anew.

Thus, each civilization in its particular way, would automatically act in self-defence. The consequence is obvious. The conceptual approach of the West, while opening up ever deeper comprehension, would at the same time become a serious obstacle to its genuine experience of the East. On the other hand the East, once it had got hold of the conceptual thought, would be able to live the life of the West but the inner reserve of non-attachment would frustrate that deepest participation which leads to creativeness. Thus, quite apart from the commanding historical evolution there is this deep structural reason which has worked toward the situation as we find it today.

The March of the Mind

The ambition of the preceding considerations has not been to lead to a final conclusion. Rather the aim has been to show some of the major problems hiding behind such terms as the meeting of the East and West, their mutual comprehension, their receiving from and influencing each other. True, the problems brought to the foreground are valid chiefly, but by no means exclusively, at the highest level. However, only there can the situation be visualized in clear light and the true standards and measures be found. Meanwhile, there is ample space for important contacts at the middle level where the main issue remains veiled and no fundamental decisions are being taken. There the influences, be they one-sided or reciprocal, are helped by the same way and manner which rule the entrance of the individual into his own civilization.

Man does not grow out of his own civilization, he grows into it. There is little doubt that an infant placed in surroundings differing from the one in which he was born will evolve as a fullfledged member of the new civilization. By virtue of his innate endowment, he will develop views and productive capacities in accordance with the new environment provided he be given the same chances as those enjoyed by the other members of the group. Even at a more advanced age the changing from one civilization to another under normal circumstances will not meet with particular difficulties. This means that on the medium level there are no obstacles in the path of exchange between West and East which cannot be overcome with goodwill and comprehension. Not so at the supreme level. There, any attempt at compromise, exchange and interpenetration would mean suicide or destruction of the other individual or civilization.

This follows clearly from what has been said about the inburst —the implosion of the structures. The great creations which in the course of the history of civilization confirm and represent the structures as they have revealed themselves in the phenomena of their inburst, are, like them, not the fruit of steady evolution. Their way of entering the world is by way of irruption, of bursting in—the eternal form in which the spirit emerges in the mind. In the minds of those men of genius who have been called upon to initiate or continue a civilization, these decisive creations are shafts of light illumining the mind as inspirations, regardless of whether they come at the end of toil or by an apparent act of grace. Even when they crown the long process of trial and error, it is not they that evolve. It is the working mind. They themselves are what they are. They burst into being like Athene springing full armed from the head of Zeus. This is testified by the very amazement of those who have been favoured by this experience. In such circumstances to designate the way of reaching the supreme level as one of growing into it would be utterly misleading. If it must be described as the act and achievement of an individual —not as a mere receiving—the designation of a breaking-through the ordinary level may be adequate.

In the sphere thus conquered, Western and Eastern mind and civilization are definitely not compatible and consistent. They constitute two separate forms of consciousness. Though both strive for the consummation of man's destination, their different aspects, methods and outlooks are comparable to parallels which meet at infinity. Whatever be the possibilities of influencing and enriching each other on lower levels, on the supreme plane, although the spirit itself remains one, the two minds sever.

* * *

In our day, with Western civilization on trial and not alone through pressure from outside, and the East torn apart, exposed as it is to the impact of two antagonistic forces, more than ever is it necessary to have the eye directed to the essence of East and West in order to keep the balance and to judge the issues. Once again the West has arrived at a turning point. Humanism, having accompanied and enlightened the new outlook on nature, just as it had been supported by the latter, seems to have left us. Now, science, as well as scientific thought in general, with their inherent indifference to value, seem summoned to take the lead in this new period of Western civilization. However, a civilization ruled by applied science would show an indisputable bend towards egalitarianism and dictatorship. And this would stand in flat contradiction to the Western structure—unity in variety. Science is not equipped to assume to itself the ascendancy over state and society. It needs the guidance of a political, religious or philosophical idea or just tradition to determine its place, its evalua-

tion and its application.[1] There is a deep significance in the fact
that science appeared, evolved and flourished in close harmony
with Humanism. Now that that close harmony between Humanism
and science no longer exists another superior purpose is needed
which will assign to science its place within the theoretical and
practical realm. This new task already arises above the horizon.

The organization of society springs up as the imminent preoccupation of the West. If this be the turn of events, it accords
with the inner logic of the evolutionary history of the Western
mind. After having striven to build human personality and to
organize the universal monarchy it turned to penetrating and
shaping the Beyond and having thus assimilated religion it then
took up nature as the object of its labour. The organization of
society will thus be in perfect alignment with the self-realization
of the Western mind. What will be the range and proportion of
this society—assuredly it must aspire at universality—it is
impossible to predict. For it will have to be achieved in the face
of a Russia where in the ancient atmosphere of a fateful mysticism
with the czar in the role of the Saviour, coupled with the logic of
the social and economic philosophy of Marxism, the indomitable
spirit of the Mongol world conquerors attempts to weld into one
people widely different nations and races. The form of Western
society, both as a whole and within its members, will insist on
unity whilst preserving and cultivating to the utmost degree the
diversity of individuals and groups. Whether this idea can be
carried to complete realization is immaterial. None of the objects
of the preceding periods of Western civilization were ever fully
realized when measured by the standard of the commanding ideas.

For the march of the mind it suffices that ideas are conceived
and that a serious effort is made to make them living realities
before the planet destined to rule the next stage rises above the
horizon. The East finds itself in an infinitely more intricate
situation. It is not enough that it is faced with the crucial problem
of assimilating a civilization which is contrary to its own. The

[1] It is highly significant that the philosophy which introduced the scientific and
technical age at the beginning of the nineteenth century, that of Auguste Comte,
finally arrives at quite another confession of faith: 'L'amour pour principe, l'ordre
pour base, le progrès pour but.' Love for principle, order for foundation, progress
for aim.

very delimitation of the term East seems to have lost its meaning amid recent happenings. In contradistinction to the West which, despite some shiftings and losses to Russia still holds its traditional territory, there is a twofold rift within what is or was the East. On the one side, China has for the time being left the orbit of Eastern mind and civilization. On the other side, Shiite Iran has moved nearer to the world of Sunnite Islam with respect to which it has so far held a jealously guarded, isolated position. In a similar move, but without loosening the ties with the West, Pakistan has drawn nearer to the other Islamic countries. What is left constituting the realm of Eastern mind and civilization, consists of Hindu India, South-East Asia and Japan, with the South-Eastern mainland living under the immediate threat of Communism.

It is not relevant for the argument of this book to weigh the political, moral and military strength of the two remaining strongholds—India and Japan. There is not even a need to form an opinion as to whether they will be legitimated to represent Eastern mind and civilizations. These questions and all others connected with the political situation, are transcended by the fact that the Eastern mind is a reality which lives on. Its visible and invisible achievements are within the reach of those who want to comprehend or to live them.

Thus, whatever may be the decision taken by the Eastern nations or imposed upon them by fate, the problem of interchange between West and East will go on regardless of whether the men of the East either desert or are forced to desert the banner under which they have fought for three millennia. If such a spiritual duel impends, the initiative will fall to the West as it has in the past. Whatever the march of fate, West and East will stand out as both representatives and champions of the two forms of consciousness that the human mind has thus far generated in the fulfilment of its destiny.

APPENDIX

The Crucial Problem of Philosophy of History

The ensuing discussion should be of interest to the general reader as well as to teachers, students and scholars. It was written in anticipation of the publication of this book and first appeared in a somewhat abbreviated form in *The Philosophical Review* in March, 1949. The courtesy of the editors in permitting its reappearance here is gratefully acknowledged. The aim and the end of this paper is to place the argument of this book in its proper niche in relation to philosophy and the history of philosophy. In a perhaps more reflective age than our own such a discussion might well have served its proper purpose by way of an Introduction.

* * *

The idea of the unity and homogeneity of mankind has not come down to us as the product of a long, gradual experience and as a result of widening horizons and multifarious fate which granted to man a better acquaintance with his kind. If theoretically such extended experience seems to result inevitably in the conception of humanity as a whole, reality flatly belies this expectation. Likewise, it is inadmissible to view this idea of the unity of mankind as an innate idea, a universal and imperishable possession of the human mind. True, the cosmogonic myths of all peoples speak of the creation of man, but what they mean, and quite naturally are interested in, is the ancestry of their own tribe.

If a dim vision of universal character can be glimpsed in these myths, such wisdom does not enter the light of consciousness. It remains undeveloped—an unfulfilled promise. More potent beliefs such as the requirements of individual and social evolution and the imperative needs of life are destined to take the upper hand.

287

What is more, for a long distance on man's way to civilization, the border-line between man and animal is ill-defined. The animal is felt to possess human, even superhuman qualities. The transmutation of men into animals is believed to be within man's power. Equally fluctuating is the distinction between man and superhuman beings. Men may arise even during their lifetime to the rank of gods or demi-gods. Beliefs such as these, the radiating effects of which may still be found in high civilizations, necessarily cause a deep feeling of uncertainty in man about his real nature. The insight into the conception of mankind as a self-sufficient unit which stands out clearly against the infra- and the suprahuman world is thus barred.

But while magic and religious beliefs favour the expanding of the idea of man beyond what shows human face and shape, his behaviour in real life reveals a basic and almost irresistible tendency to draw demarcation lines within his own species, and thus to deny in various forms the unity of mankind. The instinctive reaction to another group is one of withdrawal and defence with the corresponding sentiments of distrust and misgiving. And just as it was in primitive times, so it is at the bottom of international relations today. This contractive and self-centred attitude was indispensable for the crystallization and solidification of the group and the individual personality. But it easily suggests a disparaging evaluation of the other group as inferior and the glorification of the own group, thus establishing radical distinctions within mankind.

With all these forces opposing the conception of the unity of mankind it could not have originated and evolved as an outcome of experience. Its birthplace must be sought in another realm. This concept descended from the loftier regions of ideas. It is a product of religion and philosophy. Such an idea must itself possess the characteristics of unity and uniqueness in order to impart them to mankind. Three times and in three different original patterns did this idea take shape—twice in the form of religion and once as a philosophical thought. The religious expressions belonged to Asia, the secular one to Europe. In Judaism at least since prophetic times and in Christianity with its birth, the idea of the one God is mirrored in the idea of one mankind. This latter is created in God's image and is distinct from angels and animals in nature and in the goal assigned to it. In Persian Zoroastrianism mankind is summoned by Ahura Mazda to assist him in the eschatological fight against the forces of Evil. And in the common battle the hosts of men are led by the Persian king, this ethico-religious function being in fact the supreme legitimation of his sovereignty. But the Greeks divested the unifying principle of its religious character. They discovered the Nous—the faculty of pure reason, as separated from an intellect based upon sense-perception—and made it the distinct prerogative of man.

Particular emphasis deserves to be laid upon one fact. This is that the idea of the unity of mankind originated in one geographical sphere—in South-Eastern Europe, and in the Near and the Middle East, that is to say the Eastern part of the Mediterranean and the Iranian landbridge which connects the Mediterranean civilization with India and the Far East. This fact is all the more remarkable since the sources from which the idea sprang and the forms it assumed differ so fundamentally as to exclude mutual influence. Christianity as well as Zoroastrianism conceive of mankind as a community of salvation. The Judaic conception on the other hand is one of a community of faith. And both are opposed to the Greek mind which raises mankind to a community of pure reason capable of conceiving and beholding ideas. In India and China this idea of the unity of mankind has not been formulated and emphasized with the same clarity which particularly distinguishes its enunciation in Christian faith and Greek philosophy. True, it is virtually contained in the salvation religions of India and in the Taoist metaphysics of China and her ethic philosophy, but we will look in vain for a distinct expression. The metaphysical conceptions of India and China made the formulation difficult and in some way superfluous. In their conception of the universe man was not assigned the unique place he held in the eyes of the Greek, the Judaeo-Christian and the Zoroastrian. In the infinite realm of existence man is but a single phenomenon with all the other beings around, above and below him. The notion of the true reality in India, and to some extent in China, obliterated indiscriminately the value of existence as such. It neither admitted the cosmos idea of the Greeks, the dynamic spiritual and terrestrial hierarchy which developed in Christianity, nor the strict order of the Zoroastrian division of the universe into the kingdoms of Good and Evil.

So overwhelmed were Asia proper, India and China by the fact of existence and its connotations of impermanence, futility and mystery that they were ready to populate the realm of existence with the numberless products of their imagination. Thereby they symbolized the very fact of the senselessness and incomprehensibility of existence. And this being so, they could not persuade themselves to concede to man the exceptional place he owed to the anthropocentric *naïveté* of the Greek, the Semitic and the Persian mind. But if the indifferent absorption of man by the ocean of existence prevented the clear conception of mankind as a separate unit, social forces were nonetheless at work to produce the same result. Before and apart from Buddhism and other sects classic Hinduism linked salvation with the caste system. Thus was there erected an unsurmountable barrier between India and the rest of the world. In quite another, though less drastic, way the national pride of China, which assigned to the Chinese civilization and people the central place, kept her otherwise deeply humane philosophy from eliciting the idea of the unity and homogeneity of man.

Once this idea had descended from the realms of religion and philosophy inevitably it came to be secularized. This evolution started at the dawn of the modern world with the political and social utopias outlining the conditions of a universal state and society, from Francis Bacon and Campanella to the ideologies of the French Revolution and their socialistic and communistic offspring. Latterly, scientific thought and particularly biology and anthropology have come to pronounce themselves on the problem of mankind. There the species *homo sapiens* is well determined since all of its members interbreed but not with other species, and constitutes with the varieties of the fossil man—the Neanderthal, the *homo Heidelbergensis* and others—the *genus homo* which merges with other more ape-like forms into the family of the *hominidae*. The mental nature of *homo sapiens* seems to be as uncertain as the delimitation of his physical characteristics. Though it is now generally agreed that even the most primitive existing representatives of *homo sapiens* do not differ basically from the more advanced members in point of intellectual endowment, a unanimously recognized conclusion has yet to be reached as to whether a sharp distinction exists between human mentality and animal psychology, more particularly that of the anthropoids, and if so where that difference is to be found.

It is in the realm of religion that the idea of the unity of mankind manifests its greatest potency. In true religious faith the powers of intellect, will and emotion have not yet separated into antagonistic forces. The religious idea of unity triumphantly ignores all empirical dissimilarities between men with regard to race, standards of civilization and education, and social and economic distinctions. The fluctuating views of scientific knowledge no more prevail against this faith-rooted idea than do the prejudiced opinions based on utilitarian motives. Compared to religion, the power of the idea of the unity of mankind in philosophy is considerably weakened. This for the reason that the philosophizing mind is based on conceptual thought as distinct from volition and emotion. Therefore, the philosophical conception of the unity of mankind tends logically to its realization, but much less so psychologically. And in order to stir up the minds the assistance of social and economic trends is needed—as is amply demonstrated by the history of the French Revolution. From the spiritual realm through the philosophical sphere down to the purely theoretical scientific thought of the present day the original connection of the idea with the profound belief and will to realization has been gradually weakening. So likewise its inherent energy is waning, until finally in scientific thought it becomes totally indifferent to realization.

These conditions and their intricacies reflect upon historical science and the philosophy of history. It is in harmony with the origin of the idea of the unity of mankind that the first and most influential philosophy of history as far as the West is concerned is the sacred history of the Judaeo-Christian world. The idea of the chosen people does not prevent the Old Testament from displaying an interest at once objective and truly scientific that was unique in the ancient world in the then known racial composition of mankind. In its famous genealogy[1] it assigned with astonishing accuracy the various people to three great families named after the three sons of Noah. Nor again does it impair the veracity of the reported historical events, the realism of the descriptions, and the psychological power and impressiveness of the personalities presented. For all this is irrespective of the fact that God deigns to talk only to men of the Hebrew race and faith, and that the essence of world history consists of the dramatic intercourse between God and his rebellious people. Such is the all-too-human arsis of sacred history in which heaven and earth meet in an atmosphere of primitive *naïveté* and awe-inspiring grandeur. This picture where sacred history is narrowed down to God's relation to one people cedes the place in prophetic times to a vision of eschatological dimensions. Yet the interest in the events of secular history is limited to the extent to which they possess an immediate bearing on the spiritual mission of Israel—the conversion of the people of the earth to one God as expressed in the prophecy of Isaiah.

* * *

This, then, is a true philosophy of history. It permeates the history of mankind with a deep meaning and bestows upon it a supreme goal. But since secular history is interpreted as sacred history it is, as it were, a philosophy of history without history. This is the very spirit which permeates the Christian philosophy of history. There is a momentous addition, however, in that the historical appearance of the God-man as Saviour constitutes the *terminus ad quem* and *a quo* of history and confers upon its process quite another reality and stability. On the other hand, the incarnation of God, in emphasizing the problems of the two natures, spiritual and physical, tears the historical world asunder. Thenceforth, the kingdom of heaven and the empire of Caesar—the Thebais, the realm of anchorets and saints on the one hand, and the secular state on the other—face each other as incompatible and unequal components of the historical process. From the viewpoint of secular history, the sacred history of Christianity almost amounts to the dissolution of history proper. In the Old Testa-

[1] Gen., 10, and I Chron. 1.

292

ment the people of Israel, a distinct unit by race, faith and fate, are the backbone of world history as far as it exists. In the Christian faith—the political and national unity of Israel having been dispersed, and its ethnic and national importance superseded by the predominance of the new Gospel—the concern of sacred history then centres on the individual and the fulfilment of his spiritual goal. The historical process is thus deprived of its natural agents—peoples, states, civilizations or whatever be its subjects—and becomes the indifferent and in itself insignificant scene of the struggle of the individual soul for salvation.

Judged by the standard of secular history, sacred history, though truly universal, is biased. The Greek genius in the person of Herodotus with his disinterested and scientific curiosity in history, opened the road to secular universal history. For Herodotus mankind was indeed one. In his history he included information about all branches of humanity irrespective of race and cultural level, and the limits of his study were dictated only by the limits of the world of his time. However, if his intellectual horizon knew no limitation, yet the universality of his intuition lagged behind that of sacred history in one momentous point. In sacred history the way of mankind is alive with the same superior meaning which constitutes the essential unity of mankind. It is the eternal credit of Herodotus that no national and racial prejudice impairs his historical view. Yet he naïvely accepts the unity of mankind—he does not guarantee it by any fundamental principle. Thus the unity of Herodotus' universal history is contingent. He takes the people as he finds them, and it is but the superficial unity of space and time which holds the parts together. His universality lies in the superior impartiality with which the members of the human family are dealt with. But no dominating idea makes of these parts a meaningful reality.

Sacred history—the religious interpretation of history on the one hand, and historiography, the science of history, on the other —prepared the way for the modern philosophy of history. This evolution—the supplanting of the sacred aspect of history by secular interpretation—could only take place within the frame of a general secularization of the medieval world conception. And this process is usually linked with the resumption of the classics known by the terms Renaissance and Humanism. However, the so-called rebirth of classic and particularly Greek studies, which were never neglected during the Middle Ages albeit limited to scattered centres of higher learning, has probably had less momentum in the movement of secularization than is generally assumed. Whether the succession of a secular culture to a religious period be viewed as a necessary evolution of the mind at least in the Occident, or whether it be regarded as inevitable, since Western civilization is rooted in the secular Greek mind and for this reason the original matrix will break through as long as that civilizations exists, this much is certain: the cause of the rise of the secular cycle in the West is not to be found solely in the rebirth of the classics and still less in the extraneous incident of the entrance into Italy of the Byzantine scholars.

The flaring-up of interest in the classics is itself but the natural form in which secular civilization in the West had to express itself. It must be interpreted as the unfolding at the appropriate moment of values and forces which had never been entirely lost and had never ceased to influence the intellectual and emotional life of the Middle Ages. The mind which reanimated the classic heritage had long ceased to be that of the classic Greek and Roman. The innumerable elements of classic antiquity which were essential in building up the visible and invisible Church—the administrative body and the spiritual and intellectual life in theology and philosophy, had been imbued by a thousand years of Catholic Christianity with quite another spirit. Therefore, the minds which glorified the new period received and assimilated the treasures of antiquity in a wholly different intellectual and emotional frame. Thus, they imparted to them a meaning often at variance with the original.

Even those who more or less openly turned from the orthodox life of the Church, testified by their ideas to the deep truth of the only seemingly paradoxical words of Barrès: 'Je suis athée mais je suis Catholique.' Since Catholicism is not only a system of religion but an all embracing civilization, they could not rid themselves of the Christian matrix despite their effort to re-illumine the light of classic paganism. When, therefore, the omnipotence of Catholic faith began to be questioned and undermined, the non-religious body remained. And it is this secularized body of Catholic civilization which is the solid foundation of the Renaissance movement—more important than the resumed Greek studies themselves. The medieval world conception had only to be divested of its religious core to give birth to a secular civilization in which the transformed legacy of classic antiquity emerged in the foreground.

It is generally agreed that the decisive characteristic of the Renaissance movement is the awakening interest in nature. True as this statement is, it contains only half the truth. For it ignores the fact that nature as experienced and conceived by the man of the Renaissance differs substantially from the Greek conception. During the long painful Christian revolution the Western mind lost the immediate approach to nature as well as the belief in it as a cosmos—a self-sufficient order of all natural phenomena. In the philosophy of the Renaissance God became more and more identified with nature. In fact, nature became God secularized. That the part of the equation which profits by this identification is nature alone is evident. A genuine equalization of God and nature whereby the deification of nature does not upset the harmonious balance between the two, must always remain the privilege of a few exalted minds, and more of a mystic experience than a philosophy.

In Spinoza's philosophy alone *deus sive natura* found an adequate philosophical expression. In the new world conception as a whole, the process of secularization could only result in the disintegration of the medieval idea of God, which had to relinquish to nature some of its attributes fitting the new consummation. Thus the infinity of God was imparted to nature, thereby conferring on it qualities entirely foreign to Greek conception. The perfection of God as reflected in his wisdom found its supreme expression in the eternal laws of world mechanics—particularly in the laws regulating the march of the astral bodies. Furthermore, the halo of sanctity detached itself from the Divine Being and enveloped the whole of nature with a mystical atmosphere for which the term pantheism is in many cases an inadequate expression. This mystic aura of nature, which is distinctly different from the unorthodox magic philosophy of nature which accompanied medieval thought, to vanish only at the beginning of the nineteenth century, sprang from a definite though not a conscious desire. It was meant to overcome the medieval dualism of mind and matter and to render to nature the inner harmony it held in the Greek world conception. But the Christian faith had created too deep a cleavage between the material and the immaterial world to allow for conciliation, still less for unification. And the mystic conception of nature soon broke up into its parts and developed into two equally momentous but opposed phenomena, Western mysticism and the modern science of nature. Meanwhile, the antagonism of mind and matter, soul and body, became the central problem of modern philosophy.

The Renaissance period was not and it could not be a rebirth of Greek antiquity. It is in essence Christianity secularized in the face of antiquity and with this latter as the no longer attainable ideal. What was attainable, and was indeed achieved is this—the elaboration and the creative reconstruction of the classic elements which had been penetrated and transformed by the Christian spirit. This process of secularization was the implementation of the new world conception, and in the course of time it was destined to become increasingly alienated from the spirit of Christianity as well as from that of classic antiquity.

Modern philosophy of history too must be understood in its beginning as the secularization of sacred history. For the soul and its struggle for salvation the philosophy of the Renaissance substitutes the mind and its desire for cultural progress. To the transformation of the immortal part of man corresponds in the deep humanistic sense the formation of the mind whose immortality may or may not be assumed. The religious ideal of the saint is replaced by the secular one of the *uomo universale* who realizes in himself as a creative microcosmos the potentialities of the mind. This is called *civiltá*. For this our word civilization, worn down by indifferent use and abuse, is a misleading substitute. *Civiltá* is, therefore, the meaning and the goal of the historic process. Civilization is secularized salvation and on its plane it signifies a liberation from the fetters of barbarism just as religion aims at deliverance from the powers of evil. Both the Middle Ages and the Renaissance are individualistic. They consider human personality the exponent of the supreme values and history the means whereby it may attain the ordained perfection. Being individualistic, they are inevitably aristocratic though each in its own right. The saints constitute the true nobility of the Church but only in so far as their humility makes of them kings in serving—*servi servorum Dei* whereas the *uomo universale* is not only the paragon. He is also the creator of cultural values and the born ruler of mankind.

A pivotal point exists, however, where the analogy between the medieval and the modern philosophy of history gives way to open antagonism. Characteristically enough, this divergence concerns their respective relation to man as a political being. Even when medieval thought was not induced by the authority of the Church Fathers, above all of St. Augustine, to look at political power and the state, as the incarnation of evil, it nonetheless retained a suspicious attitude toward the state because it had to be conceived as the fatal fruit of the Fall. In the Christian philosophy of history the state is at best one of the two swords—the secular power of the Emperor and the spiritual power of the Church—and the claim to equality with the Church has been fiercely contested by the popes. The secular idea of the human personality asks for a positive relation to the state. Not only is the political community the frame of civilized life, but social and political existence itself is an essential element without which the individual cannot fulfil his destiny. If, far from being extraneous to the goal of man, political life forms a part of his secular civilization, then state and government are capable of constant improvement and subject to evolutionary progress.

During this new period the eye of the historian remains fixed with increasing attention on political data. But, henceforth, the philosophy of history encompasses the way of history as the account of mankind's evolving civilization. In truth, only thus in the genuine sense of the term could universal history originate. Political history is at best concerned with the co-operation or succession of the political fate of all known peoples and nations and their mutual encounters. But even if these millennary movements are expounded by historical laws or rendered intelligible by attributing to events and periods a quasi-teleological ultra-causal significance—even then the history of mankind remains but a summary of the histories of the parts. It is a dead letter.

The Crucial Problem of Philosophy of History

The secular philosophy of history, on the contrary, entering upon its inheritance from sacred history, filled the history of mankind with soul and spirit. It read into it a new meaning—that of the rise and progress of civilization.

*   *   *

All these new trends converge in the philosophy of history of Vico (born 1670). In his *Elements of a New Science of the Common Nature of Peoples* he encompasses in one great intuition the history of mankind. Progressing in all its branches, though not all at the same time and in the same rhythm, it marches toward the same final goal of civilization. True, Vico still emphasizes Providence as the regulator of this process and sometimes speaks of religion as the dominant driving force in the rise to higher life. But these conceptions are but a residue which do not contribute anything vital to his construction. In Vico's eyes history presses forward as an autonomous process of civilization. Civilization itself is one and indivisible though it consists of three main elements—myth, law and language, or as we would say—religion, political authority, and knowledge.

There is no reason to be amazed that some three hundred years had to pass before the themes which distinguish the Renaissance and Humanism had sufficiently crystallized to be elaborated into a great system and—to a certain degree—to be overcome. If historiography presupposes a reflective mind and an inner remoteness from its object, the philosophy of history requires these qualifications to an even higher degree. Vico is the first to recognize that after the abdication of sacred history, a secular philosophy of history could only be built upon the idea of civilization. In his work he made use of all the new conceptions, categories and knowledge which are at the base of the modern world. He went farther. Being fully aware of the shortcomings of the predominant rationalistic foundations of modern thought as represented particularly in the Cartesian philosophy, he assigned the irrational forces in man and history to their due place. And in so doing he anticipated trends which asserted themselves a century later in the Romantic period.

Salvation and civilization are the two *lumina* of the Western mind enlightening the history of mankind. Both of these interpretations of history present appropriate standards for measuring man and events. But the transcendental criterion of salvation is so inexorable and so remote from the ordinary way of life that not much will stand the test when seen against it. Also man, striving for salvation, must feel hopelessly far from and in opposition to things around him. Civilization, however, be its standard of the highest, belongs to and is rooted in this world even if it reaches out to spheres beyond. This new idea of man as the microcosmos, reflecting the perfection of the macrocosmos, implies that nothing is or should be alien to man, provided perfect harmony is accomplished among the parts. Secular civilization, therefore, is no longer subordinated to religion and is a positive value only in so far as it remains in accordance with religion. Religion on the contrary now becomes an element of civilization among others. And even if it were considered prominent it would still have to compromise with the others so as not to disturb the harmony of the various elements which compose *civiltá*. Man remains intimately connected with nature no less than with his own history of which he is the sole creator, agent and beneficiary. It was Vico's profound belief that man can only demonstrate and understand what he has himself created. And likewise it is because he makes his own history that he understands it. Confined to this world below, which man alone can make a place worthy to live in, history illuminated by a new significance, becomes truly universal.

The course of philosophy of history inevitably reflects that of the Western mind. In addition to the distinctions inherent in the ideas of the sacred and the secular, there is one point of far-reaching importance which severed the philosophy of history of the new period from that of the preceding. The sacred philosophy of history implied the exclusivism of the Christian faith. It was based not only on the supremacy of faith, but also on its monopoly as the unique guardian of truth and the only road to salvation. This claim the secular philosophy of history did not inherit from its predecessor. It runs counter to its idea of man, as well as of civilization, to assume that one race or people could pretend to any such privilege. Human civilization is one in all its variety. And each branch of the human family may and will reach the height of civilization in the form which corresponds to its genius. Vico asserted that the American Indians would evolve in quite the same way if they had not been discovered by the Europeans.

As it were, the conviction of possessing the sole religious truth and hence the monopoly of the means of grace, filled medieval Europe with legitimate pride. It felt called by God to his service and to convert the peoples of the earth. In this respect, medieval Europe continued the Israelite idea of the chosen people and of its mission as proclaimed in prophetic times. However, what has a particular bearing upon our argument is not this fact itself. It is the relation implied between the faith and those who professed it. Neither the Hebrews nor the Christian nations of Europe pretended that they owed their role as the chosen people to specific virtues of their own. Biblical history does not show the Jews in any way superior to the peoples and cultures of their time except by their faith. And even there, in their relation to God, their revolt against God and the weight laid upon them constitute the recurrent events of their history. Nor does the moral or cultural record of the Christian nations during the Middle Ages justify any claim that they surpassed the civilized people of the Asiatic world.

The sacred history of the Old and the New Testaments does not deal with the Jews and the Christianized Western nations because of their superior human standards. It deals with them because of the fact that for inscrutable reasons they have been chosen for the possession of the only true faith. And though from the religious standpoint this selection represents a sublime act of grace, in its human aspect it is, in the case of the Hebrews, an imposition, an almost unbearable charge laid upon an ignorant and miserable enslaved tribe. In like manner, the conversion of the European peoples had frequently to be achieved by means other than spiritual and peaceful and the purity of the faith maintained by drastic measures. Under these conditions, the relation between the religions of the Old and New Testaments and the people confessing the creeds—the Jews and the European nations as the first predominantly Christian people—is one of strange contingency. This must be so for this reason. According to Jewish and Christian teaching, religious truth has not been discovered,

300

still less created by man. It had to be revealed to him by divine will, and this not even by immediate inculcation into the soul, but through the intermediary of Moses, the prophets and the Saviour. Religion, therefore, had to be offered to and imposed upon man as a prepared and perfectly shaped treasure to be received, believed and assimilated.

But our interest is not to raise theological issues. Rather it is exclusively to present the psychological experience involved in the Jewish and Christian doctrines with all the implications which this experience contained for further historical development. Of the twofold contingency—that of all peoples the Hebrews and the Europeans were chosen to adopt and to proclaim the true creeds, and that the new religions did not originate immediately in the minds of man but were laid upon man through God-sent messengers, the first may be considered the more important for our arguments. And the creed retained a life of its own above and aloof from man—a phenomenon incidentally which is entirely foreign to Asiatic religions. So it is that, logically, sacred history is more—it is essentially a history of the creed rather than a history of men. In the Old Testament it is the history of God's intentions toward Israel, His revelations, His acts and His reactions to the behaviour of the Hebrews. In the sacred history of the Church the fundamental partition of history into the periods before and after Christ, the theological evolution and establishment of the faith and its fate on earth are obviously the main subjects.

With civilization substituting itself for religion, religion became one of the constituents of civilization. And though the conception of religion as a mere expression of a civilization on terms equal with the other aspects may not be found at the beginning of the new period, yet religion is no longer considered contingent— that is, imposed in the sense mentioned above—but a natural element of civilization. While no inner connection existed before between the chosen people and the religion for which they had been chosen because no particular qualifications could be held liable for the choice, such a scission seemed no longer admissible. It became evident that the link between a people and its either adopted or invented religion must be of the same nature as that existing between this people and its form of government or its art. Man became one with his civilization and the history of civilization became the history of mankind.

Vico's philosophy presents this secular aspect. For, to him Providence is nothing but what is later called the laws of the historical process, and indeed has exactly the same meaning and function. This view is in perfect agreement with Vico's assertion that man can understand only what he creates. The basic idea and experience of the new period could have found no more sublime expression than this conception. In its form, seemingly so akin to the philosophy of pragmatism, it differs from it just as deeply as in Greek philosophy, *prattein*, the practical doing with a useful aim, is distinguished from *poiein*, the mind's disinterested creative act. Man, an autonomous dynamic being, creates *civiltá*. Then civilization's various fields are but the façades of an indivisible whole which the individual personality must continuously realize in himself. To look at them as separate provinces is a later and artificial distinction. It is a dangerous deviation, equally distant from the original act and from the ideal to be attained.

In keeping with this view, Vico's philosophy of history embraces mankind in its entirety as the creator of civilization. No branch of the human family, however low its actual level, is deemed incapable of active cultural progress, provided it be left to its natural development. In the idea of an unconditioned unity and homogeneity of mankind, the new era and its philosophy of history proves to be the heir of the religious period. The eschatological hope of the final conversion of all men corresponds to the conviction that as his own saviour, man will through the process of civilization reach ultimate perfection. It is most remarkable that this same hopeful idea of man and his destination—the most hopeful yet conceived and to be fulfilled even against a pessimistically interpreted past—is the core of the ahistorical philosophy of Enlightenment, where a commonsense rationalism makes universal perfection depend upon an act of reason. By means of it, man is reinstated in his original state of plain reason and moral integrity which has been suppressed by the succession of corrupt social and political institutions.

The philosophy of progress characteristic of the last century derives from the blending of the evolutionary philosophy of history and the philosophy of Enlightenment. Its basic idea which has been formulated again and again has served to glorify technological progress and to justify the colonial policy of the great powers. All members of the human family—such is the idea—are capable of and are entitled to progress, though not all of them have been granted the enlightenment to achieve the way by their own resources. To these—not only the primitives, but also the Oriental peoples who are still far back on the path of progress— the West must lend a helping hand. It must lead them on the path of technical and cultural development of which the West is the inventor and guardian. This is the philosophy of the white man's burden, as Kipling called it—a strange compound of genuine idealistic responsibility, blindness and hypocrisy, with a strong dose of will-to-power as the basic component.

Henceforth, the philosophy of history underwent the influence of scientific and political currents which undermined the intuition of mankind as one in endowment and fate. In the first place the impact of rapidly increasing anthropological and ethnological knowledge demanded a philosophy of history more consistent with the new realities. The grotesque idea wherein at its peak the philosophy of Enlightenment had pictured man's natural state as one of innocence and perfection, and had glorified it as the paragon to be held out to a misguided civilization, was succeeded by a new social philosophy which set up an idealized picture of the masses against the condemnable aspect of the ruling classes. Also, the description given by explorers of primitive tribes as pure savages was gradually replaced by a more adequate evaluation based upon painstaking investigation. As unprejudiced study revealed in primitive society most complex institutions and highly significant religious beliefs, both of which could be proved to have influenced the life of humanity up to our own days, the remoteness of the primitives to our feeling disappeared and even turned into familiarity based upon comprehension. However, an indisputable fact remained and no fair appreciation could obliterate it. This was that there existed widespread human groups which to all appearance lacked the natural endowment for development and progress.

The Crucial Problem of Philosophy of History

A similar change occurred in the West's attitude toward an evaluation of the Asiatic civilizations yet with characteristic distinction. The conception of the unconditioned unity and homogeneity of mankind which the men of the Renaissance and above all Vico, inherited from the Middle Ages and which Vico introduced as the condition of his philosophy of history, could not admit basic differences between civilizations. The civilizations of Asia might well impress the West as strange and eccentric. But this impression related to one aspect only and the idea could not take root that it might conceal a fundamentally different kind of mind. This is clearly illustrated by the ready, and sometimes almost naïve, assumption of the homogeneity of Asiatic civilizations, particularly the Chinese and Persian, with the Western, and the recognition of their superiority in the seventeenth and eighteenth centuries. An increasing knowledge and analysis of Asiatic civilizations and a deeper comprehension of the Asiatic mind have, however, suggested the idea that the civilizations of Asia constituted a separate type of civilization, whose comparison with the West could only result in throwing the cleavage between East and West into clear relief.

In the nineteenth century the philosophy of history from Hegel to Spengler mirrors this tendency. In order fully to understand this rapid change of attitude toward the Orient and the changing evaluation of the Orient, one must not look exclusively at the intellectual process. The power which science and its appreciation granted to the West and the tremendous impulse with which the theory of evolution impregnated experience as well as the humanities, all concurred to inspire the West with a self-confidence which tolerated no rival. From the new pedestal, Oriental civilizations suddenly appeared backward and stagnant. And while in special fields, such as philosophy and art, the former appreciation was preserved and even increased, the civilization of the Orient as a whole was relegated to second place.

Equally noteworthy is it that this nineteenth century viewpoint is now undergoing a process of revision. Again, this is due not only to wider knowledge and deeper insight which tend to discover the ultimate common stratum behind the unquestionable and profound distinction, but also to a doubt of our own god-likeness.

304

Undermining the somewhat presumptuous position taken by our fathers, this opens the door to a new conception. With regard to Oriental civilizations, the attitude of the West leads, therefore, from a familiarity at once natural and naïve to separation and estrangement based upon enlarged knowledge. And from there it leads, it would seem, to a deeper intellectual and emotional nearness and affinity.

* * *

Once the idea of the unity and homogeneity of mankind was disrupted by acquaintance with the primitive peoples and the penetration of Oriental civilization, the European mind became increasingly responsive to the characteristics and distinctions of civilizations and peoples. Since the turn of the nineteenth century when the physiognomies of the Western nations were set off against each other with ever increasing clarity, the interest in the Oriental civilizations intensified and the perception of their peculiar features was sharpened. While this evolution opened up new horizons of knowledge and enriched the insight into the potentialities of man, it threatened to rend the ties which had so far held the branches of humanity together. Confusedly dispersed in space and time, one doomed to a state of unchangeable primitiveness, another definitely halted without any indication of further movement, still others having descended from a previous state of higher development and lingering on in degeneration, while a few privileged ones seemed on the way to permanent progress, human history disclosed a picture of hopeless anarchy which defied any attempt of philosophy of history to penetrate its meaning. Light came from the philosophy of nature—the forerunner of biological science—which in introducing the idea of organism had proved so creative in the philosophy of the Romantic period.

The backbone of Hegel's philosophy of history is the Aristotelian idea of entelechy. Leaving to one side all metaphysical implications and taking into account only the structure of his idea of mankind, as opposed to that held by the preceding philosophy of history, the form in which the history of mankind presents itself to Hegel is that of a living organism. Before this change humanity resembled a family whose variously aged members were all certain to arrive at maturity, passing through the same stages of development. Compared to this process, individual differences were of no avail. Even in the ahistoric view of Enlightenment philosophy, all people without exception would find the way of retrogressive movement from the corrupted conditions of the present time back to the natural state. In these philosophies the unity and homogeneity of mankind is taken seriously in a simple and absolute form. The essence of mankind realizes itself equally in all the groups of which it is composed. And what distinguishes the one from the other concerns but aspects of minor importance. In the new philosophy of history the unity of mankind is preserved. But it is the complex unit of the organism. So is the homogeneity of the branches, but with this momentous determination. Homogeneity refers only to their being parts of one and the same organism and to their functioning within and for the realization of the whole. For the rest each leads its own life.

Indeed, beginning with the Chinese, in Hegel's philosophy of history each civilized people has its determined place in the process of the self-realization of the Absolute which is history. Also, it represents another and higher stage of self-consciousness in the progressing consciousness of freedom, which is the meaning of history. In this process which is directed by the laws of dialectics, a definite place and function is assigned to each civilization. Thus, no one civilization resembles the other, although all are necessary to realize the Absolute. What we call the individuality of a civilization is nothing but the self-expression of the Absolute at a well-defined station on the road to perfect realization. Thus, since each civilization is unique in character and function, civilizations are not fungible, in strict opposition to the preceding philosophy of history, where they were theoretically exchangeable. Hegel's history of mankind is a unique process which is non-recurrent either as a whole or in part, and it derives clearly from the nature of mankind as a great spiritual organism.

Indeed, the role and idea of time in Hegel's philosophy of history is entirely disparate from that of his predecessors. With them, mankind as a whole evolves in the same way either simultaneously or in its different branches at different times. Time is but the general frame, the extraneous and formal possibility of evolution—the time of mathematics and physics. In the Hegelian philosophy of history this abstract time has no place and meaning. Just as every living organism has its own time which is not measured by standard time but depends upon its own law of growth, so in Hegel's system the evolution of the dialectical historical process is the reality which is its own measure. And its time is concrete time.

This same reasoning holds good for space. To Vico and others the place where human groups and civilizations spring up is of no importance. Space is but the mere possibility of existence. In Hegel's philosophy space is concrete space. It is nothing apart from its function of providing the possibility of meaningful situations. This means that the rank of a civilization in the universal scale is indicated by its geographical location. Beginning with the Chinese, the process of civilization as it rises higher and higher proceeds from East to West, calling upon one people after another—the Indians, the Persians, the Semitic peoples, the Greeks, the Romans, the peoples of later Europe—to fulfil their predestined functions. Space and time are concrete and significant, and so history is teleological, not causal. Never have the unity and the variety of mankind been so thoroughly safeguarded and so intrinsically conciliated. Never has the significance and goal of history been raised to such height. But in order to support the construction, his philosophy of history needed the basis of a metaphysical system. However, after Hegel's death, this metaphysical foundation inevitably discarded the common denominator of universal history—that of the process of the self-comprehension of the Absolute Spirit. With this disappearance the tie which bound the various civilizations in one great evolution was torn. In the resulting state of disintegration the elementary problem of philosophy of history came to the foreground.

In identifying as subjects of the philosophy of history the politically united peoples, Hegel had followed the example of the historians since Herodotus. This does not mean that he shared the *naïveté*, which had induced them to accept at face value the politically united peoples as such as the true subject of history. To Hegel the state was the 'moral totality'—'the reality wherein the individual has and enjoys his freedom, but only and in as far as it is the knowledge of the faith in and the assertion of the universal.' The form—and more precisely the idea of the state—expresses more clearly than any other aspect of civilization in his opinion the place a people occupies in the evolution of mankind. And this was the reason why he acknowledged the political boundaries all too uncritically, as coinciding with the distinctive units of civilization.

When he endorsed as fundamental the fact that mankind is broken up into a number of different parts, Hegel proved more realistic than the centuries before him. In assigning to each of these parts a definite role in the evolution of civilizations, he created a philosophical view of human history. And when he considered the political forms of peoples' existence to be the most marked expressions of the stage attained, he found himself in harmony with his time, which liked to measure the degree of civilization by the test of the form of government. Hegel's evaluation of the state, however, which comes near to an apotheosis, concealed a twofold danger. This danger exists much less in his system than in the nineteenth century's intellectual evolution. It consists in detaching from the whole of civilization a single part. This is then raised to so exalted a position as to become detrimental not only to the other components of civilization, but to the civilization itself. A few decades after Hegel this happened in imitation of his method—the so-called materialistic philosophy of history—the idealized economy. It happens today with the idealization of science and technology.

But what is more important for our argument than this phenomenon of the disestablishment of the components of civilization, is the growing uncertainty with regard to the determination of the true subjects of civilization. Undivided mankind or mankind evolving on equal terms in all its branches having been dismissed, Hegel conceived as the subjects of the process of civilization the politically united peoples—the states. This assignment is far from being arbitrary. With logical necessity it is regulated by his metaphysical system. Then with the disappearance of the metaphysical foundation, not only did the evaluation of the various stages of civilization lose its criterion, even the very subjects of philosophy of history became uncertain. This uncertainty was implicitly prepared by Hegel's philosophy itself.

He distinguishes clearly between Chinese and Indians and Persians, analysing their individual national personalities, but treats Syria and the Semitic East and Judaea and Egypt as components of the Persian empire because these countries were for some time parts of Persia. All these countries and civilizations are comprehended under the common title The Oriental World, to which is attributed a specific form of consciousness embracing individual variations. The Oriental World which is the prior condition of the Western world is recognized as a world of its own. It is followed by the Greek World, which though never politically united is yet considered as one. And it is found that in the disparate statehoods of Athens and Sparta the same democratic idea—in a deeper sense, of course, than the usual meaning of the term—is realized. It is only in accordance with Hegel's philosophy that in preference to the sometimes inadequate political boundaries the idea determines empirical reality because 'only in the changes which happen on the soil of the spirit the new comes forth.' The Roman world comprises West-Rome and the Byzantine empire. The post-Roman Western world is named the Christian-Germanic world, both because of the predominance of the Germanic element in the Holy Roman Empire, and because 'the Reformation restores for the first time to the Christian principle its verity and reality.'

If the coincidence of civilization and state, though upheld in principle, is thus allowed elastic interpretation in its application, this lack of precision cannot affect the structure of Hegel's philosophy of history. The reason is that individual politically united peoples, associations between them and finally the various worlds they constitute, represent the well-defined stages through which the absolute spirit arrives at complete self-comprehension. With Hegel, the philosophy of history reached its summit. He gave life and colour to history by throwing into clear relief the personalities of peoples and their civilizations. Also, he established a necessary and demonstrable connection between them as links in a great evolutionary process. This process he filled with supreme metaphysical significance. And so he exalted history as he exalted man himself. His legacy, distorted and emasculated, long influenced historians and sociologists.[1]

* * *

The decline of the philosophy of history is marked by three great names—Gobineau, Nietzsche and Spengler. This statement is paradoxical only in appearance. For while each of these three thinkers still moves within the circle of philosophy of history, in his own original way he undermines by his negative view of history its very foundation. This stands in contradiction to the unparalleled efflorescence of historical science which started with the nineteenth century. True it is that the speculative and systematic spirit in philosophy faded at the same time, and the decline of the philosophy of history itself is one of the symptoms. However, another cause of a more technical, though by no means only technical character exists to explain this decline. This has already been mentioned—the uncertainty as to the determination of the units which the philosophy of history has to recognize as the proper subjects for its constructions, an uncertainty destined to arise the moment Hegel's metaphysics ceased to be the criterion of discernment. The rapidly increasing knowledge of the European and extra-European civilizations doomed as impossible any attempt to bind civilizations to political boundaries, and least of all to confine them within the hardening prison walls of the national states. Again, this same deepening of the insight into the variety of civilizations barred the return to the whole of mankind as the real subject of philosophy of history. Against this general background, and determined by the biological interest and the nationalistic trend of his time, Gobineau's idea must be understood. This was to find in the race the subject of philosophy of history.

[1] Auguste Comte's positivistic philosophy, with its three stages—the theological, the metaphysical, the positive—through which society has to pass, reminds us in its structure of Vico's theory. Likewise it is influenced by Hegel and Victor Cousin, while the meaning and aim of the historical process shows Comte the child of Enlightenment. Herbert Spencer's system is not a philosophy of history, but the mere application of the principles of biological evolution to history. It belongs definitely more to sociology than to philosophy of history. Thomas Buckle's great attempt to discover the natural laws which regulate the history of peoples and to found these laws mainly on statistical data, is equally outside the frame of philosophy of history.

Race creates civilizations and so to each race a peculiar civilization is co-ordinated. Thus did Gobineau reason. The highest civilization belongs to the white race, of which the noblest representative is the Germanic family. Indeed, for him, the civilizations of the other races owe what is really great in them to the impact of the white race. With this view of history, the unity and homogeneity of mankind is disrupted. If Hegel too held that the summit of civilization was reached by the Germanic world, yet the other members of the human family occupied their dignified places in the evolutionary process. Gobineau proclaims the monopoly of the white race. In his essay on *The Inequality of the Human Races* there is no history in the philosophical sense. His history lacks meaning and aim and sinks to mere succession. Accordingly he presents a comparative picture of race-civilizations. And the only reason why his great intuitive view of history must be classified as a philosophy of history lies in the fact that he introduces a new subject—the race as the determinant of civilization—and maintains the category of value. In his view, both of these are constituents of the philosophy of history.

For the idea of the monopolizing role of a privileged and limited group, Friedrich Nietzsche carries off the prize. His conception is that the only goal of history is, or should be, the production of the genius—the superman. This amounts to the devaluation of history as well as of civilization, for the superman, whatever be Nietzsche's definition of him, places himself above and outside the march of history. With this view, Nietzsche's philosophy of history wilfully abandons the frame of a theoretical view and introduces an activistic element. The creation of the superman apparently is not in the line of predestined historical evolution. It needs for its realization the determined effort of enlightened minds.

However, the most ingenious dispossession of the philosophy of history, and the most effective because it springs from superior knowledge and transcendent interpretive ability, is to be found in the work of Oswald Spengler. In his theory, where the various civilizations originating like plants in their predetermined soils are secluded in themselves and inaccessible to each other's comprehension, there is no historical continuity. Nor does the mutual impenetrability of civilizations admit of comparative evaluation and gradation. This grandiose and tragic view of haphazardly rising and falling civilizations, essentially unconcerned with, because fundamentally foreign to each other, pronounces a death sentence on the philosophy of history. History there is and genuine history. Yet there is not one history but as many as there are great civilizations, each following the same stages of youth, efflorescence and decay. They are then histories of civilizations but there is no universal history of civilization. Hence, mankind becomes an empty word covering but surface and appearance. The unity and homogeneity of mankind sink to mere biological significance. Indeed, one corollary of Spengler's philosophy, one which he himself did not announce, is that man, though one as biological species, evolves into fundamentally disparate groups upon reaching the level of high civilization.

With Spengler's negativistic philosophy of history—in every respect the opposite of Hegel's system yet its equal in the grandeur of the conception—the philosophy of history has for the present time come to an end. The relevant reason, conspicuous enough in Spengler's philosophy, lies in the growing uncertainty of Western man about himself. For during the last hundred years of Western history, a deep revulsion has been shaking to its foundations man's idea and evaluation of himself.

The biological theory of evolution deprived man of his prerogatives by providing scientific arguments for his wholesale classification in the line of organic life. However, the degradation implied by this absorption was obliterated, both by the proud satisfaction caused by the unswerving march of scientific knowledge, and by the accrued power which science showered upon man. And yet the faith in his own dignity and his conviction of the meaning of life began to fade in direct ratio to man's domination of nature. True, natural science, indifferent as it is to the destruction of the traditional experience of man, pursued its advance. But speculative philosophy and the philosophy of history were doomed. They could not absorb the new conceptions of man. Dependent upon a clear and autonomous idea of man, the philosophy of history was not strong enough to stand up against the mind of a period whose prerequisites included the denial of the intellectual and spiritual prerogatives of man. This lack of a specific philosophical idea of man deprived the philosophy of history of the possibility of finding the peculiar subjects for its constructions.

For the same reason, the other constituent concept of the philosophy of history lost its specific meaning. The concept of evolution in the philosophy of history has the general significance of a directed movement which may assume various forms—the usual meaning from below to above, and the reverse, from above to below, the meaning apparent in the neo-Platonic and the Manichaean views of the cosmic and terrestrian process; the cyclic, represented in the Indian idea of the kalpas, the world periods which repeat themselves *in infinitum;* not to mention the mixed forms, as the Christian, where the downward evolution from the paradisiac state to that of sin is matched by the reverse trend, starting with the incarnation of Christ and ending with his final reappearance. The idea of evolution, detaching itself from the philosophy of history, was almost entirely monopolized by biology. Thus did the pattern of evolution based upon the principle of the survival of the fittest penetrate everywhere far beyond the biological field. As to the general cultural trend, the nineteenth century marched under the motto of progress. However, this progress-mania did not stem from a spontaneous and creative philosophy. It was merely a naïve reaction to the rapid increase of political power and expansion as well as of material welfare. This is much too thin and treacherous a basis for more than a purely emotional experience. By the end of the nineteenth century, the recognition of the futility and emptiness of the progress-ideology had already become obvious and had produced the necessary counter-reaction of disorientation and pessimism.

If it be the function of the philosophy of history to illumine man's appearance on earth with a significance that history itself is unable to confirm, man and his history must be raised from the great stream of the evolution of organic life. This stream is endless, we know not where and how it began or whither it will lead. It is void of meaning and we cannot even scientifically speak of an evolution which rises from the lower to the higher because higher carries the connotation of value with which natural science is unconcerned. And so the only testable and legitimate statement is that of an evolution from the simple to the more complex. But the philosophy of history is incompatible with an endless evolution because significance itself is limitation. The ideology which, with better reason, is called the dream of unlimited progress, is the poor bastard of organic evolution and philosophy of history. It inherits from the first the endlessness, in complete ignorance of the when and whither. From the second, it derives the idea of value, but without any definable and appropriate object to which it could attach.

Only the philosophy of history knows the genuine evolution which is peculiar to man and his history. This evolution differs from that of organic life in that what evolves and where it goes, that is to say the subject and the goal of evolution, is known. In organic evolution there is but life—an unknown magnitude, with its unknown goal. But the evolution in philosophy of history is a real unfolding of a subject—the realization of an entelechy. Thus the philosophy of progress—whether or no its advocates deceive themselves by avoiding any attempt to define one or more specific fields where progress is realized—remains a dream in the first case and denies itself in the second. Due to the lack of an evolutionary philosophy of history and to the bankruptcy of the illusion of progress, our time is marked by the uncertainty about the way of civilization. This culminates in the non-resisting and almost desperate indifference with which man surrenders to the idea of his purely animal nature and to the loss of faith in himself.

Against this background, the spirit and atmosphere of Spengler's philosophy stands clear. The great civilizations spring up at random, one after or beside the other. They look at each other with eyes that see but cannot comprehend. Each speaks its own language which is heard but not understood. And over all is the perspective of the West rushing into its inescapable fate of mass existence and serfdom. This philosophy of history turns against all the prerequisites and conclusions of everything so far known as such. It is meant to be the last word and the end of the philosophy of history—its doom, not only its necrology. There are subjects in his philosophy of history. Yet they exist for the last time, and only to demonstrate that the philosophy of history can do nothing but prove that they must be left each to itself and that no relation can be established between them. Under these circumstances, any attempt to revive the philosophy of history will have to start with a fundamental problem. It must investigate whether a new and secure way can be discovered to determine its subjects.

The problem of the subjects in the philosophy of history is strictly parallel to the problem of the species in biology though each starts from an opposite assumption. Biology, substituting the theory of evolution for the traditional belief in the separate creation of all organic species which was maintained by Cuvier, faced the task of isolating the species from the one stream of unfolding organic life besides explaining their origin. In contrast, the modern philosophy of history found itself in opposition to the idea of one and the same civilization and its homogeneous evolution. Yet, in introducing the view of various and different civilizations it had to solve the same problem as biology. For it had to determine which characteristics entitle a civilization to recognition as an authentic civilization in its own right.

So far, the philosophy of history has been speculative. Indeed, it always must be since the question of the evolution of civilization and of its meaning transcends scientific investigation. This being so, the problem of the subject in the philosophy of history has never been raised explicitly as an independent problem because the speculative systems contained the solution in themselves as one of their major elements. The answer, as it were, was given before the question arose. But this need not be so, and, it may be said, it should not even remain so. The problem of the subjects in the philosophy of history must be approached both empirically and philosophically. And the results of this effort, far from impairing the right and power of speculation, will provide a new and sound basis for its interpretation.

* * *

The evolution of the philosophy of history has thus reached this point. Any future theory, before starting off with its constructive work, will have to determine explicitly what it considers its subjects to be. In order to discover and delimitate such subjects a divining-rod is needed. This infallible criterion—*principium individuationis*—decides whether a civilization presenting an individual aspect is but a mere variety of another civilization or for that matter a composite of more than one or whether it has a claim to be admitted as an authentic and original one. The views implied in the three great philosophies of history of the nineteenth century with regard to the problem of this criterion are significative and ominous.

In Hegel's theory, statehood remains the predominant criterion. However, closer examination will show that it cannot be considered a reliable criterion in the strict sense of the term, and this for two reasons. First, the criterion is of a metaphysical character. It resides in the necessary place a civilization occupies in the evolution of the absolute mind. And of this place and rank, the statehood of the respective peoples is but the expression, though, according to Hegel, the most characteristic. Second, statehood is itself a component, among many others, of civilization and therefore unfit to serve as a criterion. As a matter of fact, the logical function of statehood in Hegel's philosophy is that of a *ratio cognoscendi*—that of a sign or symptom, but not that of a *ratio essendi*—that of an ontological datum. Statehood is only indicative of where an authentic civilization may be found. And even in this function it is by no means infallible.

The innermost meaning of Gobineau's binding together of race and civilization, for our problem, is this. He recognizes the impossibility of isolating one element from the whole of civilization so as to make of it the distinctive characteristic of civilization. So he withdraws, so to speak, from civilization as the creation of the mind and finds his criterion in the anthropological factor— the race. Then, theoretically, there are as many civilizations as there are races. But irrespective of the ambiguity of the race concept, it is particularly difficult to acknowledge the race as the criterion for the significant reason that the connection between civilization and race remains purely factual and contingent and so must lack evidence. Therefore, it is quite consistent that Spengler, just as if he wanted to turn resolutely away from the unsatisfactory solutions of his predecessors, presents his ingenious descriptions of civilizations, leaving it to them to plead their cause in defense of their authenticity and originality.

Indeed, the great insight of Spengler is to have vindicated the claim of civilizations to be self-sufficient and autonomous creations of the mind. For his statement that the great civilizations originate in certain definite geographical areas means no more than their localization in space, since the geographical situation does not claim either to condition or explain the civilizations. But from the viewpoint of the theory of philosophy of history, there is this deficiency in Spengler's philosophy. No attempt is made to determine the criterion of the civilizations presented as genuine species. Apparently, the assumption is that their analysis and description carry sufficient weight to establish their individual and incomparable souls. Even so, the scientific demand for a first principle could not be dismissed.

The march of philosophy of history itself points clearly to where this criterion may be found. If neither factors extraneous to civilization such as race, nor empirical elements isolated from the whole of civilization such as statehood, reveal the basic differences between civilizations, one way only seems to be left open. This is to find this criterion in the ground plan—the structure of civilizations—provided that such structures can be demonstrated to exist. If they do, their relation to the concrete aspect of civilizations may be compared to that of the ground plan of a building to the building itself. And just as a description of a great architectural work, colourful and complete as it may be, would not reveal its structure, so the key to the comprehension of a civilization is lacking if its description is without the knowledge of its structure. But before taking up this fundamental problem, there is still another line in the evolution of philosophy of history to be followed.

There is an unmistakable trend toward an ever more decisive evaluation of the great civilizations as autonomous creations of the mind. Quite consistently this insight finds its expression in an increasingly consummate characterization of the civilizations which are considered the subjects of the philosophy of history. Moreover, this progress in characterization is not only one of degree. It is also a change in the intuition of the nature of the great civilizations. The way leads from description to typification. For this momentous advance the widening of the knowledge of foreign civilizations as well as of our own, was not the cause. It only offered the take-off as it were, from which the intuitive act could rise to the cognizance of great civilizations as autonomous types of human fulfilment, just as with individuals the characterization of peoples starts with emphasizing a few salient features, qualities and attitudes. And albeit these are sufficient for identifying the subject and indicating the manner of approaching and the way of dealing with it, they are a long way from evoking the idea of the personality. No mere description, as this kind of characterization may be called, be it ever so striking, ever coalesces into a consummate picture of the individual or collective personality.

Such an impression can be achieved only by grasping the personal centre—the common denominator of an individual personality or a great civilization which permeates all the parts, and by making it visible in all aspects and expressions, acts and creations. Even Hegel's characterizations, particularly those of Asiatic civilizations, astounding as they are in view of the limited knowledge of his time, never transcended the level of description. For Hegel, however, the importance of civilizations to which their characterization had reference, inhered in what they signified in the metaphysical evolution of the consciousness of the Absolute. This was demonstrated by the place each of them held in the process. Besides, it must not be forgotten that in a true evolution any stage is illustrated by the stages that precede and follow. In philosophy of history, Gobineau was the first to recognize and delineate a great civilization as a quasi super-individual personality in the picture which he drew of the civilization of the white race. Spengler developed this method to virtuosity as much by the lucidity with which he envisioned the souls of civilizations as by the artistic precision with which he expounded the realizations of each civilization as emanating from the same unique life centre.

This new mode of typification must be appreciated to its full value, regardless of whether the characterizations as such or even the types isolated, are approved. For instance, it may be maintained with good reason that Gobineau's picture of white civilization is to a high degree the product of idealization, or that Spengler's tearing apart of what we consider Western civilization into two fundamentally different types, the classic and the Faustian, is not based on cogent argument. It may be objected, in other words, that both have not seen real existing types. But even if this be true, it cannot be denied that they have really seen types. And this fact—that a new and constructive idea had been introduced into the philosophy of history—is the only one that matters in these considerations.

From our specific though fundamental angle—the necessity of determining the units of philosophy of history by structures— Arnold J. Toynbee's great conception of history does not advance the solution of this crucial problem. True, his basic view that 'the intelligible units of historical study are not nations or periods but societies'—and of course civilized societies as opposed to primitive—accords with our argument. However, the determination of these units which are the true subjects of philosophy of history, remains precarious. The criterion which he offers—that a civilization is the whole without which the history of an individual country cannot be understood—is too flexible to delimit the ultimate units and to throw into clear relief their personalities. This becomes obvious when the term affiliation is used to designate the relation of Christian or Western civilization, and for that matter of Orthodox civilization, to Hellenic civilization. For this term inclines more to veil the difficulty than to solve the problem whether or not, or in what respect Western civilization includes the Hellenic.

The rise of great civilizations and the recognition of their essence are of the same importance in the history of the mind as is that of the individual personality. Both emerge out of lower strata which, though of fundamental importance, are inferior in value. Both mark decisive steps in the enfranchisement of the human mind. Obviously it is the great civilizations—the types of civilization—which constitute the pre-eminent subjects of philosophy of history. But while we may be confident that the great civilizations present themselves as types, there is still uncertainty as regards the distinctive marks of those civilizations which may be considered as types. The criterion which controls this discrimination must differ in character from those others which are the result of description and typification. To be able to determine which civilizations are entitled to the claim of being authentic types and thereby the subjects of the philosophy of history, the criterion must rise above what it is called to judge. It must be of a formal character. It must, therefore, reside in the architectural plan, in the structure of the civilizations, not in their content. Thus, wherever an architectural plan, a structure, can be found, and when it can be expressed in a clear formula and be demonstrated to permeate the concrete realizations of a civilization, then and then only may we be certain of facing a great civilization. This is an authentic type and a true subject of philosophy of history.

The way philosophy of history conceives its subjects—those entities of civilization it considers the constituents of philosophically interpreted history—leads from description to typification and from there to the cognition of the architectural structure. This scale signifies an increasing clarity of the civilizations, a burgeoning of their person-like unity, and above all the certainty as to which civilizations may be selected as the subjects of philosophy of history. At the same time, the independence of these civilizations and their nature as self-sufficient entities becomes evident. They are to be understood by their own structures and principles without recurring to data outside themselves. This does not mean that physical, anthropological and other influences do not contribute to their genesis. What it does mean is that all these influences put together are unable to explain the phenomenon of the civilization. Instead of trying to enforce pseudo explanations, the only way to come to a real comprehension is from within. This evolution is reflected by the gradually loosening links which tie the civilizations to conditions extraneous to them. At the end of the line, Spengler binds his souls of civilization to definite areas, but not as the products of either geographical or for that matter anthropological factors. True, his civilizations are immovable, incommunicable and not transferable, yet this limitation depends upon the nature of civilizations which in his eyes are unique, monad-like entities. They are closed systems existing independently of outside factors.

This review of the philosophy of history's changing concepts of the unity and homogeneity of mankind reveals that it passed

The Crucial Problem of Philosophy of History

from one of unreserved assertion to one of indifference and eventually of negation. The idea of the unity and homogeneity of mankind which Vico inherited from sacred history is as a principle still maintained by Hegel, since in his history of civilization the evolution of the human mind is the process of the self-comprehension of the absolute Spirit. But this unity and homogeneity is infringed upon by his conception of a hierarchy of civilizations in which each is assigned a definite place, function and value which it cannot transgress in order to reach a higher level. With the organic structure of Hegel's philosophical system gone, nothing is left to prevail against the recognition of the inherent differences in nature and value among peoples and their civilizations. Gobineau proclaimed this theory in its most drastic form by elevating one race and civilization to an almost monopolistic place. The idea of evolution which had been the backbone of the philosophy of history was therewith discarded. The vertical view of history was superseded by another, the horizontal. And this view, neglecting evolution and abstracting from time, looked down at civilizations as it were from above, interested only in the examination of their respective resemblances and differences. This is the standpoint from which Spengler in a spirit of perfect equanimity adjudges the history of civilizations. And so the philosophy of history is transformed into the science of comparative civilization.

This transformation must not signify that the philosophy of history has abdicated its role in man's effort to penetrate the mystery of his existence on earth. Indeed, it may have just the opposite meaning. For it may be said that the philosophy of history has come to recognize the need for broader and more solid foundations, in keeping with the extension of our knowledge and with the new problems which have arisen by the meeting and melting of civilizations. True, the philosophy of history will always have to be speculative. But the basis from which it takes off for its flight into the realm of speculative ideas must be made as strong and substantial as the implements of the day permit. To build the new basis is the task of the science of comparative civilization. Its work will have to begin with the problem of determining the true subjects of the philosophy of history. For this is the fundamental problem which emerges from its crisis.

x   321   H.D.M.

The Crucial Problem of Philosophy of History

From this angle, the ideas contained in this book are the logical outcome of the unfolding of the philosophy of history. The subjects of the philosophy of history have been determined anew. This has not meant a necessarily precarious description in reliance upon more or less arbitrary definitions of geographical, racial, political and cultural homogeneousness and affinities. Rather has it been based on the solid ground of demonstrable structures. Thus on the one hand, the comparative civilization of West and East has been presented with a secure orientation. On the other, the philosophy of history may recognize the possibility of a new start from new foundations.

Index

323

Index

139, 144, 170, 182-3, 191-2, 208, 259, 289; *see* caste system
individual, 47-8, 53-4, 125, 190, 192, 279, 293
influences, magic, 102, 105-8
inspiration, 122
instinct: 63, 96; Eastern attitude to, 64, 68-9, 75-7, 81, 82, 86-8, 199, 200-5, 214, 216, 219, 249-57, 267; Western attitude to, 64-6, 78, 79, 82, 201, 266; *see* subconscious
Iran; *see* Persia
Islam, 39, 145, 278
Israel, 53-4, 288-9, 291-3, 300-1

James, William, 238
Japan, 36-7, 61, 94, 205-7
Jeans, Sir James, *Physics and Philosophy*, 105 n. 2
Jenghiz Khan, 59-60
Jordanus Teutonicus, Chronicle of, 18 n. 1
Judaeism; *see* Israel
Jung, 111

Kang Yu-wei, 71
Kant, 41 n. 1, 124, 147, 151, 176, 253
Kautilya, 86
knowledge: Eastern conceptions of, 132, 137-8, 160-5, 171, 182, 193, 226, 231, 237; magic and modern conceptions of, 104-6, 129; Western conceptions of, 137-8, 146, 147, 160, 167, 171, 178, 179, 182, 193, 238, 271; *see* science

landscape gardening, 206
Laver, James, *Style in Costume*, 212 n. 1
law, Roman, 27
Leibniz, 147, 151
life, source of, 214-15
Lin Yu-tang, 71
logos; see reason
loneliness, in Yoga, 222, 232-3
love, 190-2

McEwan, Calvin W., *The Oriental Origin of Hellenistic Kingship*, 90 n. 2

magic, 91, 94, 96-112, 114, 116, 122, 159-61, 195-6, 209, 254-5; *see* myths
man: in magic world, 109-12; relation to institutions, 88, 89; supreme position, 53, 137, 289-90; unity of 287-91, 293, 302, 304-6, 312. *see* individual
Manichaeism, 82m, 280
materialism, 114-15
mathematics, 143, 147, 150-1, 176, 201, 203, 267-9
matter, 141-3, 146, 147, 157
Mazdak, 67, 83, 167
merchants, 74-5
Mesopotamia, 98
military class, 74-5
mind: object of its own activity, 153-4, 179-80, 266, 271, 272; place in history, 296; *see* thought
Mommsen, *Roman History*, 25
monarchy, 64, 66, 84-6, 88-95, 183-4, 195-6
Mukerji, Dhan S., *Caste and Outcaste*, 207
music, 267-9
mysticism, 152, 189
myths, 128-9, *see* magic

nature: Eastern view of, 69, 144, 205-210, 234-5, 247-9, 251, 256-7; influence on history, 305; Western view of, 30-1, 128, 153-4, 207-8, 210-11, 213, 245, 271-2, 295-6; *see* instinct, science
Near East, 53-4, 90-1, 98, 121, 273-4
necessity, 252-3
Newton, 40
Nietzsche, 310, 311

object: Eastern view of, 113-14, 116, 119, 130, 181, 185, 214, 232-3; magic and modern views of, 104-6, 109, 111-12; of consciousness, 167, 172, 186, 193, 277; objectivation of phenomena, 128, 131, 148-9, 152-5, 157-8, 170, 177-80, 207-13, 232, 245-6, 279; pivot of Western thought, 113-15, 119-20, 125, 129, 261; relation with observer, 176, 178, 201, 239; *see* materialism, subject
opposites, 55-6, 141-5, 149-51, 210, 296

325

Index

painting, 206
Paracelsus, 98, 102
Parmenides, 126–8, 146, 154, 180
patriarchy; *see* family
Pausanias, 80
peninsular, character of Europe, 12–14
Persepolis, 204
Persia, 36, 39, 50, 67, 83, 91–3, 98, 122, 125, 144–5, 204–5, 286, 289
personality, 109–11, 154–7, 166, 191, 290; *see* individual
phenomena, 97, 99, 100, 174–6, 181–2, 187, 226, 238, 275; 'saving of', 173–9, 231–2, 239, 241, 244, 256, 266, 275; *see* object
philosophers, pre-Socratic, 121, 123–4, 127–8, 131, 216..
Philosophical Review, 287
philosophy, 133–7, 139, 147, 178, 291; *see* history, philosophy of
philousia, Eastern love of essence, 134, 137–41, 152
Phoenicians, 90
physics, 175, 177–8
Plato: the Absolute, 157; deity, 155; eternity, 265; ideas, 21, 127, 128, 171, 173, 240; mathematics, 23, 134, 151, 161; opposites, 142, 146, 149; politics, 24, 67, 79, 166; reincarnation, 51, 262 n. 1; wonder, 123
Plotinus, 108, 152
polis, 23–5, 79–82
political forms: Eastern acceptance of, 57, 63, 64, 68, 72, 81, 83, 87, 166–7, 182–4; in history, 279, 308–10, 316; Western concern with, 25–6, 65–7, 73, 83, 84, 87–9, 166, 267; *see* feudalism, monarchy, *polis*
Pope, 77, 78
possession, 182, 188
present, 263–5
principle (*arche*), 126–7, 129, 134, 138, 174
Proclus, 108
progress, 16, 302–3, 313, 314
Protagoras, 247
Pythagoras and the Pythagoreans, 126–7, 134, 146, 151, 163, 166

race 14, 311, 316
rapture, 195

reality: in magic world, 103–4, 106; relation with subject in the East, 117–18, 130–4, 137, 140, 149–50, 155–6, 158, 187
reason: activity of, 128, 142–3, 146, 147; in Eastern thought, 161; political forms based on, 79, 81, 82, 266, 289, 302; Western trust in, 64–5, 87, 129, 164, 174–5, 177, 201, 260–1; *see* thought
recurrence of cosmic process, 265; *see* rhythm
reincarnation, 45, 47, 51, 262 n. 1
religion, 23, 42, 78, 138–9, 182–3, 244, 291, 299–300; *see also under specific religions*
representative government, 87
republics, 90
rhythm, 209, 248, 250, 251
rights of man, 82
Roman civilization, 14, 17, 25–6, 71–3, 77, 91–2; *see* law
Rostovtzeff, M., *The social and economic history of the Roman empire,* 81 n.1

sacrifice, 139
salvation, 82, 296, 298–9
Schelling, 147
scholars, 73–4
Schopenhauer, A., *The World as Will and Idea,* 47
science, 14, 17, 22–3, 30–5, 43, 134–6, 138, 142, 148, 154, 158, 203, 284–5, 291, 303; *see* nature, physics
sculpture, 201–2, 210–11
self, 131, 139–40, 156, 221, 259
Semitic civilization, 90; *see* Israel
sense perceptions, 128, 146, 174–6, 199, 242–4; *see* tactile sense, visual sense
Shankara, 132
significations in the magic world, 101–102, 106–7
sleep, 169–70
social forms: Eastern acceptance of, 57, 63, 67–8, 73–5, 81, 166–7, 182–4, 244; Western concern with, 65–7, 77, 78, 83, 84, 166, 267, 285
Socrates, 116
Solon, 82–3
Sophism, 127

326